Weep Not for Me

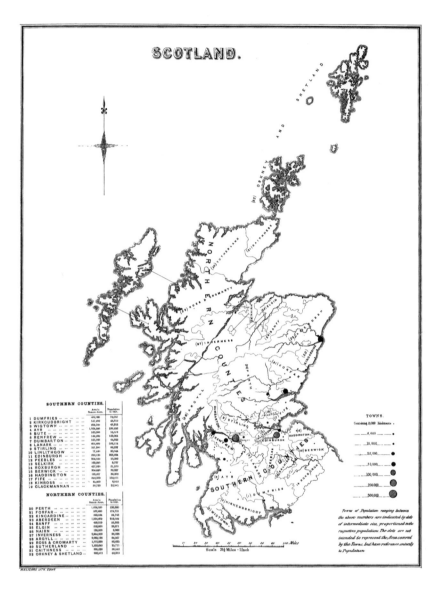

Scotland, 1862. This map uses what Scots at that time would have thought of as the names for the counties of the Edinburgh region; Edinburgh later became Midlothian; Haddington, East Lothian; and Linlithgow, West Lothian.

Deborah A. Symonds

Weep Not for Me

Women, Ballads, and Infanticide
in
Early Modern Scotland

The Pennsylvania State University Press
University Park, Pennsylvania

Library of Congress Cataloging-in-Publication Data

Symonds, Deborah A., 1951–
    Weep not for me : women, ballads, and infanticide in early modern
Scotland / Deborah A. Symonds.
        p. cm.
    Includes bibliographical references and index.
    ISBN 0-271-01616-7 (cloth : alk. paper)
    ISBN 0-271-01617-5 (pbk. : alk. paper)
    1. Ballads, Scots—Scotland—History and criticism.   2. Literature
and society—Scotland—History—18th century.   3. Women and
literature—Scotland—History—18th century.   4. Scott, Walter, Sir,
1771–1832. Heart of Midlothian.   5. Trials (Infanticide)—Scotland—
History—18th century.   6. Women—Scotland—History—18th century.
7. Women murderers in literature.   8. Infanticide in literature.
9. Heroines in literature.   10. Murder in literature.   I. Title.
PR8580.S95   1997
821'.04409352042—dc21   97-13086
                                                                                        CIP

It is the policy of The Pennsylvania State University Press to use acid-free
paper for the first printing of all clothbound books. Publications on uncoated
stock satisfy the minimum requirements of American National Standard for
Information Sciences—Permanence of Paper for Printed Library Materials,
ANSI Z39.48-1992.

For my parents,
Ann Pukish Symonds and Frank Willis Symonds,
Who always sang to me when I was young,
And still do.

Ye need nae weep for me, she says,
Ye need nae weep for me;
For had I not slain mine own sweet babe,
This death I wadna dee.
　　　　　—From the ballad *Mary Hamilton*

Contents

Acknowledgments

I have been thinking about Scots ballads since I was fourteen, when the singing of Joan Baez made me aware that there was such a thing as Child Ballad Number 173; for those album liner notes I am deeply grateful. Many years have passed since then, and many people have helped to make this book. So have several institutions. For material support, so important to scholarship, I am indebted to The Woodrow Wilson Foundation for a Women's Studies Fellowship; to the History Department at the State University of New York, Binghamton, for a Dissertation Year Fellowship; to the Women's Studies Program at the University of Iowa for a Rockefeller Fellowship in Rural Women and Feminist Issues; and to the Drake University Center for the Humanities, which has underwritten many past as well as present projects of mine. In a similar vein, I would also like to thank Julia Johnson and Marney Queen for giving me the run of their house in Edinburgh whenever I have needed it, as well as the pleasure of their company; Caroline Mackenzie for driving me all over the Highlands and the Lowlands, to many and various obscure sites; Anne Garven for research in the parish registers, and The Keeper of the Records of Scotland for the use of the court records essential to this book.

As important as the material help has been the help of many librarians, archivists, and computer-literate persons over the years. I could not have gotten anywhere without the help of the staff of the Scottish Record Office, at the Historical Search Room at Register House in Edinburgh, and at West Register House; the staff at New College Library; and the staff at Edinburgh University Library. They have patiently explained to me, over the years, what exists and what doesn't; they have found what I needed, sometimes without my asking; and even returned the pocket change I was always losing in the seats. I would especially like to thank a night watchman at the Edinburgh University Library, whose name I never knew, who let me out one night after I'd been locked in. At New College Library, Ian Hope combed through eighteenth-century sermons with me, patiently digging out whatever might apply to women. And at New Lanark, Lorna Davidson searched out material on unmarried women workers. In this country, librarians at Drake University's Cowles Library have cheerfully gotten many books for me. I am also lucky to have had the help of Angela Stone and Kristina Campbell, who typed and edited early versions of the manuscript; Missy Peterson, who did the indexing; two departmental overseers of supplies and services, Linda Wilson and Lynn Vaughn; and Denise Wicker, the graphic artist at Drake's Educational Media Services, who photographed the illustrations.

I would also like to thank all those people, friends and colleagues and teachers, who have badgered, pushed, and cajoled me over the years, making this a far better book than I could have written alone. First, I want to thank Richard Tristman for telling me what oral literature was, twenty years ago at Bennington College. Thanks also to Ian Campbell, at Edinburgh University, for tempering my zealotry as best he could; friends and colleagues at Binghamton University, who listened and put up with much; and William McFeely, for choosing to read from his life of Frederick Douglass at Mount Holyoke College some years ago, just when I needed an example of how narrative is written. There are many more people who have helped me and this work over the years, and room to thank only a few of them here: Helen Cranston Burley, Joyce Changes, Chris Lyman, Michael Pukish, John Slotwinski, and Pauline and Armen Tartanian. There have been many students, at Bucknell University and at Drake University, who have made me think critically about many of the arguments in this book, and shared their ideas about rural life and oral literature with me. My colleagues at Drake have put up with this work, or read some of it recently, especially Frederick Adams, Julian Archer, and Joselyn Ziven. There are also those friends, colleagues, editors, and readers who have gone over much of this manuscript, and done more than their share of editing, criticizing, and encouraging: John Bohstedt, Melissa Cano, Elizabeth Colwill, Susannah Driver, Linda K. Kerber, Peter J. Potter, Catharine R. Stimpson, and Mary Tartanian. But there is one person without whom this book could not have been written, and that is my friend and mentor, Elizabeth Fox-Genovese, from whom I have learned.

List of Illustrations

Chronology

Year	Scotland	Britain and Europe
1688		Glorious Revolution
1689	Battle of Killiecrankie	William and Mary
1690	Act Anent Child Murder	
1692	Glencoe Massacre	
1694		Bank of England founded
1695	Bank of Scotland founded	
1696	Last severe famine	
1698	Darien Scheme to trade in Panama	
1707	Act of Union uniting England and Scotland	
1714		George I
1715	Rebellion of 1715 (the '15)	
1736	The Porteous Riot in Edinburgh	
1737	Isobell Walker's trial	
1739		Rise of Methodism
1745	Rebellion of 1745 (the '45)	
1746	Defeat of rebels at Culloden	
1756		The Seven Years' War
1762	Agnes Walker's trial	
		Rousseau's *Emile*
1771	Birth of Walter Scott	
1775		Revolution in North America
1776	Adam Smith's . . . *Wealth of Nations*	
1784	Henry Dundas emerges as Scotland's political manager	
1789		French Revolution
1790	Elizabeth Mure's *Memoir*	
1791–92		Thomas Paine's *The Rights of Man*
1793		War with Revolutionary France
1796	Death of Robert Burns	
1798	Janet Gray's appeal	
1799–1801		Combination Acts

Prologue

In 1735 Katherine ffraser lived in the rural Highland village of Erchell, just west of the city of Inverness. She was probably a servant in one of the households there, although she might have been a small tenant in her own right, a cottager of sorts, and perhaps a widow. Late in the year she was courting, and she was pregnant on the Friday when she walked to Inverness with her lover, Duncan Buy. There they sat in a change house, or inn, for an hour or two, drinking ale and eating herring and bread. The wife of the change house keeper later described her as little, thin, and pale, and remembered that Buy called her Katherine and that she was visibly pregnant. Between three and four in the afternoon they began walking back, recrossing all the bridges that had brought them into the northern provincial city of Inverness. Several people saw them together, including a toll bridge keeper, who remembered that Buy paid both tolls.

Duncan Buy was wearing a plaid, wrapped around his waist and pinned at the shoulder, in the Highland fashion. ffraser wore a black-and-white striped gown, and a white plaid over that. They walked for hours, perhaps stopping along the road. At one in the morning, in a wood forming part of the farm of Banchrew, they struggled, and Buy beat ffraser to death with a rock. Another traveler on the road, Alexander ffraser, reported later that at one o'clock "he heard a screech or cry betwixt him and the sea," and that one of his horses startled. Buy caught up with him about a mile farther down the road, and asked if there was a change house nearby. They stopped at Rhindowie at two o'clock, and Buy bought them some chappins of ale. The servant at Rhindowie, Marion Keron, later testified that Buy "appeared confused and melancholy," drank a great deal, and "when he got the cup in his hand that he had a great trembling." While there, he kept himself well wrapped in his plaid, and put aside the bedclothes without using them. In the morning he appeared in gloves, and took his washing water out to the brewhouse, washed, and dried himself with his plaid. Keron re-

A small Highland public house, like the one Duncan Buy stopped at on the
night he murdered Katherine ffraser. From a nineteenth-century illustration
of Walter Scott's novel *Guy Mannering*.

marked later that he had refused a towel she offered. Underneath his
plaid, his shirt was soaked with blood.

While Duncan Buy was washing his hands, Katherine ffraser's body
was discovered. Three men from Banchrew, tenants surnamed ffraser
but probably not related to Katherine, were in the wood. It was four or
five in the morning; they may have been on their way to their fields, or
poaching, or returning from a night of drinking. They found the body
where Buy had dragged it, well into the wood. The oldest of the three
men looked at the body most closely. He "observed the head and face
mangled and scratched," and further noticed that her right hand was
also "mangled" and that there "were five wounds in the head," which
he thought had been given with a stone. The body was not yet cold.

Somewhat to the south, at the edge of the wood and beginning of a
marsh, they found the scene of the murder. Between two stumps lay
"severall large stones and a great deall of blood on these stones." The
ground had been trampled, and bore the mark of her head, and of her

body, dragged toward the wood. This was Saturday morning; on Sunday ffraser's body was carried to the parish church at Kirkhill.

The men from Banchrew had not recognized her. At Kirkhill her body was identified by William Roy Davidson, a tenant from Erchell. Davidson, who was either her master or her neighbor, had heard Katherine ffraser "say that she was with Child" to Duncan Buy; he also heard Buy deny it. John McEwan Oigg, also a tenant in Erchell, had heard the same words. A week before her death, she had run up to them, crying. Duncan Buy had tried to kill her, she said, when she met with him in the wood at Erchell. Before this, perhaps only a week earlier, she had spoken with two other tenants in Erchell, Donald Mckenzie and John McLean. She told each man that she was with child to Buy, also a tenant in Erchell, and begged both men in turn to speak to Buy. She did not expect marriage; but, as Mckenzie testified, she wanted to "know what provision [Buy] was to make for her," as he "was about to leave the Country." Both men spoke to Buy; with both he fell into a rage, claiming that he would have killed them had they not been his neighbors. But that did not stop him from killing Katherine ffraser. Within a few days of the murder, his neighbors were escorting him to Inverness. In May of 1736 he was tried, found guilty, and hanged.

Twenty years later, and somewhat to the south in Perthshire, the story would be repeated. Sometime between four and five o'clock on "a cold and windy afternoon" in November of 1756, Hector McLean asked his master, who was "drying a corn kilne" at the time, if he might "go to the [hill to] bring home the calfs and drive the horses to the stubble." The master, Donald Murray, a tenant farmer in Wester Buchandy, wondered at his willingness "to go on that errand," for McLean was at other times not quite so willing to go after the animals. McLean did not return for an hour and a half, and Murray was clearly put out, for he thought the work might have been done in half an hour. He testified that "when [McLean] came he was whistling and the Deponent [Murray] took notice of it that he should be so easy when he deserved a flite [blow] for staying so long." When his master questioned him, he said he had stopped at his aunt's house to comb his hair.

Shortly after this, the herdsman came to say that Isobell McEwan was missing. Murray sent him to Ann Clow, a neighbor who seems to have done his milking for him, apparently expecting McEwan to have been milking as well. But Clow sent back word that there had only

Harvesting in Perth, where Hector McLean and Isobell McEwan lived and worked. From James Beattie's *Scotland* (1838).

been two cows to milk, and that she had left McEwan at the cow fold. Murray finished what he was doing at the corn kiln, collected his two servants, Hector McLean and John Crichton, and went to the fold, a quarter of a mile from the steading.

At the fold, others had already found McEwan's body, her skull smashed and a whip tied around her head, passing between her nose and mouth. First to find her were three men, one of whom was also a tenant in Wester Buchandy. That man, William Gordon, had gone looking for Isobell at the request of Murray's wife. When they came upon the body at the cow fold, they found her on her back, "with a large Stone lying on her face." Gordon helped Murray carry the body to a barn. Someone brought candles, probably because it was dark, rather than because a wake was imminent. With candles lighted, William Gordon, twenty-four and unmarried, "perceived that she had received severall breiks upon the head and was such a dismal spectacle that he could not but with difficulty look at her."

There was little doubt in anyone's mind that Hector McLean had

murdered his fellow servant Isobell McEwan. The whip was his, and
his coat, with bloodstains, was found hidden in the barn a few days
later. He confessed to his neighbors and the sheriff-substitute, although he refused to plead guilty at his trial six months later. The jury
found him guilty, and the lords of the High Court sentenced him to be
hanged some weeks later, in July.

The cause of this sudden outbreak of violence on the multiple-tenancy farm of Wester Buchandy was Isobell McEwan's pregnancy. Not
only did the surgeon and midwife testify to Isobell's contusions and
fractured skull; they also established that she was pregnant at the
time of her death. She had come to Murray's service in March of 1756,
a few months after Hector McLean; in November, she was dead. Murray testified that he had no knowledge of McEwan's pregnancy until a
few days before her death, but that the day before, a Thursday, he had
heard "the said Isobel . . . say that if any body got the bairn [child] with
which they were then jeasting her it would be Hector McLean."
McLean was present then, but said nothing. What little he said to his
neighbors later survives only in fragments. Both Murray and the other
tenant, William Gordon, accompanied him to Perth, and heard him
admit to murdering Isobell. Only Gordon, in his testimony, made an
attempt to repeat the import of McLean's words, if not the words themselves: "that the cause of it was his having been told by her that she
was with Child by him."

Hector McLean's response was that of a trapped animal, yet it seems
doubtful that Isobell McEwan held any great power over him. Shame,
perhaps. But she had already tipped her hand to the servants and tenants in Wester Buchandy, and McLean was ill advised to kill her, for
there seems little chance that he might have gained by it. It would be
easy to imagine him a rake, combing his hair, whistling, a proud if no
doubt extremely distant kinsman of Sir Hector McLean, the clan chief
who came out for Charles Stuart in the revolt of 1745. But the anger
he left written across Isobell McEwan's face bespoke fear. And
McEwan, as a servant, was just as powerless as he in this community.
By naming him as the father of her child, she might bring about his
dismissal; her own was virtually certain, even if she said nothing. Perhaps the thought of losing his place in Wester Buchandy was unbearable. He had a relative, his aunt, in the neighborhood, and the coat he
habitually wore was a hand-me-down from his master. Perhaps finding
that he had no choices, that he was constrained, and that furthermore

he was constrained by the words of a woman he had lately seduced was unbearable.

But McLean's fury was rare, when one considers that many illegitimate infants were born in eighteenth-century Scotland, and that a number of similar conversations must have taken place in cow folds, barns, and kitchens, with very few resulting in death. Some couples married; others acknowledged their sins and made what provision they could. Women relied on their immediate families, especially if their parents were living; some men could afford to contribute; and then there were the kirk's, or church's, funds for the poor. The most desperate, or least scrupulous, of men swore oaths denying their role in the proceedings, went elsewhere in search of work, or, rarely, murdered their lovers. The most desperate of women took to the road and, finding no alternative, committed infanticide.

Neither Isobell McEwan nor Katherine ffraser lived long enough to give birth, or to commit infanticide, but their stories instruct us in the lives of village women who had to make the decision to kill or keep a child. And in the long eighteenth century of the Scots Act Anent (about) Child Murder, which stretched from 1690 to 1809, several hundred women, most of them alone, chose to kill, often at great cost to themselves. But these two stories allow us to begin by considering these women's lives in light of their relationships with neighbors, tenants, masters, and the men who fathered their infants, and in light of their positions within working households. Their world was still chiefly agricultural, with the bulk of the land worked by tenant households, usually with several tenants holding a farm jointly. Their parents, if alive, were likely to be tenants, cottagers, or servants on tenant farms. As the century wore on, a few women found employment as spinners and domestic servants in town, but most were agricultural servants, or worked on their parents' holdings. Above them were the landlords, great and small, the ministers, and the elders of the kirk. Isobell McEwan was a servant to a tenant farmer; so was Hector McLean, and perhaps Katherine ffraser. Donald Buy was apparently a tenant, but as he had no household, he was probably a cottager, valuable in Erchell for some skill, and consequently able to contemplate moving to another village or town.

These two men responded with great anger, murdering women whom they had gotten pregnant. Each obliterated the face of the woman he killed, and the violence of their assaults suggests the ex-

traordinary violence used by a few women against their own illegitimate children, presumably out of anger, fear, and frustration. McLean
showed some remorse, leaving his whip to tie him to the crime. But
Buy, whose shaking hands, bloody clothes, and unwillingness to go far
from the scene suggest that he wished to reveal what had happened,
showed more. Each man tied himself to the crime, with his whip or his
bloodied shirt, as if ambivalent about his own escape. It was not worse
than, and little different from, the ways in which some women would
leave marks of anger as well as possession on their infants' bodies.
Margaret Craigie strangled her child and threw it in a river, but could
not keep herself from wrapping the dead child in her well-known plaid
cloak; Isobell Walker tied her own kerchief over her infant's mouth and
nose before throwing him in a river; and Anne Morrison suddenly confessed and took several men to a distant field to see the child she had
beaten, strangled, and stabbed in the arms, legs, and head.[1]

These women were exceptions, for of the few hundred women who
would be indicted for infanticide in Scotland, most would think of their
own safety first, suffocating or exposing the child, leaving no marks on
its body, and few if any identifiable possessions. Virtually all of these
women, like ffraser and McEwan, would be unmarried, and for reasons
we may never know, unwilling to bear or raise their children, even as
thousands of other women in the long eighteenth century did not kill
their illegitimate children.

Introduction

I'm truly sorry man's dominion
Has broken Nature's social union,
An' justifies that ill opinion
          Which makes thee startle
At me, thy poor, earth-born companion
          An' fellow mortal!
    —Robert Burns, "To a Mouse," 1785

Katherine ffraser and Isobell McEwan, the ill-fated women described
in the prologue, died because Duncan Buy and Hector McLean both
lashed out violently when ffraser and McEwan forced them to face the
prospect of obligation, and perhaps shame. Because we cannot know
what private demons drove them to react so wildly, we are left to infer
what we can from the small worlds in which they lived. The four lived
at a time when rural couples faced increasing difficulty in establishing
households of their own, and for most young Scots villagers, a household meant a farm. Finding one meant relying on their own and their
family's connections with landowners and their agents to secure a
share in a tenant farm for themselves.[1] When Buy and McLean killed
ffraser and McEwan, both men acted selfishly, but also perhaps out of

the knowledge that they could not do otherwise. Simply put, a man without connections, a reputation as a farmer, or capital had no choice other than to remain in service, no matter what his age or inclination. If ffraser and McEwan hoped to settle as tenant farmers, they would have to marry, all the while counting on connections and reputation too.

In the seventeenth and eighteenth centuries, access to land in Scotland also depended on population, or the number of villagers looking for land in each generation, and the interest that a new breed of farmers, some of them tenants and some of them landowners, had in improving and expanding their own holdings. For young servants and subtenants like ffraser, McEwan, Buy, and McLean, the pressures created by population growth and emerging capitalist farming meant that an illegitimate birth could become a matter of life and death, threatening their reputations, their positions as servants, and ultimately their place in the village pecking order.

But it was not always a matter of life or death; most failed courtships and casual sexual encounters simply resulted in illegitimate births, which plagued various Scots communities with startling regularity throughout the seventeenth, eighteenth, and nineteenth centuries. Unfortunately, not all those children would or could be absorbed and supported by kin or by the village poor box, and it should come as no surprise that between 1661 and 1821 some 347 women were indicted or investigated for murdering their children at birth, after attempting to hide their pregnancies. For example, in Stirlingshire 15 women were investigated for infanticide there between 1693 and 1820, while 1,955 women gave birth to illegitimate children between 1637 and 1747. And for Scotland as a whole, illegitimate births amounted to approximately 5 percent of all births in the late seventeenth and eighteenth centuries.[2] While the number of illegitimate births was much larger, most people in Stirlingshire as in many other parts of Scotland would have heard of infanticide in their neighborhood over a period of roughly four generations. If murders like those of ffraser and McEwan were rare, the murder of illegitimate children by their mothers was not.

In 1690 the Scots Parliament enacted a statute defining infanticide as a reprehensible and easily proved capital crime. The statute probably did little to deter desperate young women, but it did much to make infanticide visible to their contemporaries, and it made the act accessible to us in startling detail. During the years in which the statute remained in force, from 1690 to 1809, women risked hanging for infanticide, while before and after that period the crime was difficult to prove, and investigation and trial usually led to mild punishment—a whipping in the early days and a few months in jail after 1809. But village women risked losing their lives in many ways in eighteenth-century Scotland, for during those years that the statute hung over their heads, their villages faced complex and irreversible changes that would destroy much traditional culture and social structure, turning members of small tenant families into increasingly transient rural wage laborers.

Sweeping Social and Economic Change

Those complex and irreversible changes we can now, with hindsight, refer to as the capitalist transformation of agriculture, and this book is about the impact of that transformation on rural women in eighteenth-century Scotland. Using two rich sources of information about the lives of eighteenth-century Scots village women, traditional Scots ballads and court records of infanticide prosecutions, it is possible to reconstruct the hardships of courtship and the difficulties of marriage. It is also possible to place these apparently private difficulties within the context of economic change powerful enough to dissolve the ties between villagers, and between villagers and landlords, leaving many villagers to fend for themselves. But the two sources ultimately lead us in two directions, because while the ballad tradition continued to treat infanticide bluntly, the gentlemen of the courts, and ultimately doctors and novelists as well, struggled with the prospect of infanticide and concluded that women could not kill their infants. If villagers knew about infanticide, suspected it, and continued to sing about it, by late in the century bourgeois men and women, informed by late Enlightenment ideals, erased it.

This period of change was both heralded by and provoked by Scotland's union with England in 1707. The emerging dual consciousness of many Scots can be easily seen in the Robert Burns poem "To a Mouse," which begins with the line "Wee, sleekit, cow'rin, tim'rous beastie" in Lowland Scots. But as the later stanza given above shows, Burns wrote in perfect English as well as Lowland Scots in the late eighteenth century. And his careful linguistic balancing act was one of many signs that Scotland's union with England, with all its economic and cultural ramifications, had finally taken root. That union, formalized in 1707 after bitter argument, dissolved Scotland's Parliament and Privy Council, but left the Kirk, or Church of Scotland, and the courts intact, and opened the doors to British, and especially colonial, trade.[3] Nonetheless, Scotland was still distant, isolated, and Scottish. It took four days or more for word from London to reach Edinburgh, and for forty years a vacuum of power invited rebellion by dissatisfied Scots. Rebels twice rallied to the banners of the exiled Stuart kings, in 1715 and 1745, and were beaten soundly. When that second revolt came in 1745, many Lowland Scots who found themselves caught between English enticements and Highland chiefs had made their decision, and fought beside the English at Culloden in 1746.[4] This political squabbling mattered a great deal to villagers north and south of the Highland line, for not until the new authority of London was established could the processes of agricultural capitalism begin in earnest. And in the Highlands, thickly settled tenants would not be dispensed with by their warlike landlords until it became clear, at Culloden, that the men of those households were no longer of use as fighting men.

After 1746, the hallmarks of a new Scotland began to emerge, with rapid agricultural improvement, domestic production of linen, the victory of the Moderate Party in the Kirk, and the intellectual and architectural growth of Edinburgh. The cold, hard, bare Scotland of John Knox's vehement Reformation gave way to reason, grace, and good fortune. The money came from overlapping networks of patronage and colonial trade and from the improving agricultural productivity that drove up the rents collected by landlords.[5] And the costs, inside Scotland, fell heavily on the backs of small tenant farmers and their subtenants, as the land they occupied came to be more valuable with them off it. This, then, was the world of Katherine ffraser and Duncan Buy, of Hector McLean and Isobell McEwan. They were not aware, most probably, that they lived in a society on the brink of rapid transformation, where a certain eagerness for agricultural innovation had been increasing the land's productivity and profitability, quietly and regionally, for some decades, even before 1707.

Those sometimes dramatic changes that historians have lumped together under the heading of agricultural revolution began earlier than 1746. Fields around Edinburgh were being limed (fertilized) during the seventeenth century, and by 1724 riots had broken out in the south-west, in Galloway, where land once available to tenants and cottagers was being enclosed for the new belted black Galloway cattle. The simplest explanation of the impact of these improvements on the lives of young rural men and women suggests that courtship would be complicated by couples' increasing difficulty in finding small farms or masters in need of married servants. Without a means of supporting themselves, such couples would find it difficult to marry, and courtship probably became a tougher, meaner negotiation. Young men who would have land could expect much, and women from the poorest ranks could demand little. In 1736 Isobell Walker, living with her mother and sister in a cottage in Cluden, near the city of Dumfries in the southwest, defied local midwives. She gave birth to an illegitimate child, wrapped it in her kerchief, and threw it in the Cluden Water. She was tried, found guilty, sentenced to hang, and then pardoned by royal authority. Twenty-five years later, also in the southwest, in Kirkcudbright, Agnes Walker left a newborn child no more than a stone's throw from her sister's house. The local minister found it that evening, dead, and with one leg chewed off by dogs. Within twenty-four hours Walker had been examined by several midwives, a minister, and a magistrate. She was tried and found guilty, but the verdict was so oddly written, by a jury headed by her sister's landlord, that she was banished rather than hanged.[6]

These two young women were typical of many who faced death for breaking the Act Anent Child Murder, which harshly spelled out that any woman who concealed a pregnancy, called for no help at birth, and whose child was dead or missing was to be found guilty and hanged. This was not the only infanticide statute written in early modern Europe, nor were Isobell and Agnes Walker, who were not related, the only women in Scotland to be indicted for killing newborn infants. They were two out of hundreds of women to be investigated, and often tried; they did not hang, but more than fifty women did. The framers of the Scots statute easily believed, as did most midwives in this period, that women, or at least unmarried women, could and would kill their children. Jurors sitting on cases before 1730 tended to agree. When the statute was enacted in Scotland in 1690, it marked both public awareness of infanticide, and a new will to govern resolutely, for it forced jurors to presume guilt, and to convict, even when they were shown no direct evidence of murder. It was the long arm of the king's law, and the Kirk's will, and it presumed more than guilt; it was written by men who presumed a simple, easily disciplined society, in which moral behavior was the only problem. But the statute could not enforce moral behavior on villagers who were, through marriage and tenancy, fighting for their lives, any more than it could stave off the changes that made tenant farms scarcer with each passing generation. The statute, which possibly followed a rash of illegitimate births in the late seventeenth century, and certainly followed an influx of infanticide cases before the High Court between 1660 and 1688, could only mark the changes in population growth and land distribution, which it could not change. In the eighteenth century, murdered children and illegitimate children were very probably harbingers of population growth in rural areas that were relatively inflexible in the number of households they could support. And the new statute, read from many pulpits, probably stopped few murders, just as the Kirk had been unable to control illegitimate births in the seventeenth century.

Eighteenth-century population growth, often coupled with a rise in the rate of illegitimacy, was a European phenomenon, if not as clearly a Scottish one, and historians have wrestled with the meaning of all those illegitimate children for several decades.[7] Some, cheerfully, have taken illegitimate births as evidence of a new interest in sexual pleasure, and part and parcel of the coming of systematic individualism. Others, perhaps more pragmatically, have considered the burden such children might be to single women and poor parents.[8] With an eye on the high mortality rates of children sent to wet nurses and orphanages, they have argued that illegitimate births constituted a problem, and probably represented couples who hoped to marry, but found that they could not set up a household, as the English minister William Cole recorded in 1766: "Will Wood junr, who wants to be married to Henry Travel's Daughter, the prettiest girl in the Parish, being uneasy with his Grandmother, (who can't afford to settle him), went away from her for 3 or 4 Days. The Times are so hard, small Farms so difficult to be met with, the Spirit of Inclosing, & accumulating Farms together, making it very difficult for Young People to Marry, as was used . . ."[9]

Of course, rural villagers had been struggling with constraints long before land became more valuable and landlords more inclined to capitalist innovation. Weather, disease, famine, and demands of landlords, the state, and the church had for centuries frustrated villagers. In this hard world, marriage was a necessity, both economically and demographically. But village lands were finite, and marriages had to be made with one calculating eye on the couple's access to land, through inheritance, dowry, or the goodwill of a landlord. Sometimes famine intervened, and land was available, but the struggles of these people to accommodate themselves to the land and to natural hardships were constant and old. Parents faced high infant mortality, and sometimes they must have welcomed it. Both parents sometimes, but not always, lived to see their children as adults, and complex households of stepchildren and stepparents were not uncommon. Rates of premarital pregnancy suggest that marriage often had to be provoked before it was planned, and there were always some adults who would never marry.[10]

And then in the eighteenth century the rules changed.[11] Famine and disease abated, while smallpox vaccination spread. Population grew. In Scotland, it grew rapidly after 1755, and probably grew slightly in the half-century before that, if only to replace those lost in the last great famine that struck in the 1690s. Yet as population grew, land disappeared. Not literally, of course, but through landlords' engrossment of small farms into big ones, and through their reclamation and repossession of once publicly accessible bogs and woodlands. Landlords became careful managers, while clever, literate tenants might rise to the rank of wealthy farmers as their neighbors became day laborers. Woodland was fenced, harvested, replanted; swamps were drained and fenced and planted. Tenants and subtenants lost their access to firewood, common pasture, frogs, herbs, and other necessities. At worst, they found themselves suddenly unable to renew leases on land that had rapidly risen in value, like tenants far to the south in Wigtown in the 1780s, or flatly evicted, like Highland tenants in Sutherland in the early nineteenth century. As Catherine McPhee, a cottar on one of the islands of Uist, later recalled, "I have seen the townships swept and the big holdings being made of them, the people driven out of the countryside to the streets of Glasgow."[12]

In Wigtown, leases had been literally auctioned off to the highest bidders, at prices that most of the old tenants could not imagine paying. But there were many other less obvious ways to reshape the countryside using the language of the lease. At the beginning of the eighteenth century, most tenants paid their rents with a variety of produce, including yarn and baskets, with cash, and with labor. As the century progressed, many landlords preferred to take their rent in cash, or at least to establish its value in money terms, but that was not

universally true. The great improver Grant of Monymusk rented large
farms for cash, but he demanded more and more services from his
small joint tenants and crofters. Those services included work on the
estate, but they extended to spinning and knitting, which shows that
there were indeed many ways to lose one's farm, and find oneself virtually a full-time spinner. Some of his tenants were really laborers producing yarn and stockings, and they must have held very little land
with their houses. Grant slowly converted his least productive tenants
into laborers, while they still appeared to be hanging on to some sort
of lease, and some sort of place on the estate.[13]

Infanticide

The impact of this improved farming (for the improvements that displaced so many people were, in terms of productivity, undeniably an
improvement) on the lives of Scots women in and outside these villages
forms the core of this book. Infanticide cases allow us to come face to
face with those women struggling desperately or ambitiously to make
a marriage and stay in a village, or to make a life for themselves by
refusing to give up on some vestige of companionship and community,
in the shape of their anxious partners. Their desperation and ambition
was framed by the happier lives of women who married well, managed
land, or founded businesses, and reason requires that we see the connection between Scotland's prosperity, and what an English historian
has called "the blasting of rural social structures."[14] The powerful productive logic of agricultural capitalism took its toll in villagers' lives,
and that small but steady supply of women who went to trial, and in
some cases to the gallows, for infanticide forced others to think about
those villages, and about woman's nature. There were at least fifty
hangings, far more trials, and several hundred investigations.[15] The
stories were not hidden, nor were the cases rare, and they reappeared
in ballads, and in a novel by Walter Scott.

The results of this brief visibility were astonishing, for men rushed
in, not to reform the countryside, but to deny the possibility of infanticide. Between 1762 and 1817, doctors, lawyers, jurors, and the writer
Walter Scott all scrambled to unravel the dismal story that the court
cases presented, by arguing that women did not really kill their children. What stake these men had in describing women's nature is not

simple or clear, but they rejected, almost on cue from the Enlightenment, even the most direct evidence that mothers would murder infants. Walter Scott was a vociferous Tory; the lawyers who attacked the statute in court were Whigs. Nonetheless, they joined in rejecting not only that aspect of women's behavior but also the implication that something might be wrong in their newly productive, highly rationalized countryside. During the years after 1762, convictions under the old infanticide statute dwindled to zero until the statutory punishment was changed in 1809 to no more than two years in jail. Walter Scott rewrote Isobell Walker's story in 1817, confidently blaming a vagabond for her child's death, and pushing Enlightenment views of women firmly in the direction of biological determinism and maternal nature. In this, he followed the late eighteenth-century lawyers, doctors, and jurors, few of whom had wanted to see that the evidence in front of them suggested that women killed their children, viciously and desperately.

Ballad Singers and the Ballad Heroine

The only contrary voice, apart from that of the appointed prosecutors, came from the singing of village women, village men, and a handful of landed women, who had by 1800 sung and transmitted many courtship ballads. Those ballads, which continued to be handed down by oral transmission throughout the early nineteenth century, confirm for us that courtship could be seen as a deadly and a serious business. While infanticide was being erased in court, the Scots ballads were being avidly collected and published, as cherished remnants of a disappearing old order. Ironically, many of the songs focused on courtships gone awry, describing recent problems: murder, pregnancy, jealousy, and infanticide.

One popular ballad, popular in the sense that it survived among singers in more variations than any other, was *Mary Hamilton*, which recounted the heroine's murder of her newborn child. Unlike Walter Scott's heroine of 1817, who weeps and mutters throughout *The Heart of Mid-Lothian* that she is not guilty, Mary Hamilton announces firmly and publicly that she has killed her child, and should hang. The ballads repeated exactly what the statute had announced, namely that women could and would kill, and added that women were determined to love or marry where they wished. That perspective survived on the lips of women long after the statute had fallen into disuse, and that singing stands in stark contrast to the new, polite, Whiggish erasure of infanticide, which must have struck some villagers as a mockery of the horror and tragedy with which some women continued to live. The singers knew all too well what the lawyers, doctors, and jurors refused to see, which was that women, no doubt sometimes feeling as trapped and powerless as Duncan Buy or Hector McLean, also killed.[16]

Unlike their English and American sisters, Scots women of all sorts and ranks had the figure of the ballad heroine—arrogant, powerful, canny, and Scottish—to amend the received figure of the good, maternal, and private woman. Even if they did not want to amend that figure, the ballad heroine still loomed to be reckoned with, bowdlerized, but never quite laid to rest. Even the poorest singer could alter the text of a ballad while singing it, but most of the women in a position to bowdlerize texts as they were collected and printed failed. Lady Caroline Nairne's moral and proper ballads were not popular, and Anna Gordon Brown's discomfort with ballads overcame her only after the ballads from her repertoire had been published. Luckily for us, most Scots, and especially the men who collected the ballads and rural women of all classes who sang most of them, preferred their ballads raw, blunt, and sexually explicit. And they had no qualms about publishing them, especially if they sold well.

Increasingly, urbane and bourgeois Scots women of the long eighteenth century, who ruled over drawing rooms, knew the Enlightenment as part of their lives, founded businesses, managed estates, and wrote memoirs, could escape neither the ballad heroine nor the waves of maternal sentiment that made Whigs' disgust with the statute seem more universal than partisan. They, like village women, were caught up in the transformation of the economy and ideology by which they and their neighbors lived, and they also made their ways as best they could through the new and old ideas about woman's nature that solidified and dissolved around them in the late eighteenth century. They are also part of our story, even if their struggles with change, like those of Walter Scott, are peripheral to this account of villagers, big farmers, and the law.

To reconstruct those villagers' lives, this study relies heavily on the collection of Scots and English ballads edited by Francis James Child in the late nineteenth century.[17] When these ballads were first collected in the late eighteenth and early nineteenth centuries, their collectors emended, romanticized, and sometimes bowdlerized at will, to make them marketable. And they sold well, perhaps because they allowed readers to indulge in nostalgia for a rural, honorable, dangerous, and aristocratic world slightly before that world was quite dead and buried. It became Child's life's work to restore those ballads to their original forms using the collectors' notebooks, to identify the singers when possible, and to collate them with folk themes from other national folk literatures. Needless to say, Child died before he completed his task. But his work makes it possible for us to see that most of his 305 ballads were of Scots provenance, and that most of the identified singers were women. And most of the ballads that were collected from oral tradition, as opposed to manuscripts, were about the difficulties of courtship.

If the ballad *Mary Hamilton* occurs in more variations than any other, and *Mary Hamilton* is about infanticide, the next most frequently found is *The Twa Sisters*, in which a woman, jealous of her sister's suitor, drowns her sister and marries the man herself, only to be condemned by the disembodied voice of her dead sister. As one reads, listens to, or sings more of these ballads, one consistent figure emerges, and she is the ballad heroine. She is a composite figure, shaped by the singing of village women and men, landowning women, old women moved to Glasgow from rural parishes, and their daughters who work in mills, and she can represent, as a solid, well-worn cultural product, what her singers knew or wished to say about woman's nature and woman's lot.

Court Records of Other Villagers

Village women and men who have been dead for two or three hundred years might have vanished into obscurity, leaving only a few songs, but many survive in partial but vibrant detail in the records of Scotland's High Court of Justiciary.[18] These court records, sometimes terse, sometimes awkward, are crucial, for without them, the irony as well as the true pathos of the ballads would vanish. The murders of Isobell McEwan and Katherine ffraser are recorded there, as are many of the 347 indictments and investigations for infanticide I have identified.[19]

Before 1690 there are also cases, albeit rarely, in the records of Scotland's Privy Council, and after 1800 the records of the lord advocate, or chief prosecutor, and his officials are also valuable and detailed. Legal records are often used to gain insight into criminal behavior, but the women caught in these pages seem to have been respectable enough. Some had borne illegitimate children previously; two were thought of as village idiots. And no more than a handful in Edinburgh might have been, as later police records would put it, "girls of the town." Thus the court records salvage for us not only the crime, but detailed accounts like those from the trials of Buy and McLean, describing what many ordinary villagers were doing as well as saying over a period of several days.

The ballad singing and the infanticide trials had for their background the complexity of Scotland's eighteenth century, complete with political union, economic transformation, and public discussion of old and new ideas that raged through many forums, from the sermon to essays, poetry, ballads, plays, history, philosophy, and novels. When we examine the lives of rural Scots women in this century we are, in small, engaged in a case study of the dangers and opportunities discovered by women in the great transformation, economic, political, and social, that swept through the western world between 1750 and 1850. Village women were part of that transformation, and their lives in turn affected other Scots men and women. While some historians have argued that women's history has little to do with the watershed events of textbook history, it is the purpose of this study to show that the great capitalist transformation of the late-eighteenth-century western world was just that for women, as well as for men. And just as some women did well for themselves, others would do badly, for the family landholding, and with it the family, would no longer be the basic economic unit of the rural world.

We will begin with those ballads in which village women and men described hardships that women faced, and the qualities that they found admirable in or useful to the ballad heroine. But before proceeding to some of the ballads, which will be found in Chapter 2, it is important to examine how and why the ballads were collected in the eighteenth century, who the last of the traditional singers were, and how the ballads were transmitted. Without this grounding, which constitutes Chapter 1, the ballads can easily be misunderstood.

1

Ballad Singers and Ballad Collectors

No Scottish ballads are superior in kind to those recited in the last
century by Mrs Brown, of Falkland.[1]
— Francis James Child

The Scots ballads are a unique source for historians because they come
to us from the singing of villagers, as well as from the occasional
landed gentlewoman, and they describe crises of everyday life, albeit
in the often heroic style of the ballad world. In Scotland, generations
of those villagers lived and died and left behind few records, save the
occasional inventory of their meager possessions, or statements transcribed in court records. They rarely, if ever, had tombstones in the
local kirkyard. But we know that they sang because they left behind
one of the richest oral traditions in Europe. We know what they sang,
and sometimes, with whom they sang. And we know that most of the
recorded singers, by the time the collectors came in the late eighteenth
and early nineteenth centuries, were women.

The songs those women sang are our only direct, first-person accounts of what struck them as right and wrong, as funny, and as tragic. Although we have no other autograph texts from these people, we have hundreds of ballads, many of them carefully recorded, dated, and otherwise identified, and if we understand who these singers were, how their songs were collected and often distorted, and what the songs were about, we have pried open for ourselves an extraordinary window on a past that should, by rights, have vanished from our sight. We also have very good records of who the collectors were, and what moved them to collect ballads as the eighteenth century drew to a close, and it is with them, the founders of the feast, so to speak, that our story begins.

In the late eighteenth century, collecting, publishing, and preserving traditional oral ballads became both fashionable and profitable. Beginning in 1765 with Thomas Percy's *Reliques of the Ancient English Poetry,* ballads were delivered in bulk to eager consumers, like fresh produce from market gardens. The early collections, based on manuscripts, contained a few traditional Scots oral ballads, mixed with contemporary songs, fragments of archaic verse, and blatant forgeries. But by the early nineteenth century, ballads were being carefully collected from rural villagers by gentlemen whose methods were presumptuous but whose transcriptions were probably accurate.[2] In Scotland, the rush to publish these new ballads peaked between 1802 and 1832, but appetites for traditional material were whetted and editors' tastes were shaped by the great forgeries of the eighteenth century, the poems of Ossian and *Hardyknute.* Under their faux-medieval pall, abetted by the market for gothic fiction, collectors transcribed live songs, and struggled to remake them as early modern, if not quite medieval, artifacts. Virtually all of the collector-publishers were men, and many of the singers, like Anna Gordon Brown, were women.

Before going on to describe the almost inevitable veneer of masculine heroism in which the ballads were first packaged, it is worth pausing over the simple example of Anna Gordon Brown, who was the most prolific singer of ballads that the eighteenth- and nineteenth-century collectors found. She was born in Aberdeen in 1744, the daughter of an academic, Thomas Gordon, and a country woman from the estate of Disblair. Her mother, Lillias Forbes Gordon, was one of three daughters who had inherited the family estate and who were known as the ladies of Disblair for the years before they married. The young Anna was raised in Aberdeen, but she spent time with her mother's sister, Anne Forbes Farquharson, who had chosen to marry in the country.

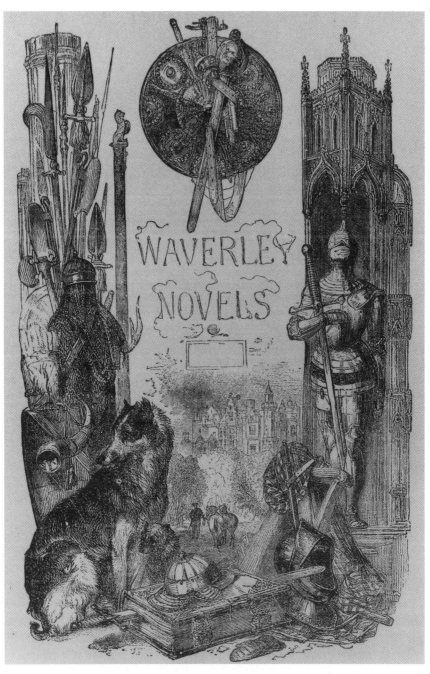

Frontispiece to a nineteenth-century edition of Walter Scott's Waverley Novels. Scott's romantic medievalism found a ready audience in his day.

Anne Forbes Farquharson learned ballads from nurses and servants on her husband's estate in the Braemar district of western Aberdeen, and it was largely from her aunt that Anna Gordon learned ballads as a young woman. But she also learned them from her mother, who must have picked them up in the neighborhood of Disblair, and from a servant in their Aberdeen townhouse. Whether Anna Gordon Brown's forty-two known ballads represent the tip of an iceberg, or whether she was particularly good at singing and composing and had a better stock of ballads than the nurses and tenants who were her ultimate sources, we can never know. But her network was quite typical, as perhaps was her interest. If she was the archetypal source, then Walter Scott was the archetypal collector; she would sing but was not comfortable with publishing, while Scott would happily publish ballads that he had not composed.

As a literate man, Scott probably had no inkling of how the ballads, as oral texts, were created and re-created by generations of singers. But Anna Gordon Brown had learned the skills of oral composition, apparently without thinking about it, and mastered the art of formulaic structuring and composition. The traditional oral ballads so quickly gathered up were, in content and structure, somewhat different from the songs and poetry of literate, urbane eighteenth-century society. Blunt, rude, and often tragic, the ballad was constructed according to strict rules, using a set stock of phrases. And its form was older than any eighteenth- or nineteenth-century collectors imagined, with roots going back to the Homeric epics. At the core of both are a series of mnemonic devices, by which a story varying in length from an eighty-line ballad to *The Odyssey* can be re-created and varied by singers over centuries without ever having been written down. Preliterate in origin, the ballads flourished in Scotland as part of the culture of traditional agricultural society, and they survived tenuously into the nineteenth and twentieth centuries. Literacy, long suspect as the solvent of oral skills, was not by itself inimical to the ballad in Scotland before the breakdown of precapitalist agricultural society, and the ballad remained a widely acceptable form of storytelling that coexisted with the bourgeois novels of the eighteenth and nineteenth centuries. But after 1750 village life changed, the distribution of chapbooks and printed songs increased, and bourgeois taste, not simple literacy, gained in power and attraction.[3]

What we now know about oral structure and formulaic phrasing

allows us to separate traditional ballads from forgeries and interpola-
tions, and what we know about this we owe to the work of Milman
Parry and Albert B. Lord. Parry, wrestling with an old problem—why
does this Homeric poetry contain so many repetitions?—turned to the
nearest living relations of Homeric singers, the traditional singers of
Yugoslavian epic tales. After watching and recording these singers,
and studying their texts, Parry and Lord, his student, made several
conclusive observations. First, they defined oral literature, whether
called tale, epic, song, or anything else, as verse, leaving European
folktales to less rigorous methods of re-creation. Second, they insisted
that oral literature was not simply any piece of literature performed
orally, as any piece could be, but a poem that was composed during
oral performance.[4] Lord, who published their joint results, described a
process rather than a product, and emphasized the role of the singer
who must know how to manipulate the stock of formulaic expressions
and accepted themes to produce songs that are simultaneously part of
a tradition and unique: "Stated briefly, oral epic song is narrative
poetry composed in a manner evolved over many generations by singers of tales who did not know how to write; it consists of the building
of metrical lines and half lines by means of formulas and formulaic
expressions and of the building of songs by the use of themes."[5] Lord
probably overemphasized the element of creativity, but he and Parry
called attention to the authorial voice and intentions of the singers,
and legitimated the variations between ballad texts. Eighteenth- and
nineteenth-century collectors, who believed that they were saving an
ancient bardic poetry from destruction at the hands of unlearned peas-
ants, would have had difficulty in seeing the singers as skilled, no matter how much they appreciated the songs.

Yet Parry and Lord did not question the older English and Scottish
collectors' belief in a male bardic tradition; the Yugoslavian singers
they studied were men with special skills, often handed down in that
culture from father to son. Yugoslavian audiences for those singers
were primarily male, in a society in which literacy was rare. While this
differed dramatically from the less formal, and often female, networks
of ballad transmission in eighteenth- and nineteenth-century Scotland, Thomas Percy and other ballad publishers and collectors had
nonetheless believed firmly in an ancient Scots bardic tradition remarkably similar to what Parry and Lord no doubt looked for, and
found in Yugoslavia. Percy, who lumped the Scots material in his col-

lection with the English, began the preface to his eighteenth-century collection by describing "our ancient English Bards and Minstrels, an order of men who were once greatly respected by our ancestors, and contributed to soften the roughness of a martial and unlettered people by their songs and by their music."[6]

David Buchan, in *The Ballad and the Folk*, followed the comparative method of Parry and Lord, and identified the telltale marks of oral composition in the Scots ballads. He also tried to historicize the ballads, but his attempt to link ballad production to historical context, brilliant in intent, lacked adequate precision, and in the end differed from the usual nineteenth-century picture of warriors and bards only in making the ballads the property of implicitly male villagers and tenants. But Buchan noticed that Anna Gordon Brown's ballads all seemed to have female heroines, which led him to speculate that

> Mrs. Brown's stock, therefore, very definitely constitutes a woman's corpus, and may perhaps represent a woman's tradition within the regional tradition. This raises the intriguing but, given the available evidence, largely unanswerable question as to how large a part women played in the regional tradition as a whole. Certainly women outnumber men as recorded sources in the transitional period between orality and general literacy, but this fact tells us little about the pre-1750 tradition. (76)

The simplest hypothesis would be that Scotland had an early period of ballad production, which resembled ballad production in the classic Parry-Lord model, during which the singers and audience were perhaps primarily male. By the eighteenth century this had changed; even Gaelic bardic tradition records a female bard by the late seventeenth century. Women sang, and as Buchan notes, they vastly outnumbered men as sources of ballads after 1750, but women did not immediately and completely transform the ballads. They did partially remake a compelling courtship literature out of epic forms centuries old, within a few generations, and this testifies to their skill, the pressure they were under to make sense of their lives, and the vitality of oral forms. If there was a shift in content from warfare to courtship, it was neither abrupt nor mutually exclusive, and one need only refer to the bride-stealing ballads, *Eppie Morrie* (C.223), *The Lady of Arngask* (C.224), and *Rob Roy* (C.225)[7] to see how easily courtship and a raid by twenty-four armed men can be combined.[8]

Wars and dynastic struggles concerned women, as Jane Porter, the nineteenth-century historical writer, attested in her long introduction to *The Scottish Chiefs:*

> But in Scotland, it is not the "pastors and masters" only who educate the people; there is a spirit of wholesome knowledge in the country, pervading all ranks, which passes from one to the other like the atmosphere they breathe; and I may truly say, that I was hardly six years of age when I first heard the names of William Wallace and Robert Bruce:—not from gentlemen and ladies, readers of history; but from the maids in the nursery, and the serving man in the kitchen: the one had their songs of "Wallace Wight!" to lull my baby sister to sleep; the other his tales of "Bannockburn," and "Cambuskenneth," to entertain my young brother . . .[9]

Not only did she describe an education that knew no class boundaries, she invoked a sympathy between herself and the servants that stood proxy for an explanation of how a young girl came to be obsessed with William Wallace, the thirteenth-century patriot who drove back the English, and with war and politics. For Porter, the warrior past was both transmitted by women, and embodied in them, and especially in Luckie Forbes, whom Porter remembered clearly:

> I can never forget that dear old woman; so shrewd, yet simple-minded, and cheerfully religious: she performed her humble duties with activity and content; her recreation, and "exceeding great reward," was reading her Bible, which she did every day. I do not recollect ever seeing any other book in her house; though she knew the history of Scotland, and the biography of its great families, as accurately as if the top of her *muckle kist* [great chest], on which her Bible lay, had been filled with historic chronicles. (11)

Forbes was joined in Porter's recollection by the old women of Edinburgh who had embodied the Scots past for her when she was a child. She saw these women, the widows of the Jacobite uprising of 1745,

Jane Porter, author of *The Scottish Chiefs*. For Porter Scotland's warrior past was both transmitted by women and embodied in them.

impoverished, behind garret windows; she glimpsed an old, distinguished woman, in long tartan plaid, crossing the square. She recalled wondering, as a child, whether this person was the Duchess of Perth, Lady Galloway, or Lady Lovatt. Porter had found, or made for herself, a history which was thoroughly male, thoroughly female, thoroughly about gentlemen, and thoroughly the property of servants. If her recollections are accurate, Porter was not the singular character she at first appears, but one of many women, including Luckie Forbes, who told stories of Wallace, and the '45, assuming them as their own Scottish history.

But the masculine tone set by earlier ballad publishers, not to mention forgers, has cast a long shadow. When Thomas Percy published his *Reliques* in 1765, he was following on the heels of James Macpherson's *Fingal, an ancient epic poem, in six books, composed by Ossian the son of Fingal; Translated from the Galic [sic] language, by James Macpherson,* published in 1762, and less directly, Elizabeth Halket Wardlaw's 1719 offering, *Hardyknute.* Macpherson's Ossianic poetry was based on his minimal familiarity with fragments of Gaelic bardic poetry surviving in sixteenth-, seventeenth-, and eighteenth-century manuscripts, and Wardlaw's *Hardyknute* was probably based on some familiarity with ballads. Both were forgeries, presented to the public as ancient manuscripts, but recently written by Macpherson and Wardlaw. Macpherson had his defenders throughout the nineteenth century, but Wardlaw was discovered as the real author of *Hardyknute* before her death in 1727. That Wardlaw's *Hardyknute* was more readily recognized as an imposture suggests that eighteenth-century readers may have been quicker to question a woman's connection to a ballad, while many were happy to accept Macpherson in the role he created for himself.[10]

Macpherson, Percy, and Wardlaw together established a taste for heroic ballads that was grounded in the Gothic paraphernalia of lost manuscripts, ancient bards, and an expectation that ballads be very old—indeed, vaguely medieval—and products of male bardic tradition. Unfortunately, there was to be a great shortage of lost ancient manuscripts, and even the Gaelic bardic tradition was not, at least by the seventeenth century, exclusively male, as the reputation of Mary Macleod (Mairi Nighean Alastair Ruaidh), bard to the Macleods, attests.[11] When collectors came looking for ballads in the late eighteenth century, they found more women than men singing. This puzzling fact was to some degree resolved by nineteenth-century folklorists' concept of a genderless, disembodied voice of the Folk, which allowed them to ignore the implications of women's active role in the transmission and composition of ballads.

The stage was set for what a recent scholar has called "scandals of the ballad," or the problems of authenticity and authorship that were endemic to the marketing of ballads. The ballads arrived on the printed page in a form created by their collectors and editors, and, often, considerably altered by those persons. Joseph Ritson, an exacting editor who died in 1803 at the age of fifty, never printed an informant's name, because he felt names were antithetical to the nature of folk poetry. The folk were a homogeneous mass, a background against which an individual like Ritson, who was both a Whig and a vegetarian, acted. Ritson, however, was scrupulous in never altering or emending the texts he collected, whereas other collectors routinely usurped the authorial position they refused others.[12] Robert Jamieson, editor and author of a collection of Scots ballads published in 1806, was appalled by Ritson: "That Mr. Ritson was most scrupulously honest, according to the letter of the law, I am very ready to grant; but I can see no extraordinary merit in that, any more than in his atrabilious, furious, and obstreperous abhorrence of forgery of every kind." Walter Scott also had "no sympathy with the noble rage of Ritson," and wrote, "If a young author wished to circulate a beautiful poem under the guise of antiquity, the public is surely more enriched by the contribution than injured by the deception." And Allan Cunningham, editor of *The Songs of Scotland, Ancient and Modern* published in 1825, later admitted in a letter that "these songs and ballads being written for imposing on the country as the reliques of other years, I was obliged to have recourse to occasional coarseness, and severity, and negligence, which would make them appear as fair specimens of the ancient song and ballad." It is no wonder that F. J. Child, who died in 1896 before he could write the essay intended to accompany his magisterial edition of Anglo-Scots ballads, did manage to leave notes on the editors' habits of improving, retouching, altering, and emending. He was clearly offended by the fumbling attempts of collectors to "improve," for he wrote that no changes in texts were "in so glaring contrast with the groundwork as literary emendations of traditional ballads."[13] He had worked for much of his adult life to compile all the ballad texts in print, first from the published versions, and later from the collectors' manuscripts. He knew, perhaps better than anyone else, the degree to which the ballads were painted and brushed up before being offered for sale, and noted every change that he suspected or could document.

The gulf between the early forgeries, Percy's luckily found manuscript, and the later collections of largely traditional oral ballads was bridged by the work of David Herd and Walter Scott. David Herd, having produced one antiquarian hodgepodge of ballads, songs, poems, and fragments in 1769, quickly began casting about for oral material to use in an enlarged edition of 1776. This early searching, beginning more or less with Herd and continued by various interested scholars and country gentlemen turned up windfalls of collections. James Skene collected thirty-two ballads from an unidentified woman known only as the Old Lady. Robert Jamieson, William Tytler, and Alexander Fraser Tytler all collected ballads from Anna Gordon Brown, who sang at least forty-two ballads from her own repertoire. Some of Anna Gordon Brown's ballads made their way into Walter Scott's *Minstrelsy of the Scottish Border*, published in 1802 and 1803.[14]

The publication of *Minstrelsy* marked a watershed in ballad collecting and ballad popularity, because the collection was Scottish and traditional, and because Walter Scott's marketing of the ballads and the Scots past was crucial to the way in which ballads would be consumed and understood. He whetted the public's appetite for the past, and satisfied it not only with ballads, but with novels and poetry. And Scott was no innocent artist; he was a rabid Tory, sensitive to his own political present, as well as a prolific writer who would recast the Scots past. Scott was able to place the ballads so convincingly not because he was a model historian but because he longed for the ancient past to which he thought the ballads belonged.[15] By 1803, when *Minstrelsy* was completely published, and Joseph Ritson had died, the ballads were, as a national literature, implicitly caught up in national politics. For a great Tory like Scott, a conservative and monarchist who hated every aspect of the French Revolution, the ballads represented a powerful remnant of the aristocratic past, and the villagers who sang them no doubt looked like good tenants, paying proper attention to the heroic lords and ladies who paraded through the ballads. But to a reform-minded Whig with extended suffrage and a more representative government in view, the ballads could also stand as proof that common people had had a literature, and an acute awareness of the maneuverings of the aristocracy, for some generations.

Scott was a transitional figure who lived long enough (1771 to 1832) to see his world greatly changed. Raised to be a lawyer of mild Whig sympathies like his father, he became a Tory and a sometime lawyer. He had the Jacobite sympathies and taste for Scots songs and tales of his mother. And he was primarily a writer, making a fortune from his novels and literary speculations, which he spent on rebuilding, out of an old farmhouse and antique bits and pieces, a Scottish baronial estate he named Abbotsford. In 1825 he lost it all and went into debt when the speculative publishing empire he delighted in collapsed. Like Abbotsford, his public face as a lawyer, sheriff of Selkirk, landed gentleman, and antiquarian was a construction built largely out of the profits of commercial publishing. And so he hid his authorship for as many years as possible, much as he hid his rigorous early morning writing schedule, and stomped about as a Tory gentleman, even after his bankruptcy.[16]

The ballad publishing that peaked in Scotland in the 1820s was conducted in Scott's shadow. This productive period began in 1819 and ended in 1833 with the republication of *Minstrelsy*, the first of Scott's books to be reissued after his death the year before. Following the first appearance of the *Minstrelsy* in 1802, four more collections were published by 1810, but between 1819 and 1832, some seventeen collections, from thirteen editors other than Scott, were printed. With the exception of James Skene, who in 1818 published a second installment of ballads collected from the Old Lady, the major collectors of this period—Robert Pitcairn, William Motherwell, George Kinloch, and Peter Buchan—had to scour villages and towns. Motherwell, for example, made an exhausting number of visits in the Glasgow area over a three-year period. What they found in this gleaning were women and men who rarely knew more than one or two ballads, in stark contrast to the older oral composer Anna Gordon Brown's forty-two.[17]

The lists of ballads sung by women and ballads sung by men between 1730 and 1896 show us that both men and women tended to avoid the older, strictly military ballads. Women and men sang more of the same songs than not; like Jane Porter, women showed interest in conflicts, feuds, and fights, and men knew some of the ballads of courtship. Nonetheless, some courtship ballads came from women only, and those ballads recited only by men are invariably heroic adventures. And we can count the singers: 173 women, and 56 men. Those women provided 438 versions of 145 ballads, while men provided 88 versions of 58 ballads.[18] While many collectors left singers unidentified, there is absolutely no reason to believe that collectors were more likely to identify women. Consequently, by the late eighteenth and early nineteenth centuries, ballad singing was very probably largely in the hands of women, and warrior ballads in the hands of printers, where they had been for a hundred years or more.

But the further lesson is that by the 1820s, the majority of people who sang or recited for collectors were not oral composers, living in communities where singing was an integral part of daily life. Most remembered, in a modern way, one or two ballads learned earlier in life, and collectors tortured themselves with the thought that there had been an earlier golden age of ballad singing. The classic statement of this despair came from William Laidlaw, Scott's land steward, ballad collector, and friend, who thought that Scott was already too late in 1800:

> . . . I had begun to enquire, and write down from the repeating of old women, and the singing of the servant girls, everything I could hear of, and was constantly aroused by vexation at two circumstances, namely finding how much the affectation and false taste of Allan Ramsay constantly annoyed me instead of what I wanted, and had superseded the many striking and beautiful old songs and ballads of all kinds that I got traces and remnants of: and again, in discovering how much Mr. Scott had been too late—from the accounts I received of many men and women who had been the bards and depositories of the preceding generation.[19]

It is hard to know what weight to give Laidlaw's rumors of a golden age, and it would be foolish to imagine a pastoral Scotland full of singing villagers, but it is impossible to ignore the evidence presented by David Buchan's literary analysis of James Nicol's ballads, which suggests that ballad content was in marked decline by the early nineteenth century. While Buchan argues ably for the corrosive power of literacy, and the deadly effects of the increasing sale of cheap printed ballads in contaminating what singers sang, it is also true that what those printed songs contained was as important as the literacy they demanded. What they brought to villages was William Laidlaw's despised "affectation and false taste," and that is quite different from the simple distribution of penny pamphlets, chapbooks, and other manifestations of the growth of a profitable, mechanized, capitalized popular culture business. The problem, or scandal, of the ballads did not lie simply with literacy, or with printing, but with the coming of new canons of taste, which we might call sentimental, or bourgeois. The new technology served new experience, and reflected the polite tastes of those who were beginning to enjoy the privilege of withdrawing from the hardness and brutality of the older life of rural villagers and land-owners.[20]

Singers stopped remembering ballads because the world the ballads had explained ceased to exist, and the misremembered ballads were often badly pieced together by singers and editors alike after 1800. But rural Scotland did not change abruptly, and some excellent and genuine oral ballads survived indifferent singing and sentimental editing. Furthermore, those ballads, given the flexibility of oral forms and oral composition, are likely to reflect the time of their composition, rather than preserving earlier cultural or social worries intact. In other words, the collectors tampered, and the singers forgot, but there are still ballads, many coming from women, that offer insight, from women's various social and regional perspectives, into the great cultural, economic, and social transition of the eighteenth century in Scotland.

Women Who Collected and Sang Ballads

Before examining the evidence we have of women's networks of ballad transmission, and their place within village or family singing, it is worth recalling that if literate men were drawn to printed songs, bawdy ballads, and ballad collecting, so were literate women. Lady Grizel Hume Baillie compiled a manuscript book of songs while in exile in the Netherlands between 1685 and 1688. This is now lost, but one song of her own composition survives; Ritson printed it in 1791 and Chambers in 1826, and it suggests that Lady Baillie had some acquaintance with traditional ballads, and used her knowledge in much the same way as did Robert Burns.[21] In 1730 Elizabeth Cochrane compiled a songbook, which contained 5 traditional ballads and 135 drawing-room songs. The first lines of three of the latter give away the contents of both:

> How long, how long, must I pine for love . . .
> Give way to pleasure, it soon will revive you . . .
> Ianthe the Lovely, the Joy of her swain . . .[22]

Cochrane included the ballads in her collection without making any distinction between one sort of song and another. Of the five ballads she knew, four were accepted by Child: *John of Hazelgreen* (C.293.A), *Gill Brenton* (C.5.E), *Robin Hood and the Bishop of Hereford* (C.144.B), and *The Lass of Roch Royal* (C.76.A). In two cases she supplied Child with A texts, meaning those he took to be the best available versions of those ballads, which is particularly impressive, for they were embedded in 135 mannered and lewd drawing room songs. Cochrane mixed her ballads with other music, and probably learned four of them from singing, which suggests that there was no clear line between the oral and the printed, or between the popular songs of village and of town in 1730.[23]

Forty years later, during the 1770s, Elizabeth St. Clair Dalrymple, living in Edinburgh and married since 1773 to Lieutenant Colonel Dalrymple, wrote out 318 pages of songs, poems, and ballads. Among her 200 pieces are 19 traditional ballads, none of which duplicate Cochrane's ballads. Both women mixed traditional ballads with printed songs and scraps of lyric poetry. Cochrane and Dalrymple seem to have come from the middling ranks, and while it is no surprise that they learned most of their songs from outside the ballad tradition, it is useful to remember that they learned ballads too.[24] When Cochrane and Dalrymple wrote down a song, ballad, child's rhyme, or poem, from memory or magazine, they participated in an old custom, that of keeping a commonplace book. But in the late eighteenth century this private usage was about to take another turn, for when Herd, Ritson, and all of Scott's correspondents began to write down ballads, they claimed them as private property, sharing jealously; and when they printed them, they re-created them as a commodity. If Elizabeth Wardlaw had been eager enough to publish *Hardyknute* in 1719, virtually no other women would follow the male collectors who published, edited, and introduced collections of ballads, songs, and scraps.

The most important women associated with the ballads were the singers Anna Gordon Brown and a woman identified as the Old Lady. The Old Lady took her identity to the grave, and Anna Gordon Brown was, by 1802, quite appalled when her name was printed in Scott's *Minstrelsy*. Gordon Brown had transcribed her ballads for collectors between 1783 and 1801, while the Old Lady wrote out hers later, between 1805 and 1818, and that twenty years' difference probably explains the Old Lady's reticence, since Gordon Brown had not been shy in using her name until 1802. Gordon Brown, whose cache of ballads was one of the windfalls of the late eighteenth century, was a literate

woman whose father was a university professor and whose husband
was a minister. Her father held the Chair of Humanity at King's College in Aberdeen. Her parents' veneer of eighteenth-century gentility,
true to the times, was still thin and brittle. Her father threatened to
horsewhip a colleague at an age when most academics might be incapable of holding a pencil. Her mother, Lillias Forbes Gordon, was one
of three daughters of William Forbes of Disblair and Elizabeth Bate-
man, an English wig maker of aggressive reputation. William Forbes
was a serious if amateur musician and a virulent pamphleteer. Bate-
man divorced him in 1704, returned in 1708, and finally left with the
three daughters and most of the estate's income, forcing William
Forbes to borrow money and live elsewhere. As Gordon Brown's father
put it in a letter to Fraser Tytler,

> An aunt of my children, Mrs. Farquharson, now dead, who was
> married to the proprietor of a small estate near the sources of
> the Dee, on the division of Aberdeenshire called Braemar, a se-
> questered, romantic pastoral country; if you ever went to your
> estate by way of the castle of that name, you are not such a
> stranger to it as to need a description. This good woman, I say,
> spent her days from the time of her marriage, among flocks and
> herds at Allanaquoich, her husbands seat, which, even in the
> country of Braemar is considered as remarkable for the above
> circumstances. She has a tenacious memory, which retained all
> the songs she had heard the nurses & old women sing in that
> neighborhood.[25]

The lesson of the Forbes, Gordon, and Farquharson households would
seem to be that ballads moved up and down through the social ranks
on an estate, and that it was easier for collectors to acquire ballads
from their friends than from old women on estates in western Aberdeenshire. The young Anna Gordon became a repository of songs
brought to her from Braemar by Anne, and from the Disblair region by
her mother, and family servants. That she mastered them, not through
notebooks, but by coming to master the techniques of oral composition,
while living in the city of Aberdeen in her father's enlightened and
scholarly household, tells us even more about how fuzzy the line between high and popular culture was in the late eighteenth century.[26]
    It was Thomas Gordon, not his daughter, who first wrote to the col-

lector William Tytler in 1783 and to Alexander Fraser Tytler in 1793, and in both cases ballad manuscripts from Anna Gordon Brown followed. She was soon known by virtually all the contemporary ballad collectors, and her ballads impressed both her contemporaries, and later scholars. When Thomas Gordon wrote to Alexander Fraser Tytler, he admitted that on first seeing a transcript of his daughter's ballads, "Both the words and strains were perfectly new to me, as they were to your father, & proceeded upon a system of manners, & in a stile of composition, both works & music, very peculiar, & of which we could recollect nothing similar."[27]

Thomas Gordon had never heard the ballads in his house, and it would be interesting to know whether Joseph Farquharson, Anne Forbes's husband, was equally a stranger to the ballads that his wife learned while living on their estate. Yet Thomas Gordon had the sense to make those ballads known, even though Joseph Ritson and Walter Scott, perhaps caught up in their own bardic mythology, were initially suspicious of Gordon Brown's ballads.[28]

Scott had heard ballads sung ever since childhood illness had sent him to his grandfather's Lowland estate, and he eventually came to respect Gordon Brown's ballads, and include some of them in his *Minstrelsy*. His early suspicion was probably founded on Gordon Brown's literacy and literary habits, which contrasted sharply with those of his informants in the countryside. Yet Scott's mother and aunt, originally the Misses Rutherford, both well-educated daughters of a physician, were important sources for him of Scots folklore, and two ballads. Scott, like most of the other Scots collectors, could turn to his family and friends for ballads; so could the collectors George Kinloch, Thomas Wilkie, James Beattie, Robert Chambers, James Hogg, Charles Kirkpatrick Sharpe, Joseph Robertson, William Laidlaw, Robert Pitcairn, and, in the 1890s, William Macmath. If an urban professional like Thomas Gordon claimed they were unfamiliar, a good many other people of middling rank knew and sang them.[29]

But that openness would not last. Gordon Brown took great pleasure in writing to collectors, but abruptly distanced herself from the published work. In 1802 she would withdraw, shocked that Scott had ventured to publish her name in connection with her ballads, which made up the bulk of the romantic ballads in his *Minstrelsy*. Shortly after both the publication of Scott's collection, and her husband's promotion to Tranent, she wrote to her collector of the moment, Robert Jamieson:

"But I am very much surprized indeed & not very well pleased to see
A Gentleman so much praised by all his acquaintance for his politeness & aimable qualities guilty of so great an impropriety as to publish
any persons name to the world without ever asking directly or indirectly whether or not it would be agreable, and both Mr. Brown & I
have been a good deal vexed at it."

The exact nature of her vexation will have to rest unexamined in the
mire of feminine propriety that made female authority and authorship
anathema in the early nineteenth century, perhaps to her husband as
much as to her. But it does fall within the continuum of her father's
anthropological surprise at discovering such songs in his household,
and it may have suited Robert Jamieson who sent Gordon Brown small
gifts in return for her help and her texts, very well. In September of
1801 she wrote to Jamieson, almost excited, to tell him that she knew
a different version of *Lamikin* than that printed in Herd's collection.
She closed by saying, "I fear myself a good deal interested in my power
to facilitate your scheme." She was dabbling at the edge of female authorship, much at the edge, indeed, but could see herself as something
of a co-conspirator in literary endeavors, with Jamieson and the better-
known Scott. It was no doubt heady, and, by 1802, uncomfortable, as
she demanded that her name be kept out of the public eye. It was not
literacy which troubled her ballad singing, but the sudden danger of
being seen as an authoress.[30]

But the business of collecting ballads was about to become far more
difficult, even though the singers' lines of transmission would remain
familiar: mother aunt, nursemaid. William Motherwell collected ballads from the textile towns surrounding Glasgow. In 1825 Miss Brown,
a sister of Dr. James Brown of Glasgow, recited *Geordie* (C.209) for
him. She got the ballad from a blind aunt, and it appears to have been
the only one she knew. On the fourth of May in that year, Rebecca
Dunse recited two ballads for Motherwell; *Little Musgrave and Lady
Barnard* (C.81) she had from her mother, who was then an old woman.
On July 18, 1825, Janet Holmes of the weaving village of Kilbarchan
sang *Fair Annie* (C.62) for Motherwell. It was the only ballad she knew,
and she learned it from her mother. Somewhere between 1813 and
1815 Betty Hoyl recited *James Hatley* (C.244) for Thomas Wilkie; she
was from Gattonside, had learned it from her mother, and it was the
only ballad she knew. Around 1825 Marjory Johnston recited three ballads for Motherwell. She was a servant to a manufacturer in Paisley,

and one of the ballads was from her "great-aunt, a very old woman." Unlike Gordon Brown, and the Old Lady, none of these women had a large repertoire.[31]

In 1826, the Widow Michael, or Margaret Patterson, sang *Child Maurice* (C.83) for Motherwell while she was living at Dovecote Ha', Barrhead. She had learned the ballads in Banffshire, far to the north, seventy years earlier. Motherwell noted that "she heard it sung with many variations, but this copy was considered to be the right way." Mrs. Storie, the wife of William Storie, a laborer in Lochwinnoch, sang five ballads for Motherwell; one of them, *Child Maurice*, she had learned from her grandmother.[32] Mrs. Thomson had grown up in Water of Leven, Dunbartonshire, but in 1825 she lived in Kilbarchan, Renfrewshire, and was then about seventy. And in that year she sang a thirty-four-stanza version of *Child Maurice* for William Motherwell, and told him that she had learned it from her mother at the age of ten, in 1765. Her grandmother also knew the song, as did "other old folks" in the village, and Motherwell chose to present the ballad as the grandmother's, presumably to give it a longer pedigree. By 1780 Mrs. Thomson had learned a different version of *Child Maurice*, *Gill Morice*, "which began with young lasses like her to be a greater favorite and more fashionable than the set which her grandmother and other old folks used to sing, under the title Chield Morice." She told this to Motherwell, but either she did not remember the newer "set," or he was uninterested, for it is not recorded. It may also not have been significantly different from the older version, which she recited—if indeed she had not combined the two by then. Of six recorded versions of *Child Maurice*, four are from the recitation of women, and their interest was not accidental.[33]

The plot of *Child Maurice* had become well known in 1756 through a play, *The Douglas Tragedy*, written by a soon-to-resign minister of the kirk. In the ballad, Lady Barnard is to meet Child Maurice in the woods, but suspecting a lovers' tryst, her husband goes instead, beheads Maurice, and presents the head to Lady Barnard. She confesses that Maurice was her illegitimate son, gotten on her by her father (or a visiting English lord), and that she will now die. Her husband curses her for hiding the child, insisting that he would have treated him as his own. After the play appeared, there was something of a revival of interest in the ballad, which very probably appeared in print. Mrs. Thomson's new version, *Gill Morice*, was likely learned by those lasses from a printed copy, which demonstrates neatly how a story might move from ballad to the Edinburgh stage, and then generate new ballads. Both *The Douglas Tragedy* and *Child Maurice* turn on illegitimacy and secrecy, and the popularity of both suggests that urban and rural preoccupations were similar when Mrs. Thomson was growing up.[34]

As Motherwell's collecting shows, women like Mrs. Thomson moved from rural areas to the new textile towns like Kilbarchan, and many cited mothers, grandmothers, and aunts to the exclusion of other sources. The increasing frequency of one-ballad singers after 1832, with many of those single ballads coming from a mother or grandmother, suggests that with migration ballad sources for many women shrank from community to family of origin and that while ballads may have survived some disruption of the agricultural community, they did not survive transplantation to mill towns. The communities of Lanark, Paisley, or Kilbarchan did not become ballad communities, even though disparate women and men in them knew ballads. In contrast, Airds of Kells, Kirkcudbright, where Jane Webster learned seventeen ballads in the late 1830s, remained a singing community even though extensive improvement greatly altered the earlier structure of sturdy small tenants. Webster learned ballads from women and men, and her ballads allow us to consider the role of men as singers, and the further question of whether men and women sang the same songs, and sang them differently.[35]

Men also sang, and women also reported learning ballads from their fathers. Agnes Lyle, who recited eighteen ballads for Motherwell between 1825 and 1827, mentioned that she had learned *Lord Derwentwater* (C.208) from her father (1731–1811), who was of Anna Gordon Brown's generation. But she also said that her father sang a different version of *Geordie* (C.209), without, unfortunately, mentioning how it differed from hers. The Widow Michael, or Margaret Patterson, told Motherwell in 1825 that she had learned *Child Maurice* (C.83) seventy years earlier, in Banffshire, where she had heard it in many variations. An old woman in Buckie, Banffshire, who recited three ballads for William Christie told him that her father had been "a noted singer." She died in 1866, and had been born in approximately 1786, so her father was also of Anna Gordon Brown's generation. Perhaps she was too old to remember more; her father's penchant for ballads was otherwise apparently not transferred to her. One other woman, "an old cottar-woman" near Kelso, mentioned, in the 1880s, having learned her one ballad, *The Twa Sisters* (C.10), from her grandfather.[36]

Men were more likely to mention learning ballads from fathers or grandfathers; women were more likely to mention mothers, grand-mothers, and aunts. Thomas Wilkie, the son of the blacksmith in Bowden, Roxburgh, remembered hearing his father sing a fragment of *The Baron of Brackley* (C.203). He communicated this to Scott, adding that his father remembered it from the singing of a Lady Brigs from that county. Before his death in 1838, Wilkie filled four notebooks with songs, ballads, and rhymes, most of which he collected himself, carefully leaving notes of his sources. Robert Sim, a weaver in Paisley who sang one ballad for Robert Motherwell in 1825, said that he had learned it from his father, "a great reciter of heroick ballads." And James Nicol, the most prolific of male singers, with twenty-one ballads to his credit, claimed to have learned them from many people, when he was young.[37]

If these scraps of information offer a tantalizing suggestion of what ballad singing and village culture might have been like, one woman left a perfect record of how she learned ballads, and of who in her village sang. Jane Webster, a spinster aunt of the ballad scholar William Macmath, knew seventeen ballads, and left a perfect record of where she had learned sixteen of them. First approached by Macmath in 1886, she claimed to have learned fourteen of her ballads in 1836 as a girl in Airds of Kells. Three came from her mother, two from her aunt, one from a nursemaid, one from the wife of a cotman, and one from another villager, Roseanna McGinnies. But she learned six more ballads from men, five of whom lived in the same village. Two came from Samuel Galloway, one from James Smith, one from John Coltart, one from James McJannet, and one from Thomas Duffy, a joiner in Parton. This is a far more human and useful record, showing a young woman active in her village, and a village where both men and women sang ballads. And while she learned ballads from five men and eight women, both in and outside her family, she was apparently selective, taking only one or two ballads from anyone. Outside the village and in later life, she learned two more ballads, both from women.

Where Jane Webster learned ballads means a great deal more when reinforced by the content of those ballads, especially *The Jolly Beggar* (C.279), which she learned in two versions, from her mother, Janet Spark, and from the joiner in Parton, Thomas Duffy. *The Jolly Beggar* is a slightly lewd, virtually classic tale of a young traveling man who seduces farmers' daughters; a variant, *The Pollitick Beggar-Man*, can be found in Samuel Pepys's seventeenth-century collection of English broadside ballads.[38] This kind of song, in print for many years, probably belonged to a male public house or coffeehouse audience. Not surprisingly, the version she learned from her mother is a fragment of two stanzas, in which the beggar, seen from a housewife's perspective, is a pushy guest who insists on sitting near the fire.

> He wadna lie in the barn, nor he wadna lie in the byre,
> But he wad lie at the ha-door or the back
> O the kitchen fire.
>
> (C.279.B.c)

In Thomas Duffy's version, the beggar seduces the daughter of the household, in language closer to ribaldry than balladry.

> It's fare ye weel, gudewife, an it's fare ye well gudeman,
> Ye hae a gude fat daughter, an I rattled her pan.
>
> (c.279.B.d.)

Of the six ballads Jane Webster learned from men, four, including Duffy's version of *The Jolly Beggar*, have sexual comedy at their core, in which the joke is always at the expense of a woman. But nine of the ten she learned from women belong to the older, or at least more serious, discourse of dynastic struggle played out in deadly courtship, raid, and battle. Jane Webster learned most of her ballads by 1836, too late to be included in the heyday of ballad collecting, which peaked in the 1820s. But her experience provides a good glimpse of ballad transmission in a village, and Macmath's account of Webster's singing shows that while both men and women in Airds of Kells knew and exchanged ballads, the women had a slightly firmer grasp on the tradition in numbers of ballads, and a much firmer grasp on the old tradition in the quality of their ballads. Nonetheless, we should remember that Webster preferred, or at least remembered, Duffy's version of *The Jolly Beggar*, but largely forgot her mother's, and that in 1836 she had presumably gone out of her way to learn Duffy's version. The lesson of her mixed bag of ballads is clear, if ironic; the lines drawn between men's and women's

singing are both evident and tenuous, subject to any singer's prefer-
ences.[39]

That dichotomy between men's and women's singing, which may also
reflect the dichotomy between printed songs and oral ballads, was evident earlier. In 1802 Anna Seward, the English bluestocking, wrote to
Walter Scott complaining that the version of *The Twa Sisters* (C.10.L)
that she knew was terrible: "The Binnorie of endless repetition has
nothing truly pathetic, and the ludicrous use made of the drowned sister's body is well burlesqued in a ridiculous ballad, which I first heard
sung, with farci[c]al grimace, in my infancy (1747), thus . . ."
(C.IV.448). The version she knew from her childhood in Derbyshire
was much closer to the English bawdy tradition than to the Scots oral
tradition, and ran, in part, as follows:

> O it was not a pheasant cock,
> Or eke a pheasant hen,
> But it was and a gay lady,
> Came swimming down the stream.
>
> And when she came to the mill-dam
> The miller he took her body
> And with it made him a fiddling thing,
> To make him sweet melody.
>
> (C.10.L)[40]

Anna Gordon Brown's Scots version is, instead, about a drowned
woman's revenge. Two sisters love one man, who courts the elder but
loves the younger. The older woman drowns her sister, and the
drowned woman's body floats until stopped by a mill dam, where a
harper takes her hair to use as harp string. Once reembodied as a harp,
she makes the harper do her will.

> He's taen three locks o her yellow hair,
> An wi them strung his harp sae fair.
>
> The first tune he did play and sing,
> Was 'Farewell to my father the king.'
>
> The nextin tune that he playd syne,
> Was 'Farewell to my mother the queen.'

The lasten tune that he playd then,
Was 'Wae to my sister, fair Ellen.'

(C.10.B)

Both are versions of *The Twa Sisters*, which exists in twelve versions
from women's recitation, and one version from men's, along with numerous older printed copies. That it was sung in the 1750s as far south
as Derbyshire, England, and in Aberdeenshire in 1783, suggests that
its popularity depended both on broadside copies and on various versions' appeal to both men and women. The broadsides, or printed copies, were cheaply printed and sold from stalls or peddler's packs, and
often consisted of hack writers' versions of older ballads.

At two extremes, the ballad could be about a lusty, fiddling miller,
or about a drowned woman's need to speak, and to avenge herself. The
persistence and popularity of both, as in the case of *The Jolly Beggar*,
illustrates the interlocking of print and oral culture, and the inimical
sources that women were apparently both drawing on and rejecting, to
develop ballads. Seward, an educated woman, a poet, and a bluestocking, reacted with distaste to the stall-ballad version, with its salacious
underpinnings, for she refers to "the ludicrous use made of the
drowned sister's body," which is not the case in the Scots oral versions,
where the fiddler is used by the dead woman. Yet her solution, a complaint to Scott, was far less effective than that of the eight Scots women
who simply sang it differently.[41]

Throughout the eighteenth century ballads made their way from village to townhouse with some ease. But in the century's closing decades,
ballad collectors began the work of drawing a line between what they
saw as their contemporary culture and the ballads. Nor were they altogether wrong to see the ballads as endangered, for villages were
shaken and altered by new farming practices, the use of wage labor,
and migration of the dispossessed to textile towns. Armed with an almost righteous sense of timeliness, Scott, along with all the other men
who collected, emended, and altered ballads, largely in the name of
rubbing off the rough edges of a literature they barely comprehended,
committed some sins. But without them, and their copybooks, curiosity, and desire to make a little money in publishing, we would not have
most of the ballads now collected in Francis James Child's volumes. In

their eagerness to glean what they could, they never managed to erase the importance of women, either as singers or heroines, despite their firm belief that the ballads had originated in a male bardic tradition. The bones of the old singing showed through their editing, and we can glimpse the patterns of transmission, the importance of women singers, and the interest of men and women in many of the ballads. The collectors saved enough to allow us to weigh the probably endemic presence of ballads in Scots-speaking communities, if not in the Gaelic north, and at least speculate on the importance in Scots culture of the old figure of the ballad heroine. The drowned sister in *The Twa Sisters*, who will be heard, dead or not, is one of her milder manifestations. The heroines of the ballads considered in the next chapter, still in command of their own lives and bodies, ride, fight, kill, and die on their feet. In their bluntness, fury, and calculating canniness, they are the antithesis of bourgeois sentiment, and we know them only through the bumbling, earnest, and arrogant efforts of men who were for the most part conservative antiquarians, but also sentimental conservatives clinging to vestiges of the warrior past.

2

The Ballad Heroine

"Oh are ye blind, Willie?" she said,
"Or do ye no weel see?
I think ye micht see my heart's blude
Come rinning by my knee."
　　　—Lord Thomas and Fair Annet
　　　　　(C.73.B)

The ballad heroine lived in a ballad world that was both mythic and grimly material, both ancient and contemporary to the singers' lives. As villagers sang about her adventures, they drew on remnants of older tales and songs, but they did not simply repeat them. The Scots ballad *Babylon* is a good example of one with cognate Scandinavian tales, but in the Scandinavian tales the heroine does nothing heroic. Like Little Red Riding Hood, she must be saved by an older male figure. In the Scots ballad, three sisters go into the woods to pick flowers; each in turn is accosted by a banished man, an outlaw or "outlyer," who demands of each either her maidenhead or her life. The first two sisters' responses, given below, are identical, and lead to their deaths. After two such exchanges, the third sister breaks the pattern by refusing to answer the question, talking about her brothers instead.

There were three sisters, they lived in a bower,
Sing Anna, sing Margaret, sing Marjorie
The youngest o them was the fairest flower.
And the dew goes thro the wood, gay ladie.

The oldest of them she's to the wood gane,
To seek a braw leaf and to bring it hame.

There she met with an outlyer bold,
Lies many long nights in the wood so cold.

"Istow a maid, or istow a wife?
Wiltow twinn with thy maidenhead, or thy sweet life?"

"O kind sir, if I hae't my will,
I'll twinn with my life, keep my maidenhead still."

He's taen out his we pen-knife,
He's twinned this young lady of her sweet life.

He wiped his knife along the dew;
But the more he wiped, the redder it grew.

The second of them she's to the wood gane,
To seek her old sister, and to bring her hame.

There she met with an outlyer bold,
Lies many long nights in the wood so cold.

"Istow a maid, or istow a wife?
Wiltow twinn with thy maidenhead, or thy sweet life?"

"O kind sir, if I hae't at my will,
I'll twinn with my life, keep my maidenhead still."

He's taen out his we pen-knife,
He's twinned this young lady of her sweet life.

He wiped his knife along the dew;
But the more he wiped, the redder it grew.

The youngest of them she's to the wood gane,
To seek her two sisters, and to bring them hame.

There she met with an outlyer bold,
Lies many long nights in the wood so cold.

"Istow a maid, or istow a wife?
Wiltow twinn with thy maidenhead, or thy sweet life?"

"If my three brethren they were here,
Such questions as these thou durst nae speer."

"Pray, what may thy three brethren be,
That I durst na mak so bold with thee?"

"The eldest o them is a minister bred,
He teaches the people from evil to good."

"The second o them is a ploughman good,
He ploughs the land for his livelihood."

"The youngest of them is an outlyer bold,
Lies many a long night in the woods so cold."

He stuck his knife then into the ground,
He took a long race, let himself fall on.

                            (C.14.D)[1]

The ballad ends with the power of the third sister's revelation, as her brother recognizes her, and then kills himself. *Babylon* shares some of the admonitory stiffness of the Scandinavian tales. But the youngest sister's self-possession, amounting to agency, is unique to the ballad. In the Scandinavian tales, all three daughters die, and are avenged by their father.[2]

Basic prescriptions—do not go into the woods alone, do not give up one's maidenhead—stand behind both this ballad and the tales. However, in *Babylon* the absolute power of the Scandinavian fathers is displaced by the heroine, the youngest daughter, whose facility with speech, and willingness to claim her "outlyer" brother, as well as the minister and the ploughman, mark her as different from her freely sacrificed dull sisters (C.I.174). But the youngest sister's agency is a complex phenomenon. It depends in part on her own boldness, in part on family membership, and also on the possibility that she has no virginity to lose. If the latter were true, one could easily see why the woman would have been well practiced in turning and avoiding questions. Women accused of infanticide had often displayed equal skill in denying their pregnancies. The third sister is like the heroine of an eighteenth-century novel, even though she is related to Cinderella and Little Red Riding Hood.[3]

More forthright than the third sister, Eppie Morrie wrestles her would-be suitor into submission in the course of a Highland bride-stealing raid.

> They have taken Eppie Morrie,
> Since better could nae be,
> And they're awa to Carrie side,
> As fast as horse could flee.
>
> When mass was sung, and bells were rung,
> And all were bound for bed,
> Then Willie an Eppie Morrie
> In one bed they were laid.
>
> "Haud far awa frae me, Willie,
> Haud far awa frae me;
> Before I'll lose my maidenhead,
> I'll try my strength with thee."
>
> She took the cap from off her head
> And threw it to the way;
> Said, Ere I lose my maidenhead,
> I'll fight with you till day.
>
> (C.223.8–11)

Her struggle with the raiding would-be husband is the core of the ballad, told from her point of view, but what has been stolen in *Eppie Morrie* is the heroic male perspective usually at the center of such an exploit. Eppie Morrie, minus father and brothers, takes center stage, and her story replaces Willie's. Here courtship is plainly a battlefield, albeit an indoor one, but *Eppie Morrie* is unique, a lone story preserved in only one text.[4]

Two key texts, found in many versions, seem to stand at the center of the network of courtship ballads: *Lord Thomas and Fair Annet* (C.73) and *Child Waters* (C.63). Together, they share many formulaic structures and themes with other ballads, perhaps because they elaborate the two possible results of courtship in the ballad world, marriage and death. In the B text of *Lord Thomas and Fair Annet*, the protago-

nists appear as Sweet Willie and Fair Annie, and their courtship is
broken when Willie, with advice from his family, chooses the brown
bride instead of Annie. This version begins with a conversation suddenly broken.

> Sweet Willie and Fair Annie
> Sat a' day on yon hill;
> Though they had sat til the leventh o June,
> They wad na got their fill.
>
> But Willie spak a word amiss,
> Fair Annie took it ill:
> "I'll neer marry a tocherless lass
> Agen my ain friends' will."
>
> Then on she lap, and awa she gat,
> As fast as she could hie:
> "Fare ye weel now, Sweet Willie,
> It's fare ye weel a wee."
>
> Then he is gane to his father's ha,
> And tirled at the pin;
> Then up and rase his father proud
> And loot Sweet Willie in.
>
> "Come riddle us, riddle us, father dear,
> Yea both of us into ane;
> Whether sall I marry Fair Annie,
> Or bring the brown bride hame?"
>
> "The brown bride she has houses and land,
> And Annie she has nane;
> Sae on my blessing, my auld son,
> Bring ye Brown Bride hame."
>
> Then he is to his mither's bouer,
> And tirled at the pin;
> Then up and rose his mother dear
> To let Sweet Willie in.
>
> "Come riddle us, riddle us, mother dear,
> Yea baith o us into ane;

Whether sall I marry Fair Annie,
Or bring the brown bride hame?"

"The brown bride she has gowd and gear,
Fair Annie she has nane;
And for my blessing, my auld son,
Bring ye Brown Bride hame."

Then he is to his sister's bouer,
And tirled at the pin;
And wha sae ready as his sister dear
To let her brither in.

"Come riddle us, riddle us, sister fair
Us baith yea into ane;
Whether sall I marry Fair Annie,
Or bring the brown bride hame?"

"The brown bride she has horse and kye,
And Annie she has nane;
But for my love, my brither dear,
Bring hame the fair woman."

"Your horse may dee into the staw,
The kye into the byre,
And ye'll hae nocht but a howther o dirt,
To feed about your fire."

Then he is to Fair Annie's bouer,
And tirled at the pin;
And wha sae ready as Fair Annie
To let Sweet Willie in.

"You're welcome here to me, Willie,
You're welcome here to me":
"I'm na welcome to thee, Annie,
I'm na welcome to thee,
For I'm come to bid ye to my wedding,
It's gey sad news to thee."

"It's gey sad news to me, Willie,
The saddest ye could tell;

It's gey sad news to me, Willie,
That shoud been bride mysel."

Then she is to her father gane,
And bowed low on her knee:

. . . .

"Come riddle us, riddle us, father dear,
Us baith yea into ane;
Whether sall I gang to Willie's wedding,
Or sall I stay at hame?"

"Whare an will be your frien, Annie,
Twenty will be your fae";
"But prove it gude, or prove it bad,
To Willie's wedding I'll gae.

"I'll na put on the grisly black,
Nor yet the dowie green,
But I'll put on a scarlet robe
To sheen like onie queen."

She's orderd the smiths to the smithy,
To shoe her a riding steed;
She has ordered the tailors to her bouer,
To dress her a riding weed.

She has calld her maries to her bouer,
To lay gowd on her hair:
"Whare e'er ye put ae plait before,
See ye lay ten times mair."

The steed Fair Annie rade upon,
He bounded like the wind;
Wi silver he was shod before,
Wi burning gowd behind.

And four and twenty siller bells
War tied til his mane;
Wi ae blast o the norland wind
They tinkled ane by ane.

And whan she cam unto the place,
And lichted on the green,
Ilka ane that did her see
Thought that she was a queen.

"Is this your bride, Sweet Willie?" she said,
"I think she's wondrous wan;
Ye micht have had as fair a bride
As ere the sun sheend on."

"O haud you tongue, Fair Annie," he said,
"Wi your talk let me abee;
For better I loe your little finger
Than the brown bride's haill bodie."

Then out and spak the nut-brown bride,
And she spak out of spite:
"O whare gat ye the water, Annie;
That washd your face sae white?"

"O I gat een the water," quo she,
"Whare ye will neer get nane;
It's I gat een the water," quo she,
"Aneath yon marble stane."

Then out and spak the nut-brown bride,
And she spak yet again;
"O whare gat ye the claith, Annie,
That dried your face sae clean?"

"O I gat een the claith," quo she,
"Whare ye will neer get nane;
It's I gat een the claith," quo she,
"Aneath yon bouer o bane."

The brown bride had a little penknife,
Which she kept secret there;
She stabbd Fair Annie to the heart,
A deep wound and a sair.

It's out and spak he Sweet Willie,
And he spak yet again:

"O what's the matter wi thee, Annie,
That ye do look sae wan?"

"Oh are ye blind, Willie?" she said,
"Or do ye no weel see?
I think ye micht see my heart's blude,
Come rinning by my knee."

Then Willie took a little sword,
Which he kept secret there,
And strak the brown bride to the heart,
A word she neer spak mair.

And after that a' this was dune,
He drew it through the strae,
And through his ain fair bodie
He causd the cauld iron gae.

The last words that Sweet Willie spak,
His heart was almaist gane;
"May never a young man like me
Have sic a sad wedding.

"For gear will come, and gear will gang,
And gear's ae but a lend,
And monie a ane for warld's gear
A silly brown bride brings hame."

Sweet Willie was buried in Mary's kirk,
And Annie in Mary's quire,
And out o the ane there grew a birk,
And out o the ither a briar.

And ae they grew, and ae they threw,
Until the twa did meet,
That ilka ane micht plainly see
They were true lovers sweet.

(C.73.B)[5]

For an audience or a singer immersed in the ballads, many of these
stanzas recall other ballads. The repeated "Come riddle us, riddle us,"
resembles both *Riddles Wisely Expounded* (C.1) and *The Elfin Knight*

(C.2).[6] The outlyer's questions in *Babylon*, which test the heroine, are like *Lord Thomas and Fair Annet*, where the power and danger of language begin the ballad ("But Willie spak a word amiss, / Fair Annie took it ill" [c.73.B]).

But the difficulties of courtship represented by the initial quarrel are rapidly shown to have a material basis. Fair Annet, or Annie, has no tocher, or dowry, while her competitor, the brown bride, has houses and land, gold and gear, horses and cows. Consequently, the riddle Lord Thomas, or Willie, puts to his relations is no riddle at all. His father and mother advise him to marry the brown bride, but his sister tells him to bring the fair woman home, for the brown bride's horses and cows may die. Nonetheless, Lord Thomas, tells Fair Annet that he will marry the brown bride.

With Lord Thomas and Fair Annet, we have more than a simple representation of the heroine; we have competing systems of values. While Annet and the brown bride draw on the old, transhistorical polarities of wealth and poverty, and beauty and repulsion, something more complex is being played out in their confrontation. The obvious reading would be that Annet is impoverished but noble, and the brown bride rich but common. In that case, the ballad mourns the passing of old, titled families, who would seem to have a real claim to innate superiority. Annet is acknowledged by all who see her as a queen, by her complexion and bearing, as well as by her old trappings. But under closer scrutiny a very different sensibility, more in keeping with the 1790s, emerges. The brown bride has land, houses, and beasts, and these are the dowry of a great heiress. That she holds it irrespective of her personal worth is typical of the workings of noble inheritance, and opens the door to criticisms of a social order where the gulf between her property and power and her personal qualifications is so great. Annet, on the other hand, has only labor to command, as her hair is dressed and her horse shod with silver. While we might be tempted to read these as the trappings of gentility, specifically the loyalty of old family retainers, what Annet really has, when dressed and mounted, is herself. What little wealth she has is congruent with her character, while the brown bride is doomed to the incongruence of ugliness masked by wealth. When they face each other, the brown bride is cowed by Annet's presence, and by her face, not by the sudden display of gold in Annet's hair, or on her horse.

In the A text they have a short encounter, in which Annet makes clear that her complexion is the result of her parentage, not the use of cosmetics, much as she did at greater length in the B text. In the B text, Annie answered the brown bride's questions about her washing water and the "claith" that dried her face by telling the brown bride that they came from, respectively, "aneath yon marble stane" and "aneath yon bouer o bane." Both the marble stone and the bower of bones refer to graves, presumably those of her parents, and the brown bride, whose money might have bought her rosewater and towels, but cannot buy her new parents, promptly kills Annie/Annet in both texts.

> Up then spak the nut-browne bride,
> She spak wi meikle spite:
> "And whair gat ye that rose-water,
> That does mak yee sae white?"
>
> "O I did get the rose-water
> Whair ye wull neir get nane,
> For I did get that very rose-water
> Into my mither's wame."
>
> The bride she drew a long bodkin
> Frae out her gay head-gear,
> And strake Fair Annet unto the heart,
> That word spak nevir mair.
>   (C.73.A.23–25).

The bitterness of the bride's comment, as well as Annet's reference to her mother's womb as the source of her beauty, coupled with the bride's almost immediate reliance on "a long bodkin" with which to kill Annet, suggests that she could not avoid recognizing the power of this unanswerable insult to her color, cows, land, gold, and gear. If Annet's powerful presence still signified aristocratic birth to some singers and listeners, it was soon to be the property of the bourgeoisie, made manifest in a long line of novel heroines with virtue radiating from scrubbed faces. By the 1790s Annet's pale face and worthy manner might mark the face of any decent woman, as well as a queen.[7]

Annet is at once an aristocratic heroine, self-possessed and seductive when she appears at the wedding, a penniless Romantic heroine, driven by her desire, and a proper bourgeoise, bleeding quietly and saying little. It is Lord Thomas and his bride, with knife and sword

quickly drawn, who display aristocratic tempers. What is most striking
about Annet is precisely the difficulty of sorting out her multiple bourgeois and aristocratic aspects, and confronting the degree to which her
shining natural presence has been built out of the trappings of
queenship. Insofar as the ballad heroine could be used to debate problems of class as well as gender, it is easy to see that she would interest
both men and women, as singers and audience.

Desire and marriage contracts often ran at cross-purposes in the ballads, with the heroine coming down firmly on the side of desire. In *The
Earl of Errol* a tocher, or dowry, was disputed when the bride claimed
that her husband could not consummate the marriage.[8]

> Up spake my lord Carnegie [father];
> "Kate, is your toucher won?"
> "Ye may ask the Earl of Errol [husband],
> If he be your good-son.
>
> "What need I wash my petticoat
> And hing it on a pin?
> For I am as leal a maid yet
> As yestreen when I lay down."
>   (C.231.A.10–11)[9]

Even though the Earl of Errol fathers a son on a servant, so he can
claim the tocher, the definition of "sufficient man" remains in Kate
Carnegie's power.

> I'll swear before a justice-court
> That he's no a sufficient man.
>   (C.231.A.14)

The ballad ends with the Earl's defensive and angry last words:

> "You may take hame your daughter Kate,
> And set her on the glen;
> For Errol canna please her,
> Nor nane o Errol's men;
> For Errol canna please her,
> Nor twenty of his men."
>   (C.231.A.25)

But there are happy marriages, significantly coming only when the heroine has her way, and marries a man who appears to be poor. In *Willie o' the Winsbury* (C.100) the young man turns out to be a Scots noble; in *The Kitchie Boy* (C.252) they exchange tokens, and he returns when he has made his fortune; and in *Richie Story*, she marries her farm servant, or footman, remarking,

> "O what neads I be sad, sister,
> An how can I be sorry?
> A bonny lad is my delit,
> And my lot has been laid afore me."
> (C.232.B.9)[10]

The ballad heroine uses desire to find value in men who appear ordinary, which must have been something of a radical proposition. It differs greatly from the self-control urged on daughters by Dr. Gregory, author of *A Father's Legacy to His Daughters*, as a means of protecting them from seduction by "men of the first rank." Instead, the ballad heroine chose for herself, with a self-possession that reeked of precisely that superiority that a concerned and politically progressive father like Dr. Gregory detested.[11]

But the ballads are more often brutal, and the road to marriage, or sexual pleasure, is often blocked by violence. The ballad heroine must be wary, and even in her own house she faces danger, as do her chosen men. Male relatives will kill her lover in *Earl Brand* (C.7), *Erlinton* (C.8), *Rare Willie Drowned in Yarrow* (C.215), *The Three Ravens* (C.26), and *Clerk Saunders* (C.69), as well as others. Her husband will kill her lover in *Old Robin of Portingale* (C.80), *Little Musgrave and Lady Barnard* (C.81), and *Child Maurice* (C.83). And these are not much different from ballads in which the woman finds herself married to the wrong man and desperately hoping that her lover will come for her, such as *Lord Saltoun and Auchanachie* (C.239), and *Bonny Baby Livingston* (C.222). Brothers stop weddings by killing their sisters in *The Cruel Brother* (C.11), *Sheath and Knife* (C.16), and *Lady Maisry* (C.65). The motive in two of these songs is incest, and the brother may, as in *Sheath and Knife*, kill his sister because she is pregnant, or he may kill her to stop her from marrying.[12] The ballad heroine rarely kills the male protagonist, but in *Clerk Colvill* (C.42) she does away with an admirer by means of a curse, in *Babylon* (C.14) she reveals his crimes

and he commits suicide, and if she is the poisoner in *Lord Randal*
(C.12) she uses newts. The ballad heroine can kill, and the brown bride
cannot be ignored, for she too can kill.

The heroine's constant companion is premarital pregnancy. If she is
married to another, as in *Lord Ingram and Chiel Wyet* (C.66), Lord
Ingram discovers that his bride is already pregnant. In *Lady Maisry*
(C.65) her family burns her for being pregnant, and in *Fair Janet*
(C.64) she dies giving birth to Willie's son while she is being married
to an old French lord. But in *Child Waters*, part of one text of which is
given below, the heroine refuses to be separated from the father of her
child.

> Lord John stood in his stable-door,
> Said he was bound to ride;
> Burd Ellen stood in her bowr-door,
> Said she'd rin by his side.
>
> He' pitten on his cork-heeld shoone,
> An fast awa rade he;
> She's clade hersel in page array,
> An after him ran she.
>
> Till they came till a wan water,
> An folks do ca it Clyde;
> Then he's lookit oer his left shoulder,
> Says, Lady, can ye wide?
>
> "O I learnt it i my father house,
> An I learnt it for my weal,
> Wenneer I came to a wan water,
> To swim like ony eel."
>
> But the firstin stap the lady stappit,
> The water came til her knee;
> "Ohon, alas!" said the lady,
> "This water's oer deep for me."
>
> . . . .
>
> The nextin stap the lady stappit,
> The water came till her pap;

An the bairn that was in her twa sides
For caul begane to quake.

"Lye still, lye still, my ain dear babe,
Ye work your mither wae;
Your father rides on high horse-back,
Cares little for us twae."

O about the midst o Clyden water
There was a yeard-fast stane;
He lightly turnd his horse about,
An took her on him behin.

"O tell me this now, good Lord John,
An a word ye dinna lee,
How far it is to your lodgin,
Whare we this night maun be?"

"O see you nae yon castle, Ellen,
That shines sae fair to see?
There is a lady in it, Ellen,
Will sunder you an me.

"There is a lady in that castle
Will sunder you and I":
"Betide me well, betide me wae,
I sal go there an try."

"O my dogs sal eat the good white bread,
An ye sal eat the bran;
Then will ye sigh, an say, alas!
That ever I was a man."

"O I sal eat the good white bread,
An your dogs sal eat the bran;
An I hope to live an bless the day,
That ever ye was a man."

   . . . .

O four an twenty gay ladies
Welcomd Lord John to the ha,

But a fairer lady than them a'
Led his horse to the stable sta'.

   · · · · · · · · ·

Whan bells were rung, and mass was sung,
An a' men boun to meat,
Burd Ellen at a bye-table
Amo the foot-men was set.

"O eat an drink, my bonny boy,
The white bread an the beer":
"The never a bit can I eat or drink,
My heart's sae full of fear."

   · · · · · · · ·

But out it spake Lord John's mother,
An a wise woman was she:
"Whare met ye wi that bonny boy,
That looks sae sad on thee?

"Sometimes his cheek is rosy red,
As sometimes deadly wan;
He's liker a woman big wi bairn,
Than a young lord's serving man."

   · · · · · · · · ·

"Rise up, rise up, my bonny boy,
Gi my horse corn an hay":
"O that I will, my master dear,
As quickly as I may."

She's taen the hay under her arm,
The corn intill her han,
An she's gane to the great stable,
As fast as eer she can.

"O room ye roun, my bonny broun steeds,
O room ye near the wa;
For the pain that strikes me thro my sides
Full soon will gar me fa."

She's leand her back against the wa;
Strong travail seizd her on;

An even amo the great horse feet
Burd Ellen brought forth her son.

Lord John's mither intill her bowr
Was sitting all alone,
Whan, i the silence o the night,
She heard fair Ellen's moan.

"Won up, won up, my son," she says,
"Go se how a' does fare;
For I think I hear a woman's groans,
An a bairn greeting sair."

O hastily he gat him up,
Stayd neither for hose nor shoone,
An he's doen him to the stable-door,
Wi the clear light o the moon.

He strack the door hard wi his foot,
An sae has he wi his knee,
An iron locks and iron bars
Into the floor flung he:
"Be not afraid, Burd Ellen," he says,
"Ther's nane come in but me."

Up he has taen his bonny young son,
An gard wash him wi the milk;
An up has he taen his fair lady,
Gard row her in the silk.

"Cheer up your heart, Burd Ellen," he says,
"Look nae mair sad nor wae;
For your marriage and your kirkin too
Sal baith be in ae day."

                                    (C.63.B)

As it stands, the ballad is a test, like the "outlyer's" questions in *Babylon*. But this test is physical, and like Eppie Morrie, Burd Ellen must do something, in this case master both the journey and childbirth, while disguised. Disguise may have reflected the efforts of many women to hide pregnancies, and the journey exaggerated the effort required, quite literally, to keep up while pregnant. Or disguise may simply have represented toughness, just as Fair Annet dressed to represent her superiority, and then rode hard. Physically exhausted and notably wan, Ellen is rewarded, just at that moment when other women, alone, might have chosen infanticide. Lord John breaks down the door, which Burd Ellen must have locked from inside, and claims both his son and Ellen. Once she proves a stubborn and serious companion, and a mother, he becomes a willing mate. Yet most fathers of illegitimate children did not, and could not, behave to this standard, as many Scots knew.[13]

Mary Hamilton, the Infanticide Ballad

At twenty-nine versions, *Mary Hamilton* (C.173) stands as the most popular ballad in all of Child's collection, and in it Mary Hamilton finds herself pregnant, kills her illegitimate child, is discovered, tried, and condemned to hang. Like Fair Annet, she is alone, and like Annet again, she chooses to make her stand in public. Mary Hamilton was the quintessential ballad heroine, worthy kin to the third sister in Babylon, Eppie Morrie, Fair Annet, and Burd Ellen. She could speak, she could ride like a queen down Edinburgh's Canongate, she could face death with equanimity, and in her ballad she shares center stage with no one.[14] Early ballad collectors presented this ballad to their audiences without echoing the contemporary problem of infanticide, by pointing a finger at earlier court society and locating illicit sexuality, disorderly women, and infanticide securely in that limited quarter. Walter Scott, despite exaggerated Tory sympathies, cited John Knox's descriptions of the shameful behavior of women at Mary Stuart's court, and concluded with Knox's ringing condemnation, "but yet was not the court purged of whores and whoredom, which was the fountain of such enormities."[15] Scotsmen were for the most part extremely conservative, and it is instructive that Scott could so unself-consciously locate this sort of evil in a royal court.

But *Mary Hamilton* was not a plausible evocation of "the times of Mary Stuart," for the ballad shows off a domesticated court, where a queen imposes moral standards on her dependents, who were Presbyterian in the sixteenth century and bourgeois in the nineteenth. This moral voice is particularly clear in Kinloch's version of the ballad, where Mary Hamilton speaks impersonally about herself, in the third person, as if she had learned the language of a new world.

> "Sae, weep na mair for me, ladies,
> Weep na mair for me;
> The mither that kills her ain bairn
> Deserves weel for to dee."
>
> (C.173.H.22)

Only in this version of *Mary Hamilton* does she say she deserves to die. In the Old Lady of Annandale's version, Mary Hamilton says, "For had I not slain mine own sweet babe, / This death I wadna dee." In a version collected by Motherwell from an unidentified singer, Mary Hamilton says, "It's all for the sake of my puir babe, / This death that I maun die." In Mrs. Crum's version, Mary Hamilton says, "For it's all for the sake of my innocent babe / That I come here to die." In these, Mary Hamilton accepts that she will die, but not that she deserves to die. In Kinloch's text, the emphasis on her just deserts has displaced those phrases common to that stanza: poor babe, sweet babe, innocent babe. These words make it clear that Mary Hamilton did not want to kill the child; without them, in Kinloch's version, Mary Hamilton becomes a simple murderer, without any suggestion that she felt forced to act in spite of her sympathy with the child.[16]

But the editors and collectors, earnestly looking for the court, and the queen, and Mary, missed the point. The rural men and women who sang the ballads were not parrots, existing to hand on traditional lore to Walter Scott, all the while with Scott complaining of a text of *Mary Hamilton* "that the tale has suffered great alterations, as handed down by tradition." He was irritated that they hadn't got their facts right, that they had strayed from Knox's tale.[17] But of course they had, because they had never been telling Knox's tale. The court shrank to a household, and a female one at that, because that was what the Old Lady in Annandale, or Mrs. Crum of Dumbarton, Nancy Hamilton, Mrs. Gentles, Jean Macqueen, or Mrs. Trail understood to be the interior of anyone's house, castle or not. The site of the murder moves from the dramatic "And she's thrown it in the sea" (C.173.A.a.3) to the usual, sad, poor, domestic:

> They sought it out, they sought it in,
> They sought it but and ben,
> But between the bolster and the bed
> They got the baby slain.
>
> > (C.173.E.9)

But and *ben* refer to the two rooms of the typical tenant farmer's cottage. To hide the child's body in the only space a servant might control, her bed, was also typical of the behavior of young female agricultural servants cited in court records.[18]

But the collectors were not fools to ponder, albeit too literally, the court and the queen. The royal trappings of *Mary Hamilton* meant something to the villagers who sang the song. No doubt they knew of Mary Stuart, or a local laird's daughter; or perhaps Queen Caroline. But the queen in *Mary Hamilton* is merely a respectable older woman exercising a moral rather than political authority with some grace. She speaks as any bourgeoise or tenant wife might, asking for the child she heard cry, and then telling Mary Hamilton to prepare to ride into Edinburgh, or in some instances, Glasgow. It is only for Mary Hamilton that the full weight of noble presence is twice invoked in the ballad.

In the first instance, the nobility invoked for Mary Hamilton is that of the fairy queen, and of Fair Annet. And it is invoked by the formulaic language of two stanzas in which the queen commands Mary Hamilton to dress for a journey to Edinburgh, to Glasgow, or to see a wedding. In the singing of Nancy Hamilton and Mrs. Gentles, the wedding is ironically to be Mary Hamilton's own.

> "Busk ye, busk ye, Marie Hamilton,
> O busk ye to be a bride!
> For I am going to Edinburgh toun,
> Your gay wedding to bide.
>
> "You must not put on your robes of black,
> Nor yet your robes of brown;
> But you must put on your yellow gold stuffs,
> To shine thro Edinburgh town."
>
> > (C.173.D.11,12)

In the singing of the Old Lady of Annandale, the wedding has disappeared, but Edinburgh remains:

> "O Marie, put on your robes o black,
> Or else your robes o brown,
> For ye maun gang wi me the night,
> To see fair Edinbro town."
>
> "I winna put on my robes o black,
> Nor yet my robes o brown;
> But I'll put on my robes o white,
> To shine through Edinbro town."
>
> (C.173.A.c.6,7)

A good listener within Scots oral culture, or a familiar reader of ballads, would follow this reference to other processions, specifically those in the ballads *Tam Lin* (C.39) and *Lord Thomas and Fair Annet*. Child did note the connection with *Lord Thomas and Fair Annet*, but only as a repetition of lines, not as a contribution to how meaning is created in *Mary Hamilton*. Yet within a living oral culture, meaning must have come not only from the narrative established in a particular ballad, but also from the network of formulaic phrases within the ballads. Sometimes these references must have been accidental, but a good oral composer-singer could have used such resonances in creating meaning that ranged within and between ballad texts.

In *Tam Lin* the ballad heroine finds that Tam Lin, the father of her child, has been stolen by the fairy queen. But on Halloween, when the "Queen o[f] Fairies" leads her people in procession, she may steal him back, if she can recognize him.

> "But how shall I thee ken, Tam Lin,
> Or how my true-love know,
> Amang sae mony unco knights
> The like I never saw?"
>
> "O first let pass the black, lady,
> And syne let pass the brown,
> But quickly run to the milk-white steed,
> Pu ye his rider down.
>
> "For I'll ride on the milk-white steed,
> And ay nearest the town;

> Because I was an earthly knight
> They gie me that renown."
>   (C.39.A.27–29)

What has been borrowed for Mary Hamilton is not the identity of the heroine Janet in *Tam Lin*, but the reference back to a magical world, and to those who ride with the Fairy Queen; this will resonate behind the subsequent description of Mary Hamilton riding up the Canongate with what might otherwise be taken as mere bravado.

> "I'll no put on my robes o black,
> No nor yet my robes [o] brown;
> But I'll put on my golden weed,
> To shine thro Edinburgh town."
>   (C.173.C.9; 1825, Mrs. Crum)

Mary Hamilton's abbreviated ride is a short version of Annet's journey in *Lord Thomas and Fair Annet*. Determined to go to what should have been her wedding, the tocherless Fair Annet orders smiths and tailors and ladies-in-waiting, dresses in scarlet and mounts a horse shod with silver and gold, and everyone who sees her mistakes her for a queen. This is not wealth hidden from Lord Thomas to test his love, but Fair Annet possessed of a splendor that is no longer material.

> "I'll na put on the grisly black,
> Nor yet the dowie green,
> But I'll put on a scarlet robe
> To sheen like onie queen."
>   (C.73.B.20)

Fair Annet and Mary Hamilton both ride, fearlessly well dressed, for the public gaze. Both die. But Mary Hamilton was not created as a heroine by villagers as a means of embodying, or preserving, an older world, but so that she will have the power to speak. It is hard to imagine a young woman of the tenant, cottager, or day-laborer classes sufficiently self-possessed to speak as well in public, after a trial, and it is Mary Hamilton's task to speak after being condemned, and to begin by addressing an audience of other women who have been reduced to tears by her plight, as she was.

When she gaed up the Cannogate,
She laughd loud laughters three;
But whan she cam down the Cannogate
The tear blinded her ee.

When she gaed up the Parliament stair,
The heel cam aff her shee;
And lang or she cam down again
She was condemned to dee.

When she cam down the Cannogate,
The Cannogate sae free,
Many a ladie lookd oer her window,
Weeping for this ladie.

"Ye need nae weep for me," she says,
"Ye need nae weep for me;
For had I not slain mine own sweet babe,
This death I wadna dee.

(C.173.A.c.13–16)

The presence of mind required for a gallows speech is something we more easily associate with lords on a losing side, highwaymen, and religious martyrs, as in the hangings of Isabel Alison and Marion Harvey in 1681. Both were Cameronians of "humble life," in their twenties. On the scaffold in Edinburgh with five women condemned for child murder, these two Protestant martyrs had no trouble speaking out, as they had throughout their trials. One called the king "a perjured bloody man," and both sang the Twenty-third Psalm loudly enough to drown the "curate's" voice. Harvey sang the Eighty-fourth Psalm from the scaffold, read the third chapter of Malachi, and then addressed the crowd. Her address ended only when the Provost told the hangman to "cast her over." Alison repeated the performance. Not one of the five women condemned for infanticide seems to have spoken, although the minister assured them they were far more likely to be saved than the "fanatic Covenanters."[19]

The Cameronian women could no doubt speak more easily because they were part of a community, and one that valued speaking, and provided models with every sermon. Young women condemned for child murder were likely to feel themselves outcasts; besides, they had prob-

The Canongate, part of the ancient main street of early modern Edinburgh, down which Mary Hamilton rides in her ballad.

ably been committed to denying their pregnancies and were not in a position to speak with authority. That is Mary Hamilton's task. The great opening stanza, like the first line of Genesis, makes it clear that some words are powerful, not intellectually, but because material consequences follow.

> Word's gane to the kitchen,
> And word's gane to the ha,
> That Marie Hamilton gangs wi bairn
> To the hichest Stewart of a'.
>
> (C.173.A.c.2)

At first, Mary Hamilton must work against that word, denying that there is a child. The Old Lady in Annandale sang, "There was noe babe untill my room"; Nancy Hamilton and Mrs. Gentles sang, "O hold your tongue, Queen Mary, my dame, / Let all those words go free!" Mrs. Crum sang " 'O hold your tongue now, Queen,' she says, / 'O hold your tongue so free!' " Having refused to acknowledge the child, she then refuses the queen's instruction to dress in dark or unlucky colors, choosing white, gold, or, rarely, scarlet. Mary Hamilton fights the word for possession of herself, and unlike Fair Annet, whose clothing constituted a revelation, Mary Hamilton initially struggles to conceal her recent pregnancy, partially by means of cutting that same impressive figure as she rides.[20]

> But Marie mounted her milk-white steed,
> And rode foremost thro the town.
>
> (C.173.A.c.12)

Mary Hamilton's ride ends not with a wedding, but with a trial before the High Court that brings her to tears.

> But when she cam down the Cannogate
> The tear blinded her ee.
>
> (C.173.A.c.13)

And the trial allows her to return to speaking bluntly, as she had when alone with the infant, in the Old Lady of Annandale's text.

> "O sink ye, swim ye, bonny wee babe
> You'll neer get mair o me.
>
> (C.173.A.c.4)

But the trial slips between the interstices of the heroine's procession as she rides from the old Parliament building to the Tolbooth, Parliament Close, the Canongate, and the Netherbow Port, and the focus is on the heroine, the public procession, and her last speech.[21]

Ignoring real time, the procession brings her almost directly to the gallows, with weeping companions in the street, and references in the three A texts to women watching from windows. With an audience, the end of the ballad becomes Mary Hamilton's gallows speech, direct, stylized by toasting, built around her demand for a bottle of wine, or a cup.[22]

> "Ye need nae weep for me," she says,
> "Ye nee nae weep for me;
> For had I not slain my own sweet babe,
> This death I wadna dee.
>
> "Bring me a bottle of wine," she says,
> "The best that eer ye hae,
> That I may drink to my weil-wishers,
> And they may drink to me.
>
> "Yestreen the queen had four Maries,
> The nicht she'll hae but three;
> There was Marie Seton, and Marie Beaton,
> And Marie Carmichael, and me."
>
> (C.173.A.c.16–18)

Moving from the royal court to the juridical court to the open streets of the city, she can confess, and she can be reconciled with her community, calling for wine, recognizing her "weel-wishers" in a network that spreads beyond the "four Maries" and "upon the sea" to include her parents.

This frank speech and reconciliation must have been rare for most women accused of infanticide. Only a very small number of women confessed; the rest had to live, or die, with whatever truth they admitted to themselves. By the time the Old Lady of Annandale recited her

Condemned Covenanters in the West Bow, duplicating the path taken by convicted criminals in Edinburgh, from the Tolbooth to the gallows in the Grassmarket.

version in the early years of the nineteenth century, the crime had become a misdemeanor, and thus necessarily something with which one lived.[23] And it is precisely the decline in indictments under the old statute of 1690, and the meager punishments meted out under the new statute of 1809, that fueled the ballad's popularity. Given that the ballad did not appear in collections before 1790, and seems to belong to the five decades spanning the period from 1790 to 1840, it is arguable that the ballad appeared exactly as capital punishment declined, and misdemeanor prosecutions rose. Also on the rise was the popularity of a song about confession and, let us emphasize, capital punishment. In the ballad, singers took seriously the full tragic dimensions of infanticide, and while the new law of 1809 saved women's lives, it did so at the cost of dismissing their actions and their children's lives as inconsequential. The law was powerfully cosmetic, and collectors were quick to label the ballad as a very old and quite singular story (C.III.394–95).

But the ballad allowed singers to create a heroine who confronts her own death, and through that, the death of her child. Like the suicide note, itself a new object of interest in the eighteenth century, the ballad set the record straight, showing a murdered child and a young woman, pregnant and far from her parents, facing death.[24] Almost all versions, both long and fragmentary, retain the invocation of one or both parents. The stanza below, from 1876, is virtually the same as one by Burns in 1790:

> "Oh little did my mither think,
> The day she cradled me,
> What road I'd hae to travel in,
> Or what death I'd hae to dee!"
> (C.173.N; Burns C.173.R)

At this distance, we can only speculate as to why, over perhaps a hundred years, women in Dumbarton, Paisley, Largs, Annandale, Old Deer, and the "north country" recited the ballad of this particular woman, who faces the task of taking leave of the world she knows with all the accumulated grace and wisdom of the ballad heroine. Infanticide was not all that common, but perhaps the experience of leaving home and facing unknown trials was. To face those unknown hardships with equanimity was no doubt a valued skill in the early decades of the nineteenth century, and the ballad heroine offered a tough, honorable, sexual, and utterly secular model of what a woman could be.

3

Reconstructing Rural Infanticide

There was an old woman who lived in a shoe,
She had so many children she didn't know what to do.
So she gave them some broth without any bread,
And beat them all soundly and put them to bed.[1]
                                        —Mother Goose

Hardship was probably synonymous with life for a great many European villagers for many centuries, but in the seventeenth and the eighteenth centuries, in one region after another, life took a particularly difficult turn. Improvements in agricultural production coincided with population growth, and we will never know how many newborn infants in early modern Europe were suffocated, strangled, burned, stabbed, abandoned, or otherwise murdered by their mothers. Infanticide is older than the early modern European world, of course, as the figure of Medea in Greek drama, and the works of early Christian moralists remind us. But in early modern Europe, statutes tailored to the quick and unforgiving prosecution of unmarried women for this crime appeared in 1624 in England and in 1690 in Scotland, and during the seventeenth and eighteenth centuries hundreds of single women in

Scotland and England were prosecuted for this capital crime.[2] With infanticide thus linked to illegitimacy, which plagued eighteenth-century Europe, we cannot fail to acknowledge that we are confronting, through court records, a problem that caught up a great many ordinary Medeas, and was in some respects beyond their control.[3]

That problem, apparently, was marriage. What we know about European rural households from the late Middle Ages on suggests that marriage, perhaps for many more accurately described as household formation, was a complicated process, in which village customs, the kirk, landlords, and innumerable relatives and friends played a part, and in which many things could go wrong. Because the household was still the site of production, marriage was an economic as well as personal institution, and couples' business was literally the business of the community. Children were equally subject to economic necessity, and high infant mortality among married couples no doubt included some victims of infanticide. Nor could the conception of a child by a courting couple force a marriage at an inauspicious moment, and illegitimate children were sometimes common enough in England and Scotland. They were often fitted into rural communities, where their presence may well indicate temporary crises that led to the suspension of marriage plans, but not the complete disruption of local life.

But the infanticide we are dealing with in Scotland between 1661 and 1821 was, like its English counterpart, of a new sort. No longer the discreet custom of hard-pressed married parents, or the by-product of what Scots termed notorious adultery, this new infanticide became increasingly visible. The murders were carried out by young, single women, sometimes abetted by their mothers, and occasionally by the fathers of the children. The small bodies hurriedly buried or hidden in bedclothes indicated a new despair, unlike the earlier and continuing efforts of families, villages, wet nurses, and orphanages to absorb, or discreetly eliminate illegitmate or unwanted children.[4] The exact sources of that despair are harder to locate, because the economic underpinnings of a community rarely appear in court cases to explain why a couple, a mother and daughter, or a particular woman acted in lonely desperation. But one conclusion is that they saw themselves as separate, as individuals within a community that could punish, but could not help them. This, of course, flies in the face of the old historical presumption that they were so bound to their communities by shame that they were effectively forced to kill the children. But that was a nonsensical use of shame, and religious compulsion, for any community with so great a hold over its members would surely have bound them to higher moral standards, such as abstinence, or raising the child. Self-preservation at any cost comes to communities that are falling apart, not tightly bound.

Indications of the economic forces that might explain why some villagers could not easily marry, and why they killed their children, remain.[5] In a Scotland largely worked by tenant farmers and their subtenants at the beginning of the eighteenth century, dependence, favor, and access to land mattered a great deal to those setting up a new household. The dominance of landlords and favored tenants still mattered, and mattered so much that those women who acted on their own were either utterly desperate, or had gotten a heady glimpse of themselves as individuals. Most of these women, as well as their families, were affected by three great, and for the poorest villagers, humbling and infuriating changes in the eighteenth century. The agricultural revolution sparked land hunger among those with capital; population growth fed on increased agricultural production; and a newly visible cultural interest in sex, which was hardly a new interest to anyone, tied sex to romance, seduction, free choice, and ultimately, freedom.[6]

That population growth brought with it more illegitimate children, over much of Europe. And even though Scots figures show what appear to be older, regional, and somewhat more sporadic outbursts of illegitimate births, the two great explanations of European illegitimacy that have emerged bear on our ability to understand why illegitimate infants should have been murdered in Scotland. One focuses on a new sexual individualism, showing people disinterested in marriage, while the other describes illegitimacy, and, implicitly, infanticide, as the result of failed courtships among people eager to marry, and driven by economic necessity.[7] Despite debates between the proponents of both explanations, the two arguments were not mutually exclusive. Tenants who harbored hopes of sexual satisfaction might also hope for economic success, especially in a world where courtship and marriage had been the traditional road to both sorts of adulthood, sexual and economic. Consequently the new infanticide of the late early modern period should be seen as the result of a complex matrix of forces, including sexual adventuring, threatening economic pressure, and a hope of modest success in the rural economy. Given the nature of Scots rural economic enterprise in the eighteenth century, with its opportunities for the best tenants and eviction for many, including the worst, and the ideological currents of individual sentiment and even revolution, it would seem unwise to exclude either desire or despair from the minds of eighteenth-century Scots women and men.[8]

It would also be unwise to exclude faith, and the still-rigorous doctrines of the Kirk. Even so, illegitimacy and infanticide, together with the struggles of church and state to define and control clandestine marriage, tell us that the old paths to marriage and productive adulthood were becoming overgrown, and the old structures of village authority were decaying. The Kirk, that once-powerful church founded by John Knox, was losing its struggle to control marriage and sexual behavior in the eighteenth century, and the Kirk was losing control that parents had already lost, or never had.[9]

The overwhelming majority of Scots women prosecuted for infanticide between 1661 and 1798, or investigated for concealment of pregnancy between 1809 and 1821 were unmarried and acting alone.[10] They acted alone because the path to marriage eluded them, if they were hoping for that, and even the paths to simple help and consolation seemed closed to them. If some women thought of themselves as free spirits breaking with convention, for the sake of love, or pleasure, or marriage, it is certainly easier to see most of them as women trying to cross bridges that gave way beneath their feet. Between 1661 and 1821, at least 347 women were investigated on complaints of infanticide or, as the crime was known after 1809, concealment of pregnancy.[11]

Most of these women were villagers. Some 86 were either the daughters of tenants or servants to tenants; 11 were wives or widows on tenant farms; and another 35 were agricultural servants to big farmers, mains tenants, or the gentry.[12] Compared with these 132 women who worked on the land, there were 25 domestic servants, most of them serving in working urban households, not big houses, and 24 daughters in urban working households. The last and most anomalous group includes 23 women listed as indweller or residenter, which is a vague category, comprehending people who were masterless without being independent, but compared with the 3 women who were simply wandering through the countryside when caught, they had addresses, and probably some means of supporting themselves.[13]

The numbers tell a very small part of the story, but they force us to recognize that in counties with repeated prosecutions, such as Aberdeen, Dumfries, Fife, Edinburgh, Lanark, Perth, and Stirling, there would have been stories circulating among every generation in the eighteenth century. But one case that was well recorded and well prosecuted can open a door for us into eighteenth-century rural society and legal thought. The story that follows, Agnes Walker's, allows us to examine the workings of village society in 1762 and to evaluate a verdict that became an important legal precedent in 1798, when two cases were appealed and the statute's power was broken.

On the eleventh of May, 1762, Mr. George Heron, minister of the gospel in the parish of Terregles, "was coming home from his Workers in the Evening." On his way, he noticed a dog at the side of the highway eating part of "a Carcase," as he first put it. As he drew nearer to investigate, "he perceived it was a Child that had been laid there in a hole which was at the root of the Dyke and seemed not to be much larger than the Seat of a Hare." The dyke enclosed part of a tenant farm, Halmyre, and the farmhouse nearby. Without touching the child, Mr. Heron sent for three people, including his servant, the town beadle, and a midwife, and left any actual examination to them. He then left the scene, hurrying to inform the magistrate, Mr. Dalyell, magistrate of Kirkcudbright.[14]

John Sloan, the beadle, described his first sight of the child primarily in terms of the hole it had been in, and the amount of dirt that had been scattered over it, which "could have been contained in a Bonnet or the Crown of a hatt." He went so far as to admit that he had touched "it," but when asked how long he thought the infant had been buried, answered that "he imagines it could not be very long in regard the Weeds that had been thrown upon it appeared to be still green." Mr. Heron had not looked closely at the child that evening, either, for all he could recall was color: "as much of the Skin as was unsullied by the Earth appeared fresh-coloured, but when he saw it next day it was all discoloured."

While he was calling on Mr. Dalyell, Marion Jardine, the midwife, joined Sloan and Smith by the dike, where she picked up the child's body, "wrapt it in a Cloth and Carried it into the Minister's barn." She inspected the child that night and again the next day. In contrast to the men's testimony, she described the body in detail, but ignored the site. She noted that the left leg had been torn off, that there was a scratch behind the left ear, the throat was black and blue, the right leg was disjointed at the knee, the nose flattened, and that something like blood was coming from the nose. She did not particularly remember the small hole or the loose dirt as did the men at the scene, for she thought the child had lain in the ground only a day or two, but could only refer to some loose grass "which was not withered," an indirect expression. In contrast James Smith, Mr. Heron's twenty-five-year-old servant, had said nothing about the child's body, but had been struck by "a Sort of hole beside which it was lying, which did not seem to be dig [sic] but seemed to be Scratched out by fingers at the root of a Thorn bush."

James Smith, John Sloan, and several elders of the parish sat up with the child's body for some time, when Smith and Sloan left and the elders agreed to stay until morning. In the morning, perhaps five—no one remembered exactly—young women were summoned to the barn, to be examined by four midwives under the eyes of Mr. Heron and Mr. Dalyell. This was the magistrate's idea, Mr. Heron reported, although he was reluctant to yield all credit and authority to him. Heron admitted that "he was desired" to make these arrangements, but implied that the plan was made "in Concert."

Of the midwives, Marion Jardine was eighty, a widow, and by her own words not a professional midwife, but had assisted many women in childbirth. She lived within half a mile of Halmyre. Elizabeth Paterson was fifty-one, the wife of a tenant farmer in another parish, and called herself a midwife, but noted under questioning that she had "no regular education in that way, having taken up the trade at her own hand." She had had eight children. Janet Irving was fifty, the wife of a local tenant farmer, and said she was not a midwife, but had had thirteen children. Agnes Kennedy, the fourth woman called on by Heron and Dalyell to examine the dead child and the young women, did not testify.

Meeting in Mr. Heron's barn on the morning of the twelfth, the four women first inspected the infant's body. The midwives'—for they were all certainly thought of as that by Heron, Dalyell, and, later on, members of the court—testimony agrees pretty well in facts and in language. The judgments that midwives were called on to make in these cases were based on relatively simple observations, or at least so they appear through the formulaic language of the court. The child was come to the full term, was a ripe child, for it had nails on its fingers and hair on its head. All concurred that it had been born about eight to ten days before, and had been in the ground no more than two. Marion Jardine offered as her opinion that the child had been strangled. Elizabeth Paterson's description of the child concurred with Jardine's, but she believed that the nose had been flattened by pushing the child into its hole under the bush, and the leg eaten off by the dog. She refused to make any judgment on the child's bruised throat. Janet Irving offered no judgments with her description, until she came to mention the bruised throat, which occasioned her damning comment: "That there was a bruise upon the throat of the Child, which [she] and the Women that were with her imputed to its being Strangled."

Paterson, the only woman claiming to be a midwife of the three, was most aware of the authority of her voice in giving evidence, of the burden she bore, and of the fragility of her position as authority.[15] It was late in her testimony, under questioning from the court, that she admitted to having no formal education as a midwife. She stubbornly declined to give opinions beyond the observed facts, testifying that "there was a Bruise upon the throat, but whether that was owing to violence, or had happened accidentally by the Child being thrust into a hole where it was found [she] cannot possibly say." By contrast, the willingness of Irving and Jardine to conclude for strangling, without any doubt, points to a conflict of either skill, morality, or sympathy. As the one admitted midwife, Paterson may have been more careful of her reputation, or more sympathetic.

Dalyell and Heron were in or near the barn as the suspect women were examined, as they had been for the examination of the child's body. Elizabeth Paterson, always professional, remembered examining exactly five women, "who were brought into the Barn where the Child was laid."[16] The midwives would have attempted to draw milk from the suspects' breasts, and then inspected their outer genitalia for signs of distension or discharge. Only Agnes Walker showed signs of being recently brought to childbed, for in her "breasts there was green milk, and She had all the other Symptoms of a green Woman." *Green* means freshly delivered of a child, not literally green, and is the usual language used to subsume the bitter details of these examinations, as well as present them to a public audience. Dalyell immediately took down a statement from Agnes Walker, and probably committed her to the Dumfries jail to wait for the coming of the circuit court in the fall.

Certainly Paterson bore the brunt of the lawyers' and even jurymen's demands for precise judgments during the trial that followed in Octo-

ber. She had presumably seen enough individual variation in childbirth to know that she could avoid citing precise responses of the
female body, or precise cause of death in an infant, but those were
exactly what the all-male court, unfamiliar with childbirth, wanted. In
failing to satisfy them, her own professional competence was on trial.
Jardine and Irving were far more willing to revel in their sudden elevation to the role of expert by the court, and damn the child's mother by
their testimony. They also came from Terregles, while Paterson did
not.

The ruthless efficiency of the rural community in discovering illegitimate mothers in their midst is clear, as is the willingness of older
women to provide damning evidence. The village ties that so easily
caught Agnes Walker were typical, as was the fact that those formal
ties, among neighbors and between village, church, and state authority, were invoked only by the discovery of an infant's corpse. Agnes
Walker was identified and committed for trial within twenty-four
hours of the minister's inadvertent discovery of the dead infant.
Brought to misfortune, she was probably a stranger to the village, although she had a sister and a brother living there. Rumors of her pregnancy had preceded her arrival, possibly by as much as a month. Both
the minister and his servant, James Smith, could not help noting that
the child was found near Halmyre, and, as Smith put it, within "a
penny stone throw" of the house. Everyone knew that Agnes Walker's
elder married sister, Janet Walker, lived there, and that Agnes had
been staying there. Smith was even able to detail her movements about
the parish for the two weeks that she had been in Terregles; he let slip,
perhaps with some envy, the fact that Halmyre was "a single house,"
no doubt in a parish where most lived in multiple tenancy farms, or
may have been cottagers. The parish seems to have been a baited trap
set for her arrival.

Terregles is a small parish in the south of Scotland, flat and arable,
at the convergence of the rivers Nith and Cluden; it lies just outside
the port town of Dumfries. Agnes Walker had been in Terregles just
twelve days when she was committed to the jail by Stewart Substitute
Dalyell. She was a stranger to most of the villagers there, with the
exception of her brother and sister, both of whom were raising families
on tenant farms. During the preceding winter, she had been in service
at a farm in the parish of Crossmichael, the Crofts. Most likely she
walked the fifteen miles northeast from Crossmichael to Terregles

knowing that she was about to deliver. She arrived on the doorstep of her sister on May 1, and stayed with her for about a week, coming and going between there and her brother's house a mile away. After that she moved on to work nearby at James Sloan's, and it was from Sloan's house that she was taken to the barn on the morning of May 12.

Her decision to move from Crossmichael to Terregles suggests that she intended to conceal the pregnancy as best she could, and escape the rumors flying about Crossmichael. She chose to rely on her family, but she may or may not have told them the truth. According to the testimony of her sister, brother, and sister-in-law, she denied being pregnant to each one of them, and they looked at her carefully, and believed her. But she was confronted by questions as soon as she arrived, because rumor had preceded her. Her brother, James Walker, insisted that "he Interrogated her whether She was with Child or not, many a time, but She put off his questions by a wavering way of Speaking." This was damning testimony, but he also backed down, and said that "as far as he could Image of the Pannel [Agnes] by looking at her She did not appear to him as if She had been with Child." Janet Walker, who had also heard reports of her sister's pregnancy, asked Agnes, only to hear a story of mysterious inward pains and stitches. James's wife, Mary Thomson, heard rumors of the scandal some six weeks before Agnes came to Terregles. As she put it, "She mett her about the door and asked her about the truth of this report but that the pannel denied it, and said that it was her Dame that had raised this Story. That She brought her into the house and again Strictly inquired if it was true, but that the pannel still persisted in her denial."

James and Mary reported being convinced that the defendant did not look pregnant. Mary Thomson claimed that "She put her to all manner of work like a young Girl," and that "She took all manner of Observation and Saw her several mornings upon the floor in her Shift and observed no appearances of pregnancy." Finally, Thomson said, "She appeared to be Straight and supple and that She was very unlike the Deponent who was then big with Child herself."

For twelve days in Terregles, Agnes Walker lived with constant confrontation and observation. She probably gave birth on the Monday night after her arrival on Sunday, suggesting that she timed her disappearance from Crossmichael carefully, or that her delivery was hastened by the fifteen-mile walk. In either case, observation of her in the succeeding days could not have revealed the already completed pregnancy. The most telling evidence that she persisted alone in all this is the infant's grave outside the yard dike of her sister's and brother-in-law's house. Had her sister acted as her accomplice, surely Janet would not have left the body half buried, practically on her own doorstep.

By the midwives' calculation, the child had been born around the second of May, if not earlier, but not put in the ground until the ninth, when Walker took work just down the road at Sloan's and left her sister's roof. Presumably the child had been hidden indoors for several days, and Agnes Walker hastily buried the child in a hole she scratched out with her hands, with a bush and the yard dike for cover, and then walked on to James Sloan's house to begin work. A birth and a child kept in such proximity to the house suggests her sister turned a blind eye, but felt unable to do more, until the trial began.

Why was there no help for her before the trial? She probably refused to admit that she was pregnant, and perhaps she never fully acknowledged it to herself. Many Scots women before and after her chose to give birth outdoors, out of sight, and preferably neither in one village nor another, as if they could then say, truthfully, that they had never borne a child in the village. They were engaged in a bitter struggle for survival, a struggle to maintain their identity in the community. Morality and economics must have been much the same thing in most villages, especially in Scotland, where subsistence meant living closer to the bone than in many more temperate areas of Europe. Their repeated denials of pregnancy were half that struggle: to retain the consciousness of an innocent woman. To retain the physical shape of an "unfurnished" woman was presumably impossible, but there was little that could be done about that. Preindustrial rural communities allowed the individual little privacy, but we have come to believe that the rewards of interdependence far outweighed the disadvantages for several centuries' worth of subsistence farmers, male and female. When these communities began to break down, however, their ability to enforce marriage, through gossip, ministers' visits, and fines by the kirk, broke long before their ability to know who should be shamed disappeared.[17]

The parish of Terregles lies in the Stewartry of Kirkcubright, on the southwest coast of Scotland. Most of the land is better for animals than crops, although there is good arable land in the eastern side of the county. The west became one of the earliest cash-producing areas in

Scottish agricultural history: Black cattle, with strains imported from Ireland, were raised there in increasing numbers in the seventeenth and eighteenth centuries, always for market just across the border in England. The western half of the county was crisscrossed with drove roads, some of which swung across the southeast, and into England. Terregles lies at the far eastern border of the county, on low, arable hills, near the Cluden Water, and on a main road into the major southern market and port town of Dumfries.[18] Agnes Walker ended up there, but she probably came from the parish where she was working as a farm servant, and where her father still lived, Crossmichael. She had, at least, been there for four years prior to her appearance on her sister's doorstep, as the minister from Crossmichael testified at her trial.

Crossmichael is in the center of the parish, perhaps roughly at the border between cattle land and the arable farms of the eastern side of Kirkcudbright. It makes sense to assume that the older Walker children, in marrying and finding small tenant farms for themselves, had had to move into an eastern parish. In the cattle areas, mixed subsistence farming had been threatened since 1724, when tenants rose up, dismantling dikes to the west and north of Crossmichael. These anti-enclosure riots meant that landlords' interest in their cattle was beginning to surpass their interest in their tenants.[19]

Both of Agnes Walker's settled siblings may have been newcomers to Terregles, although their spouses probably were not. James Walker ended up in the multiple-tenancy farm of Kirkland; his wife had the same surname as the other identified male tenant, Robert Thomson. Janet Walker, five years younger than her brother, had married well. She and her husband had Halmyre, which seems to have been a compact single-tenant farm. They also had a young female servant, which her brother did not. She was Winnifred Thomson, probably yet another of the Thomsons at Kirkland. The two families were connected to each other, not least via dealing with the same, or related, landlords, but Janet was undoubtedly better off.[20]

Janet and James were at odds over their troubling sister, offering rather different testimony, taking sides that probably stood for deeper resentments. Both siblings were old enough to have heard about Isobell Walker, tried for infanticide twenty-five years earlier in the neighboring parish of Irongray, condemned, and saved at the last minute by royal pardon.[21] While no one had reason to speak of it at the trial, it was certainly within living memory for the adults, and a baleful memory for any related Walkers still living in Irongray. Janet clearly went out of her way to protect her sister; James had little good to say of her, and bitterly qualified the few positive remarks he found himself forced to make.

The urge to clear Agnes, like the urge to condemn her, tied both of her older siblings to wide networks in their community, not simply to a private history of family morality and pride. They could not have made decisions about their sister without also understanding that they were making strategic decisions that would affect their places in the community. Janet Walker chose to insist that nothing had happened, either in her house or to her sister. James Walker seemed willing to throw in his lot with those who wanted his sister to hang. We cannot know if Agnes Walker understood or expected relatives and strangers to take the sides they did when she was examined, and then tried, but with hindsight we can see that her life depended on the power of those for and against her, and not on her guilt or innocence.

She was almost undoubtedly guilty. The fatal convergence of village suspicion, midwives' examination, and blue marks on the child's throat had sent many women to the gallows before her, accurately and remorselessly. The minister, his servant, and his beadle, and two of the three midwives—the two who were actually from Terregles, that is— upheld the old moral voice of the community. Her brother, James, a cotenant in Kirkland, next to the kirk and manse, leaned toward their side. He was unwilling to directly accuse or condemn his sister, but he mentioned her "wavering way of Speaking." He also gave the crucial information that he had sent for Agnes on the first Monday evening that she was in Terregles, and that he was told that she was "Indisposed" but would come on Wednesday morning. His own wife, Mary Thomson, had gone into labor that Monday, adding an ironic detail, for that must have been when Agnes Walker gave birth as well.

The midwife whose testimony was most damaging, Janet Irving, also lived in Kirkland with her spouse, Robert Thomson. It was Irving who let slip the information that during the examination of the child's body, three of the midwives had agreed that the child's bruised throat was to be "imputed to its being Strangled." Irving had heard the rumors of pregnancy before Agnes Walker got to Terregles, so she had kept her eyes open: She had seen Agnes at her brother's, once sitting with Mary Thomson, once coming in to light her pipe at her brother's fire while Irving was washing a child of James's and Mary's.

The other midwife, Marion Jardine, was an eighty-year-old widow; her testimony was damning, but she did not appear to have gone out of her way to make it especially so. Jardine lived alone in Terregles-town, a group of houses east of both Kirkland and Halmyre. She was called out to the corpse that night because Terregles-town was no more than half or a quarter of a mile from Halmyre. The beadle, John Sloan, probably also lived in Terregles-town. The prosecution's witnesses were drawn from the minister's manse, from the nearby multiple-tenancy farm of Kirkland, and from Terregles-town, a group of houses probably still leased with farmland.

Where were Agnes Walker's defenders? To begin, Janet Walker and Robert Lockhart, her sister and silent brother-in-law, lived in Halmyre, where the child was found. They did not attend the parish church in Terregles, but walked further down the road to Irongray; it has an impressive seventeenth-century church, surrounded by even more impressive monumental gravestones, commemorating the wealth of artisans, farmers, and professional men. The midwife who persistently avoided coming to any conclusion, Elizabeth Paterson, came from Irongray. Her husband, Edward Walker, was a tenant in Cluden, the same multiple-tenancy farm from which Isobell Walker was dragged to trial in 1737.

The defense also called Nathaniel McKie, the minister of Crossmichael.[22] He explained that three or four years earlier, Agnes Walker had confessed to an illegitimate pregnancy, taken care of her child, done penance, and the child was, he believed, still alive. He also acknowledged the recent rumors in Crossmichael, and confirmed that elders had visited Agnes Walker. Local women, he said, had refused to examine her, as none of them were practicing midwives. It is hard to understand why Walker left such a lenient parish, but worth noting the defense tactic of countering Mr. Heron's authority by calling in McKie, and capitalizing on the kirk's fragmentation.

In an ambitious display for 1762, the defense presented five other witnesses. Two women, not living nearby, and a physician from Dumfries were asked to corroborate Walker's claim that the milk found in her breasts was residue from the four-years-previous pregnancy. They were not convincing, but the effort taken to find them suggests a strong will at work in Agnes's behalf. May and Jean Sloan, daughters of James Sloan in Terregles-town, made it clear that Agnes did not have a child while in their house, but kept to her spinning every day, as they did. They were in their mid-twenties, and both seemed fond of Agnes, or at least sympathetic.

Agnes Walker's defenders were drawn from at least four parishes, and most of them were women.[23] Her best alibis came from her sister, who explained patiently what work Agnes had done for her on every day of the week she had stayed there: On Sunday, she took care of the child while her sister went to church in Irongray; on Monday she went to her brother's to do heavy housework; on Tuesday, she dressed the child, and "swingled [scotched] lint"; on Wednesday she was back at her brother's, baking bread for the christening; on Thursday she was there, preparing the christening dinner; on Friday and Saturday she swingled lint, and on Sunday watched the child again while Janet walked to Irongray. Her sister-in-law, Mary Thomson, refused to side with her husband, perhaps remembering her help, and insisted that Agnes had worked "like a young girl." The sympathetic midwife from Irongray, perhaps a friend of Janet Walker's, clearly went out of her way to counter the local assumption that the child had been viciously strangled. The Sloan daughters outdid themselves in praising Agnes's work.

Although the men in these households are, perhaps not surprisingly, silent, Walker's support came from three households—that of Janet Walker and Robert Lockhart, Halmyre; of James Sloan and his daughters, in Terregles-town; and of the midwife Elizabeth Paterson and Edward Walker, in Cluden. Within the parish, they were opposed by the minister, and presumably his elders, the tenants in Kirkland, and some of the tenants in Terregles-town. Agnes Walker was banished to a plantation in America instead of hanged because her lawyer was very smart, and because the jury handed in such an oddly written verdict that the court had trouble interpreting it. The foreman of the jury, chosen by the other members, and always as a mark of respect, was John Maxwell of Terraughtie. He was Janet Walker's and Robert Lockhart's landlord, and if he lived at his home farm of Nether Terraughtie, he lived about two miles south of Halmyre. We cannot know if he intentionally engineered the writing of an uninterpretable verdict, but he was certainly in a position to influence the writing of that verdict. Agnes Walker's salvation most probably lay in having a sister and brother-in-law who were favored tenants in a good farm, who, in other words, had a foothold on the right side of the agricultural transformation, and a landlord willing to protect them and theirs. Many other women were not so lucky; without friends, they would go to the gallows in the high street without a word of sympathy from the anxious, powerless villagers who had regained some sense of control by sending them there.

Those who sent them to the gallows were villagers much like those of Terregles: a minister, often with the elders of the kirk; older women, midwives, and often, if the accused woman was a servant, her mistress. Infanticide was a woman's crime, and it was suspected by women and usually brought to light by women. Only as rumor and gossip would it affect men, forcing or inviting ministers and elders to discipline fornicators, investigate, and send for magistrates or baillies. But men rarely investigated at first hand, unless, like George Heron, they stumbled over the body. Behaving with propriety, they sent for women, usually including at least one midwife, and often women married to elders of the kirk. Usually the women had gotten there first, but not always.

In the parish of Garvock in 1715, the minister and his elders, formally gathered as the kirk session, sent one of the elders, David More, along with three women, to draw the breasts of Jean Larry at her stepfather's house. He ordered Larry out of bed; she refused to get up, unless he would go to the door, so that she might clothe herself. Once she was out of the bed, More searched it while one of the women held a candle for him. He found a child, dead, wrapped in "a Linning cloath upon the Straw of the bed."[24] He may or may not have then stayed to watch while Katharine Law drew Larry's breasts. The investigation seems to have been in his charge; none of the women claimed the authority of midwife. All three women were wives or widows from tenant farms; More was a tenant farmer, but only he testified that the child was a full-term child.

From the kirk's point of view, this case probably represents an ideal, if we ignore the obvious ideal, in which the minister's exhortations or private lectures stave off fornication, or at least convince Larry to raise her child. Unfortunately for the kirk, More's enthusiasm was atypical. The kirk's moral rule was very often superseded by an older right to discipline and punish, which adult, married, childbearing women felt had been vested in them. Often these women were good members of the kirk, married into respectable tenant households. But a good midwife could speak with some authority, with or without such stability. When, in 1714, Lady Barras called an elderly widow from a nearby joint-tenant farm to look at a dead baby found in her grounds, the old

woman, unwrapping the black silk kerchief thoughtfully provided by
Barras, had no trouble flatly pronouncing it a "three-months child."[25]
While Lady Barras had asked her the right questions—was it a full-
term child, were there any marks of violence on the body—Barras apparently could not recognize that it was the body of an extremely premature fetus. Perhaps Lady Barras never looked at the body at all.
The case against a young servant, on her way back to her mother's
house from Aberdeen, was dismissed. The elderly widow in Lumgair
had no credentials from the kirk, but had had fifteen children herself,
and twenty years' employment as a midwife.[26]

Ministers and elders, like good hunting dogs, had an eye for move-
ment in the landscape. Women who had taken to the road were therefore likely to attract the attention of the kirk, and various godly
villagers. Margaret Minna, the daughter of a tenant farmer in Berwick, had walked—from Coldingham in Berwick, or from some employ-
er's household—some thirty miles south into Roxburgh. In the town of
Eckford she gave birth, in the house of a midwife, the spouse of a
weaver. She left there apparently later the same day, in the company
of an elder, who escorted her to the house of the minister, Mr. Johnston. The elder, Henry Oliphant, testified that he led her there "thinking it not proper that she should go out of the Parish untill the minister
had seen her." She told Johnston that "she was married to James
Young weaver in a factory in Edinburgh and that the said James Young
because his trade was low had gone to Berwick" and "she was going to
him."[27]

Her explanation may not have convinced her hearers, for it certainly
didn't explain why she was in Roxburgh. Nonetheless, the minister was
all too eager to get rid of her, and put her and her child on a horse
behind his servant, with instructions to deliver her in the next parish
to the north, and from there deliver her to Berwick. As the minister's
wife put it, "Her Husband being of opinion that when once [Minna]
was out of his parish he had no further Concern with her." Unfortunately she was probably not on her way to her husband, but had simply
been making her way south, probably with a vague intention of somehow returning without the child. Perhaps she intended to disappear
into England briefly, but went into labor at Eckford. In any case, once
at Hightown in the next parish, she insisted that she preferred "to go
on foot," if only someone would walk half of the way with her, to a John
Dickson's house.

That evening she was back at Eckford and stayed in the miller's house, in bed with his female servant. The next morning suspicion was aroused. She had no child with her, and left behind a "Linnen Cloth in the shape of a young Childs shirt." Confronted, she told them where to look for the child: in Coatland Puddle, just south of Eckford Mill, wrapped up in a kerchief with a three-pound stone. Worldly enough to make her way south, and face down the minister, she was not worldly enough to walk away from Coatland Puddle, or any other suitable ditch. It was her own guilt and misery, not the kirk, that stopped her.[28]

Twenty years earlier, in 1733, Janet Stewart, the daughter of a quarrier in Elgin, was sighted entering the parish of Knockando. The minister, Hugh Grant, could recall in April that "she came first to this paroch about the middle of March last with Child; I called for her Testificate but she made not Account of herself, only told me she had come from the paroch of Keith."[29] She was followed by "a Stranger Fellow," named Donald Sutherland, "whose Mother is married at Present to her Father." This was enough to alarm the minister; when he "was informed that these two Strangers Lodg'd together, the Session appointed them to Remove." They took themselves off to another village to be married, and they seem to have wandered in the neighborhood, for "their Residence was not fixt in any place."

When a child's body was found, partially eaten by dogs, in Knockando, Grant spoke for the community when he said "but a Woman who was a stranger here having been observed to be bigg with Child sometime before . . . our Suspitions fixed Jointly upon her." He sent people searching for her, and discovering that she and Sutherland were in the next parish, Inveraven, he sent someone "Express" to the minister there at nine o'clock at night. His earnest desire for her return is somewhat illuminated by his account of her questioning. She did, he said, "prevaricate and entangled herself with a Vast Number of Dissembling Falsehoods." But in the end she told him something that he wanted to hear; "after attacks made upon her by Different Persons from Eight in the Morning til Five at Night I did at last obtain her Confession." He immediately had her repeat it to the assembled kirk session, who must have been waiting nearby. Even though the High Court had as recently as 1690 resorted to confessions made under torture, the gentlemen of the courts were appalled by the methods of the kirk in 1733, and the case never came to trial.[30]

Rarely did lairds act like ministers, but in 1738 Sir William Maxwell of Barsalloch took over an investigation begun by the kirk session of Mochrum, in Wigtown. When Sir William threatened "to put her in Irons and other ways to punish her," Agnes McGuffock confessed. What exactly she confessed has not survived, but she was let off with a whipping, which means that the court found her guilty of very little, or disliked Sir William's method very much. Lairds, as in Terregles, were far more likely to join in by sitting on juries, and saving young women from kirk, neighbors, and statute. What rough questioning there was usually fell to ministers, midwives, and mistresses.[31]

Ministers and elders might have it their way, or they might not. Margaret Mayne was hanged in 1700, and the only evidence against her was her own confession, delivered before a minister, elder, and baillie in the Inverkeithing jail.[32] But by 1752, Sarah Quarrier, held in jail for five months, petitioned to be set free, claiming that she was held "in Consequence of a groundless malicious Information" given to the Dumfries sheriff by "One of the Elders of the Parish of Kirk-mahoe."[33] One of His Majesty's lawyers examined the case, and threw it out, refusing to indict Quarrier. Obviously, the roles of ministers and elders depended on the strength of the godly community in a parish, the character of the minister, the shifting mood of the kirk itself in the eighteenth century, and the degree to which minister and elders competed with other local worthies—lairds, magistrates, and eventually physicians—for authority in these cases. And villagers might appeal to a minister, north or south, simply because he seemed the appropriate figure to contact a magistrate.[34]

In cases of infanticide, ministers must often have been frustrated, not only by the deaths or the illegitimate births, but by their own shrinking roles in their communities. In 1761, Jannet Heatly was brought to trial and hanged without one mention of minister or elder. One evening Heatly took to bed early, telling her mistress, Jannet Finlay, that she had begun to menstruate again after an inexplicable lapse of several months. She was followed to bed by another servant, Margaret Waugh, who slept in the same bed, as the servants and master and mistress all slept in the kitchen. Waugh claimed to know nothing of a birth, and to have suspected nothing. Yet next morning Jannet Finlay found blood on the doorstep; she went out with the dog, which discovered an afterbirth in a drystone wall near the house. As Finlay had not yet had a child, and the afterbirth was "a very unseemly sight to her," she went to get her mother, Isobell Fowler. They were followed back by two other women, Isobell Steel and Katharine Ritchie. With these women, accompanied by Finlay's husband, James Ross, and probably Waugh, Jannet Heatly recovered the child's body, which she had thrown into a ditch full of water. She insisted that the child fell from her body onto the stone doorstep and was killed, but she admitted knowing she was pregnant, by weeping in desperation as she asked a woman in the next parish to persuade the father of her child to speak to her. Her admitted desperation, and her failure to call for help from any of the people sleeping in the same room no doubt hanged her.[35]

The work of discovering and enforcing fell heavily on women of the household and of the neighborhood, willing or not. Jannet Finlay, only twenty-three herself, probably confronting a woman of about the same age, went for her mother. The women who cornered Isobell Walker in 1737, ripped off her clothes, tried her breasts, and forced her to hold the dead infant showed considerably more taste for their work, and an unshakable sense of purpose.[36] Christian Trin's mistress, sitting by her fire, smelled something "nauseous." She poked in the fire with her tongs, until she saw blood on them, at which point Trin took the tongs from her. The mistress left, and returned with two other women, to find that Trin had something wrapped in her apron. There was a struggle, and the women took the body of an infant, its arms and legs burnt off, from Trin. Her mistress then examined Trin's bed, found it to look like childbed, and promptly sent word to one of the elders. She was not summoning him, however, but sending word that he should summon "officers and midwives" from Aberdeen.[37] As in the Heatly case, not only were women competent to investigate, but by mid-century the authority of the kirk seemed somewhat abated, perhaps especially in proximity to the larger cities. It was all too often the familiar face of a mistress or midwife that bespoke conviction, and less often, that of a minister or magistrate.[38]

The Fathers of the Children

But there is one face, and that an important one, that is rarely visible in the court record: the father of the child. It would be easy to speculate that women who committed infanticide were those whose pregnancies were forced on them by masters, relatives, or prostitution. That is not borne out by what record remains of their lovers. Jannet Heatly, before giving birth, went to a nearby village, which she called New Miln, and, weeping, asked a woman there to ask the father of her child, Mungo Ochiltree, to speak to her. Apparently he never came, or she chose to conceal that conversation. They had been servants together at another tenant farm in a parish contiguous to the one in which Heatly gave birth. Her old master testified that he had observed "indecent familiarities" between them just before she left service there, and Ochiltree's master said the same.[39] It is hard to say that Heatly was luckier than Isobell McEwan, but Heatly was to some degree in control of her fate. Of course, McEwan, who was mentioned in the prologue, may also have thought that she was in control of her life.

These women probably saw these men as likely husbands, and no doubt some doomed children were conceived under promise of marriage. Whether the men saw these women as likely wives we cannot know. Even masters might conceivably have married their servants, for most of the masters we see in the court records are not small landowners or gentlemen, but tenant farmers, often in multiple-tenancy farms. Few masters seemed to have formed attachments, as it was said, with servants without being able to offer them some protection; the case of Adam Wilson, below, is something of an exception.[40] Far more dangerous, it seems, was courtship with a man of similar class, who could be, in many respects, as economically helpless as a female servant. And worst of all was the casual prostitution that sometimes fell to the lot of a woman attempting to support herself, for then there was little hope of the man's protection or intervention. Janny Stewart, a sewing mistress in the village of Corstophine in 1770, could say only that the father of her child was a man whom she had met near Edinburgh, on the road from the port of Leith.[41] Perhaps her pupils' fees were often not enough, or she found the requisite celibacy unsupportable.

In 1747, a bit north of Loch Leven in Kinross, Megg Arnot became pregnant by her master, Adam Wilson. Wilson, a portioner in Wester Balgeddie, was a small farmer who worked his own land, with the help of a young boy and Arnot. She returned to her parents in the winter of 1746, but was back with Wilson in the spring. Evidently he promised to help, and to some degree made good his promise, for he went to surgeons in two nearby towns, Kinross and Leslie, seeking "druggs" to bring on abortion. He was refused. He sent Arnot, and she was also refused. She testified to telling one surgeon that half a crown was too much to pay; he of course disclaimed having made such an offer. When she was brought to bed, through a Saturday evening and Sunday, the door to their house remained closed, and Wilson ventured out only once on Sunday to water his horses. On Sunday afternoon she gave birth, with Wilson as midwife. The child was not seen by neighbors until it was dug out of Wilson's cornyard five weeks later, after an investigation initiated by the elders of Orwell Kirk, with midwives and Arnot's mother participating, and finished off by magistrate's order from Kinross.[42]

No one will ever know what happened in that house while the door was shut that weekend. After the body was discovered, both Arnot and Wilson were jailed. They gave conflicting accounts of the child's birth. Arnot, who would be tried first, shifted the blame to Wilson, saying that he had prevented her from calling midwives, that he dashed the child on the ground, and subsequently buried it. She said she had heard the child give a "weak cry" before he "threw the child upon the ground." Then Wilson went out the door, and she "fell into a Swarff and did not know what she was doing."[43] Wilson, for his part, insisted that he had offered to go for women when her pains came, and that he had left a living child with her, only to return to find the child wrapped in Arnot's apron and deposited in a bucket of water.

When Wilson's second cousin, an unmarried man of thirty, visited or confronted them in jail, he was able to watch them argue, and report their words. Wilson said, "Megg when your pains Came upon you I proposed to Call your Mother and Jannet Miller." As Wilson continued, Arnot agreed with this, and "Said she was so filled with Shame that she would Chuse to Suffer [the] Utmost that would happen to a woman in her Condition rather than to be seen by Women." But as the conversation continued, they could not agree over when the child had died: Arnot said to Wilson, "Adam don't you Remember that I gave you a Living Child" and Wilson replied, "You did not give me a Living Child But I left a Living Child with you when I went out, and when I Came back again I found it in the Bucket among the Water."[44] At this point the cousin, David Ireland, no doubt in some frustration "observed that it was Strange they did not Glorify God by telling the truth."

Wilson stuck to his story that day, and Arnot finally yielded slightly, reiterating her exhaustion. She said to Wilson, as the cousin remembered it, "if you left a Living Child with me I was in Such a Condition in body and mind that what my two hands did to the Child when you was out No Mortall can know, annexing for her reason that she was so much troubled in body and mind that she could not know herself what she did with the Child."[45]

While at first it appears that Arnot was about to accept blame, that was not the result of her repeated descriptions of her exhaustion and incompetence. She was withdrawing into that description, perhaps increasingly so as time passed, and as she withdrew she left Adam Wilson alone on the stage, and alone to take the blame. He confessed while in jail, about a month after the child had been born, saying to one of his elders that he could have no peace until he did so.[46] It would have been so much easier, and safer, and respectable to have married Arnot. She probably returned from her parents', where she had gone after becoming pregnant, with some hope of establishing a household with Wilson. But instead, he obsessively locked the door, giving the story its Gothic overtone, and then buried the child in the cornyard. Whatever happened in the house was thus framed by Wilson's control, and all too easily interpretable by neighbors and jurors as a story of male control, or presence, and female helplessness, or absence. Wilson's presence threw into relief Arnot's distress and confusion and exhaustion, and allowed outsiders to construct a story in which a strong masculine hand throttled the child. Perhaps it was true, but the verdicts confirmed that jurors held Arnot responsible for the child's death. Perhaps, after failing to obtain abortifacients in November, their intentions were not clear, even to themselves. Both tried to absent themselves, Arnot by saying she fell into a "swarff," and Wilson by walking out the door immediately after delivering the child. Both probably intended to see—or not see—that the child did not survive, but only Arnot hanged.

What Wilson could do for Arnot was based on his control of that property. He could lock the door, he could bury the child in his yard.[47] He could deliver the child. Most young men had no such protection to offer their lovers, nor could they think of protecting themselves by such measures. With such help as Wilson's in disposing of the body, many women who hanged probably could have weathered local suspicion, or at worst been banished before trial, for lack of evidence. It is quite probable that the large number of women banished escaped hanging precisely because they had had help from family, friend, or lover. Wilson's help, on the other hand, came to naught, probably because he lacked the status of a laird, and couldn't get away with locking his house and his and Arnot's lives away from public view. It took considerably more authority to successfully bar the door.

The masters and mistresses who appear in most of these cases were rarely powerful, propertied people.[48] If they had been, they probably would have protected their servants as a matter of course, assuming the right to direct the lives of their people. One exception was Douglas of Inveresk, who in 1753 "thrust out of the family" one Isobell Kilgour, who was at that time pregnant by his son. His son "left the Country." Kilgour left her child to die of exposure on Leith Links and took service with a smith there. When a repentant Douglas came to claim his grandchild, boys playing on the Links discovered the dead child, and Isobell Kilgour was found guilty of exposing her child, and publicly whipped. This, clearly, was a case where there was at first glance no question of marriage between a servant and a substantial landlord, even though Robert Douglas relented toward the child. But the line separating the Douglases from Isobell Kilgour was perhaps not absolute either. Elizabeth Mure remarked on "improper attachments" in the first half of the eighteenth century, which she believed resulted from the isolated "small society" of the rural world, and the habit of allowing children from big houses to grow up with the children of tenants and servants. But by 1753, in a wealthy farming parish just outside Edinburgh, the line between a servant and a wealthy, but working, farmer was becoming clearer.[49]

So little evidence remains to indicate the identity of the men who fathered these children that it is impossible to go very far with any one generalization. Most often they must have been men near to hand, living in the same household, either as servant or master. Ann McLeod, on the island of Skye, was pregnant by Donald McLeod, and both were servants to Ensign Norman McLeod of Gillon. In 1763 Marjory Russell was with child to her master Charles Lumsden, a tenant farmer in Cabrach, in Aberdeen. It was her second child with him, and he managed to save her, in part by locking the child's body in a chest, and joining her in defying the local kirk. Mary Mackenzie, servant to a tenant farmer in Knocknafanoch, Ross, had less about which to be sanguine. She had been gotten pregnant by her master's son, and told a female friend "that tho he had got her with Child he was to marry her, to which the [woman] made answer, are you to believe him?" The friend, who was twenty-eight and may have been older than Mackenzie, was dubious about Alexander Simpson's promise because Mackenzie was at least the third servant Simpson had "used" in that fashion. And then there was Mary Pearson, a widow in a tenancy on her own, who became pregnant by the neighboring tenant; Isobell Walker, the daughter of day laborers, who became pregnant by a neighborhood tenant farmer at midsummer; and Bessie ffisher, servant to John ffisher, a married tenant farmer, who was gotten pregnant by him.[50]

But in most cases the men were simply not there, not in the court record or on the farm, which was of course the problem in a nutshell. Whether the man left for London, like James Gray, a twenty-one-year-old barber who had gotten a respectable widow pregnant under promise of marriage, or he refused to speak to the woman like Mungo Ochiltree, or he purged himself by an oath before the kirk, the man was usually absent. Katherine Ramsay lived in one room with her parents near the Devon Works in Clackmannan, the three of them subsisting on her father's army pension. In 1814 she gave birth to a child in that room, dressed it in a mutch (cap) and "a piece of an old shirt," and locked it in a chest. Two days after giving birth, she met the child's father, James Johnston, near the Devon Works, and he told her to dig a hole and bury the infant. Three men found her freshly dug hole beside the river, brought the child back to Ramsay, and forced her to give a statement. She knocked a hole in the jail's wall and escaped, presumably having understood that the advice she got from Johnston was of little value, and that she was on her own. Johnston did not want to be seen in company with Ramsay; Mungo Ochiltree would not come when called, not even in secret; men with greater prospects found themselves sent to distant cities to take up a trade. Adam Wilson could do more, but he could not or would not unravel the complexities of his position, or Megg Arnot's, so far as to offer marriage. Only a man in the position of Douglas of Inveresk or Maxwell of Terraughtie could keep a child or dominate jurors.[51]

Women probably killed their children only when there was no help for it. A few had already had one or two illegitimate children, like Walker; they may have exhausted their immediate resources, or their friends' patience. They tended not to mention their partners' names, perhaps because a woman's struggle to survive was a lonely business, or perhaps because their only defense was to deny the pregnancy. While they necessarily acted alone in concealing their pregnancies, or had the help of one confidante, they were rarely alone, living in small communities where they were closely observed. If they ran, they risked being marked as strangers, and accused and condemned by ministers, elders of the kirk, and most important of all, the often suspicious midwives and mistresses. Those who had the power to help, like Maxwell of Terraughtie in 1762, were distant, elite men.

Help was scarce early in the century. From 1690 until about 1720, local godly folk, the gentlemen of the juries and men of the court usually acted in unison, and most of the women who were hanged went to the gallows in those years. But in 1740, women indicted for infanticide began to be banished, sometimes as indentured servants, without facing trial. By 1750, this was the most common outcome of an infanticide indictment, and between 1740 and 1809, when the statute was revoked, 111 women in Scotland were banished. This marked a clear change in the courtroom, if not in villages, for as indictments increased after 1750, hanging became rare, as did trials. Of the 347 women inves-

Scots women at work in Benawe, Argyllshire. Left, a woman spins wool outside her house. Right, a woman tends children as a man carts timber.

tigated for infanticide between 1661 and 1820, fifty were hanged, all but a handful of them before 1750. After mid-century, hanging, as well as the arbitrary punishments of whipping or labeling, virtually ceased. Local people, like midwives, ministers, and especially elders, were likely to see their accusations come to little, as the lairds and burghers of the juries balked at hanging women, and lawyers like the one who saved Agnes Walker from the gallows in 1762 found new arguments to use against the statute, and prosecutors seemed eager to banish women quickly and quietly. After Walker, only seven more women would hang, and her case, with its clever defense argument, would be cited as a precedent in Janet Gray's appeal in 1798, after which the statute was finally toppled. After that appeal, there would be no hangings, and in 1809 the law was changed to describe the crime as concealment of pregnancy, and punished with no more than two years in a local jail.

What happened in the courtroom is an important story, for it implies that in 1690 ministers and lawyers found it all too easy to believe, as did midwives and sundry other villagers, that a woman alone could and would kill an illegitimate child. It also implies that between 1720 and 1750, when convictions declined and banishment became common, lawyers and jurors found it increasingly difficult to accept the reality of infanticide. But what happened in the courtroom, which represents an important aspect of evolving beliefs about motherhood and woman's nature in the eighteenth century, did not alter what happened in villages like Terregles.[52] Agnes Walker's story, like those of the other women mentioned briefly here, remained typical, even as fewer villagers, and very few gentlemen of the courts, would acknowledge the economic, social, moral, or emotional realities of those women's lives.

4

Women's Work in the Transformation of the Scottish Economy

Loyalty and devotion butter no parsnips.
—J. E. Handley

Work consumed the lives of Scots village women, just as it did the lives of urban women trading in the streets or from shops, or gentlewomen managing estates, and it is difficult to know what attention these women might have paid to the more spectacular hardships of those few neighbors who became entangled in child murder.[1] It is equally difficult to know how much attention they could have spared to think about changes in village, parish, and regional economies, even though, in the course of the eighteenth century, their work and the work of those about them began to change dramatically. As J. E. Handley implied, loyalty and devotion would disappear from rural communities, as ties between tenants and landlords, and then between neighbors, faded, chiefly because those parsnips would be buttered, for some if not for others, in unheard-of quantities by the end of the eighteenth century.

In the scramble to get rich, which was also a scramble to use land well, and defeat famine, many villagers would find themselves losing land, and sliding down into the ranks of cottagers and day laborers. Others would do better, leasing the new, compact farms that had been created out of many families' holdings. Women might continue to shear sheep, harvest grain, or lead carts, but they too would hope to see their families do well. Some would even initiate improvements in bleaching linen, or raising calves. But it would be a precarious hope, as Agnes Walker and her two siblings must have known.[2] In that shifting world, women's work differed from men's, but the necessity of constantly performed labor drew men and women together in the service of the land, the animals, and the households, and that rural, seasonal work must have provided some reassuring continuity for both villagers and those who observed them.

Work, together with the seasons and the weather, structured villagers' days, shaped their courting, and framed the moments at which they conceived their children and gave birth. When Ann Blair was raped in 1792, the court recorded that "a man had attacked her on the road as she was coming from Shearing." When Henrietta Manson was questioned about the infant she buried in the dirt floor at the foot of her bed, she described the work she had done on the day the child was born: "The Declarant went before Breakfastime to the Moss of Bronzay for a Burden of Peats. That on her way to the Moss she called at the house of Anthony Cormack in Akergill where she left three Purns of Yarn. That on her Return from the Moss she Called again at Anthony Cormack's where she laid down her Burden of Peats and Reeled her Yarn and after doing so she took up her Burden and Carried it home."

Manson gave birth at some point on this journey, carrying the child's body home with the peats. When love, or sex, figured in these lives, it must have slipped in among the tasks that they, and their lovers, performed daily. When Hector McLean and Isabell McEwan came to grief over their unborn child, he killed her behind their master's barn. Presumably they had met there before, and it had been one of the common sites of their courtship, and their work.[3]

Most of Scotland was worked by tenant farmers at the beginning of the eighteenth century, many holding farms jointly with as many as eight other families. More families lived on their land as subtenants and cottagers, and young people from all these households customarily went out to work as servants, like Manson, McLean, and McEwan, until marriage. Much of the land was still in runrig, which is to say that it was divided up into many strips, with each tenant holding strips all over the farm. It was an old system, supposedly guaranteeing each tenant a share of all the qualities of land in the farm, and allowing tenants to survive with little capital, sharing valuable plows and draft animals. Land and children, in effect, were shared, and the land thickly subtenanted, no doubt resulting in complex communities.

Their houses, built in groups, were almost universally bad, without real windows or doors, divided into two rooms at best, and perhaps housing animals during the winter. Floors were of dirt, and roofs were variously covered with local material, thatching or turf, and leaked, often into the fire built in the middle of the floor. Any low place on the floor was liable to fill with rain water. Peat fires smoked badly, and holes left in the roof, or in a sidewall, instead of chimneys, did little to help. Animals and people entered by the same door; hens and rats scratched on the roof, and nested in the rafters; sooty water dripped down in bad weather, and worms fell from the turf in dry seasons. Not far from the door there would be a pile of human and animal manure, carefully saved to dung the fields in the spring. By 1700, the exception would have been among tenants around Edinburgh, who possessed better two-roomed houses, with a chimney in the public room, and perhaps a floor in the inner room.[4]

The women were as work-hardened as the men, as English travelers noticed for several centuries. In 1825 an officer reported from Haddington, a much improved parish near Edinburgh, that "The women were extremely ugly and nasty, having dirty clouts tied round their heads, falling about their shoulders . . ."[5] His account differs little from one published in 1662 by John Ray, a naturalist traveling through Dunbar, on the southeast coast. Ray noted that "the women generally seemed to us none of the handsomest. They are not very cleanly in their houses, and but sluttish in dressing their meat[.]"[6] If the English noticed the women, it was, as Handley put it, because "the women [were] like all peasant women grown old before their time with hard work and exposure, who showed plainest the ravages of disease and dirt."[7] They showed those ravages so plainly because the observers were already familiar with wealthier farming families, where wives and daughters worked indoors if they worked at all. The contrast between women who worked indoors and those who still worked outside seems to have consistently led observers to stare, always more shocked by the sight of women, who were tan and muscled from heavy labor. Thomas Pennant, in 1774, reported that "The common women are in general most remarkably plain, and soon acquire an old look, and by being much exposed to the weather without hats such a grin and contraction of the muscles as heightens greatly their natural hardness of features."[8] Not only would heavy outdoor work eventually fall exclusively to men's lot, but the idea would spread more rapidly than its realization, and so Pennant saw the effects of weather on women as the mark not only of work, but also of masculinity.

We cannot follow them through the fields, but we can glimpse the insides of their houses, and understand that even indoor work was heavy and difficult. When Moses Morgan, a well-off tenant and estate official for his landlord, Sir Archibald Grant of Monymusk, died in 1738, his estate was inventoried. He left behind four rooms and one closet full of the heavy implements and coarse cloth of that family's relatively good life. The most valuable items were a horse, a pair of cows, and a copper kettle; each was valued at about £20 Scots. Besides the kettle, the main or "fire room" contained three pots and a brass pan, a bed, a long table and a folding table, one armchair and one without arms, three stools, fireplace tongs, a wool wheel and a yarn winder, a large chest, a girdle [griddle] and other baking equipment, a meal peck, a corn peck, and a handbarrow. This is not the equipment of comfortable living, but of a working household, with few entertainments and little leisure.[9]

The simple work of the household meant washing and cooking for the family, including the servants. It meant cutting and carrying peats for the fire; milking the two cows, making butter, and cheese if the milk was abundant; daily baking and making porridges, and, less frequently, meat broths; brewing ale for daily consumption; preserving meat; managing fowls or pigs; carrying water, and heating it for laundry; spinning, swingling lint, sewing, knitting; watching children; running errands; or directing the inevitable one or two young servants to do any of this. At harvest, women would be expected to help in the field, or feed the ravenous harvest gangs whose wages included meals. Morgan's wife may have been spared fieldwork, but probably not, even though her household was physically different, and more demanding, than those of ordinary tenants and cottagers. Among ordinary tenants and cottagers, women were drawn out of the house to do the odd jobs of farming: cutting whins, leading a cow to a neighboring farm to be

bred, or leading a cart. There was less work to keep these women indoors, in two rooms, beyond the making of porridges and stews that
required little preparation.

Rural women lived their lives in a series of households. The first
household was that of their parents, the second that of master and
mistress, and the third, with luck, was their own, entered by marriage.
Most were agricultural servants by the time they were in their early
twenties. And most understood their households as linked to their
neighbors', but also tied to the will of the landlord, and the temper of
the estate's officers. The landlord's needs impinged on tenants' lives
chiefly through the conditions of the tack, or lease, which tied tenants
to landowners. At the beginning of the eighteenth century, tacks were
often verbal, and probably negotiable in bad years. By the end of the
century, tenants had secure, written, long-term leases, often with
rents measured in money, even if they were still partly collected in
produce. These contracts were less likely to be negotiable. In either
case the agreements tenants reached with landlords effectively structured much work in the household, but the later contracts were often
the tools of landlords who were becoming aggressive managers.[10]

The Monymusk Example

At the heart of rural women's experience in the eighteenth century lay
the decisions made by landlords, and many of those men left behind
excellent records of their struggles to improve and dramatically change
their estates. In the hands of Archibald Grant of Monymusk, the lease
was a flexible and powerful tool, which he used to reshape his estate
and alter his tenants' lives. In 1714, before Grant took over, one Monymusk tack demanded some money, plus meal, beer, corn, one hog,
peats, linen yarn, geese, capons, hens, and a variety of services, mostly
carriage of grain to nearby Aberdeen. By 1748, Grant would demand
less produce, more money, and even more labor, in the form of prescribed services. If grain had to be carried to market in 1714, by 1748
there was timber to move, and quantities of lime, and slate, and this
came on top of the old demands for "cariage and hariage" [transporting
produce], and harvesting and plowing.[11]

But these tacks applied to ordinary tenants, most of them joint ten-

Villagers herding cattle near Castle Campbell, Perth. Work, together with the
seasons and the weather, structured the days of rural Scots villagers.

ants with six to eight other families. Grant also offered classic "improved" leases, in which a substantial money rent freed the tenant
from an onerous round of services, but these were reserved for important tenants, holding large farms. In 1735 Grant "let the whole farm &
lands of Afforske" to James Moore of Stoneyfield, Younger, Esq., for
five or fifteen years. The annual rent was £25 sterling, there were no
services, and there were to be no subtenants, except one crofting family. Moore was bound only to maintain the current advanced practices:
timber plantations, crop rotations, and bringing new ground under the
plow. Afforske was a new farm, cleared of tenants and subtenants for
the farmer lucky enough to get it, and in the 1740s Grant was busy
clearing other farms. He used tacks to create large farms, like Afforske
and Todlachy, out of jointly-tenanted farms. Todlachy was by 1741
made up of two consolidated holdings, consolidated without surveyors,
simply by specifying contiguous strips of land in each tenant's tack. If
all the old names of fields and meadows remained, they were no longer

At harvest time, women were expected to help in the field or feed the ravenous harvest gangs, as in this scene of Coldstream.

distributed among six or eight families, but two. The other families would also have tacks, but would find themselves moved to a cottage, or a house with a few acres.[12]

The estate papers from Monymusk can tell us a good deal about this small world, controlled by Archibald Grant from Monymusk House. Grant had twelve single tenants by 1755, with the tenant in the Mains farm paying £1000 per year, and the others much less. As Grant converted some farms into single tenancies, he seems to have stocked other farms with the excess tenants as time passed. The farm of Coullie had six tenants in 1741, one of them a woman; in 1755, there were twenty, and four of them were women. This suggests that Grant negotiated the social difficulties of clearing his best land by making other farms tenant-intensive; the Coullie tenants and subtenants persisted as a community until the end of the eighteenth century.[13] But by 1755, the tenants were not equal partners in terms of the rents paid. The four women paid from £6 to £17; most of the men paid between £30 and £50, and William Middleton paid £113. Apparently Coullie was partly engrossed to Middleton, and partly divided into small holdings for those who could not, in good conscience or good management, be dismissed. But women were not always among the lesser tenants. At Kirktown, two of the four major tenants were women, and however they got their farming done, they paid a substantial portion of Kirktown's rent (128).

The changes Grant wrought were constant, as were the conflicts that arose. He removed tenants, and he pushed his tenants to remove their subtenants, as one line in his Memorandum Book for 1746 reveals: "All useless in Kirktown, Cowley, etc. settle [them] in brae touns." "Brae" towns probably meant landless cottages. In 1761 he recorded another resettlement, "Tombeg to remove all his subtenants to Brownie's Hill upon each side of the road." The subtenants may have gone without a whimper in 1761, but forty years earlier, when Tombeg Moor was drained, Grant's officer reported that he found "little or no oposition tho the wifes in the neighbour head the day before had threatened to attack us" (84). Over the years, the constant transgressions in the Baron Court record had been all of a piece: cutting and stealing peats; poaching salmon, hares, and birds; sending animals to graze on someone else's grass; resisting carriage services. No doubt it was not simple starvation at work here, and if want figured in this list, so did habit, and a bitter resentment of Grant's reshaping of their world. Grant's 1756 memorandum to his tenants, asking them to plant trees, was by turns cajoling, paternal, and threatening.

> Such of you as are diligent misapply it and won't take advice from those who know better, nor will you follow good example when you see it has good effects, but will keep straitly to the old way. But also a great many of you are idle and trifle away a good deal of your time. Many hours of it are often spent in idleness and sauntering about upon trifles; and when you are at work you don't work with life and spirit, but as if half dead or asleep, and many half hours which you don't value, might be made good. As to your poor living I am sorry for it, but it is your own fault. (lxx)

Grant was relentless but not ruthless, and he met with difficulties. In 1735 his factor, or estate manager, had written to Grant insisting that he could not remove tenants, for "our tenants are such lawiers" (128)

that he, like his predecessor, was in danger of being indicted for proceeding improperly.

The women and men living in Monymusk must have been well aware
of who was doing well, and who was behind in rent. The amount and
quality of land a family held would have been obvious, and little was
private, as the tenants' resistance to Grant's plans shows. If we can
extrapolate from this community, which was exceptional at the time,
but probably typical within a few decades, we can begin to imagine
the problems of courtship in a community where a couple might have
difficulty picturing just where and how they would live. And for
women, we must remember, a future meant marriage, for they had
little access to land if they did not marry. The women on Grant's rent
rolls were almost undoubtedly widows, continuing in their family holdings. If they had the labor of children to command, along with servants
or subtenants, they could produce rents indistinguishable from those
of male-headed households. If they had no labor to command, aside
from their own, they would have a croft or just a cottage, and pay their
rent by keeping hens, or a cow, knitting or spinning, perhaps watching
and teaching their neighbors' children. They belonged to their communities, but they had earned the right to a bit of ground by years of
work, and probably at least one marriage. For young women, there was
service, or marriage.[14]

Christian Gellan has left us some record of what an old woman
might hope to have. She died in 1752, leaving behind on her two-and-
one-half-acre croft her few possessions: two chairs, a bench, a stool, a
small table, a stand bed, a quarto Bible, a cow, several chests, and
tools. She had wool combs, a large wheel for spinning wool, a water
stoup, crooked tongs, a griddle iron, cheese hook, and pruning chisel,
and two piles of fodder for the cow. The cow accounted for half the
income from the sale of these things, which totaled £48. She could afford a respectable burial, since some £9/18 were spent for a coffin,
shroud, and candles, and a man who spent a day inviting the guests,
who were treated to gin and honey. Christian Gellan was lucky; she
was perhaps also industrious, and related to other good tenants in Monymusk.

In Monymusk in 1719 Ann Lunan had taken the lease of a croft in
her own name; she may have been a widow, but she may also have
taken possession as an individual, or as an agent of her parents or
siblings, extending the family holdings. Sons were known to join their

fathers in leases, but if unmarried daughters acted for themselves and
their families in this way, it must have been rare, although it cannot
be ruled out. In Atholl the Widow McInroy competed with all comers
in 1758 to keep possession of Balledmond, which she and her sons had
greatly improved. Given the struggles landlords faced with tenants, a
capable woman may sometimes have been quite acceptable. But that
never emerged as a regular practice. In 1758, Grant obtained a "de-
creet of removing"—an eviction order—against seven of his tenants.
Five were women, one recently widowed. Lone women would not hold
land without difficulty.[15]

Rising rents, population pressure, and evictions probably combined
to make some tenant communities increasingly unstable. It may also
be true that the Scots farm towns, or tiny villages of multiple tenants,
had been fragile to begin with, owing as much to mortality, ambition,
and quarrels as to landlords' eagerness to find "new farmers."[16] If we
move from Grant's records to the experience of tenants, we can see
another dimension of that instability, namely the animosity that sometimes existed between tenants. The rivalries and antagonisms of tenants with each other and members of their own families were apparent
in the witch hunts in Scotland, and survived after the hunts had ended
in the 1690s.[17] If some of that was constant, there must also have been
regional peaks, driven by various fears.

Antagonism Between Tenants in Graystane

In 1753 William Selbie, an unmarried tenant farmer in Graystane,
outside Aberdeen, was hanged for having intercourse with one of his
cows after six of his neighbors testified that they had watched him
"bull" the cow in the very ineffective privacy of his cow barn. Of the
men and women who testified, four had previously been in service with
Selbie. The youngest three had found new places for themselves, two
with great landowners, one with another tenant farmer. The fourth,
Peter James, was fifty, which was old for a servant, and only when he
rose to the status of tenant himself, by marrying the widowed Janet
Taylour in Graystane, did the case come to court. None of Selbie's current servants appeared in court, so it seems that the people who knew
him best felt obliged to move before raising the evidence with a magis-

trate. The family formed by James, Taylour, and her son by the previous marriage became the respectable, older core around which the younger, complaining servants gathered, and together their evidence was damning. But they never went to the local minister, Walter Sim, who played no part in the investigation.[18]

Janet Taylour, apparently a tenant at Graystane for some years, and Elspet Webster, one of Selbie's servants, had discussed Selbie for four years; Taylour remembered watching Selbie through the "muck holl" of his barn, and seeing "cows shern" [vaginal discharge] on the front of one of Selbie's shirts, just before Webster washed it. Webster said she once saw him coming out of his cow barn "with his coat the fore part of his Britches and one of his Legs besmared with Shern." Selbie's servant William Bonnar reported that while feeding the cows, he saw Selbie coming out from behind one cow, and testified that she "was Slyming [sliming] as if She had been with a Bull, but there was no Bull there."[19]

Selbie's predilection was certainly no secret, for Bonnar reported that a year before the trial, he and other servants had refused milk from that cow. Their fears must have seemed plausible to the court, for Elspet Webster, who milked the cows, was asked about the milk, and the clerk recorded that "she was in use to milk the Cows & did mix that Cows milk with the milk of the other Cows." The other witnesses were Janet Sutherland, who had been Selbie's servant, and James Smith, Taylour's son by another marriage, who had been thirteen when he watched Selbie through "a holl in the door, the same being Shutt and not much worth." It is hard to know where to draw the line between animosity and fascination, if those are the right words, since it seems that these people watched Selbie regularly, for several years, rather than turning away in disgust.[20]

In the face of his servants' disapproval, Selbie mastered his tenancy in the old style, willfully ignoring his women, copulating with his cow, and forcing his servants to drink what they believed to be tainted milk. He might, of course, have abused his female servants and abandoned them with far less risk to himself, but he did not. In 1753, the balance tipped against him, perhaps because Peter James became a tenant, or perhaps because Selbie failed to marry Taylour, or Webster, or Sutherland, or any woman. If we are tempted to imagine, from the example of the witch hunts, that only gender could predict vulnerability, Selbie's demise serves to remind us of just how fragile, how carefully constructed, and how complex a villager's position could be. Selbie was hanged, and the cow may have fared even worse.

Why did they act only after watching him for years? James, Taylour, and the younger servants understood that they lived with constant constraints on their lives, to which William Selbie had set himself as an exception. All of the women knew they would have to marry to live decently, from Janet Taylour, who perhaps had to remarry to remain at Graystane, to the younger servants, who may have hoped to marry Selbie. Knowing that he could choose not to marry, and hold his place, while leaving his barn door in sorry repair, as Taylour's son remarked, must have stood as a challenge to his neighbors. If Selbie's preference for the cow irritated, or threatened, the women of his community, the men found him terrible as well, especially if they had to drink that cow's milk, or if, like young James Smith, they were of an age to start reckoning their chances of getting a tenancy. If this unnatural relationship no longer smacked of witchcraft, and made little impression on the local minister, it may still have been too much to bear for servants and neighbors whose anxiety about their own status was reflected in their censure of Selbie's cocksure flaunting of his.[21] Selbie had the great bad fortune, not only to be bulling his cow, but to be doing so at that moment that most historians agree marked the beginnings of rapid, and visible agricultural transformation, 1750. Morality alone cannot explain his neighbors' actions in seeing him tried and hanged, because they had watched him for four years. Something must have made them less tolerant, more powerful, or more determined to secure his land for another tenant.

The New Managers of the Agricultural Landscape

But changes in farming began before 1750. There were fewer crop failures, particularly after 1660, and the export of grain reached significant proportions in the late seventeenth century.[22] Edinburgh and Glasgow doubled in size, small communities sprang up in the central Highlands, and between 1660 and 1707, 246 markets and fairs were authorized outside the burghs. Those new rural markets constituted 58 percent of all markets in existence in 1707, testifying to expanding and shifting centers of marketing.[23] Nonetheless, the population was ravaged by one last great famine in the 1690s, after which wages for farm servants rose, and no doubt some landlords increased the labor dues they specified in their leases.[24]

The weakness of the new system told rather quickly in that last great famine, when lime alone, and lime used only in some advanced regions, could not save the population it had nurtured over the seventeenth century. The real problem was that only small areas of arable land were limed, just as the black cattle raised for market were still a localized specialty.[25] The grain surplus that fed the growing cities and was shipped abroad apparently came from counties around Edinburgh, where liming was reportedly well understood as early as 1627, and from estates along the northeast coast, where coastal trade made disposal of surpluses easy. But the rest of the country's farming was unimproved, and the famine carried off many people.

After the great union of 1707, the continuing threat of Jacobite rebellion slowed the spread of new techniques, but by 1750, with a bloody peace secured at Culloden, the profitability of farming became both visible and undeniable, if still quirkily understood. This was Grant of Monymusk's world, which he busily shaped with an iron hand (xxxviii). The question that remains is why some landowners improved, while others did not. The answer does not lie wholly with grain and cattle prices, even though the low prices and constant threats of glut could not have been much of an incentive.[26] That explanation assumes that seventeenth- and eighteenth-century Scots landowners thought like capitalist farmers, when their relations with each other, as well as with their dependents often must have been more feudal than contractual, profiting them in things other than cash. Elizabeth Mure, speaking in 1790 from her experience in a landed family, recalled her grandfather, born in the 1660s, in language that is properly patriarchal.

> Their manners was peculiar to themselves, as some part of the old feudle system still remained. Every master was revered by his family, honour'd by his tenants, and aweful to his domestics. His hours of eating, sleeping, and ammusement, were carefully attended to by all his family and by all his guests. Even his hours of devotion was mark'd, that nothing might interrupt him. He kept his own sete by the fire or at table, with his hat on his head; & often perticular dishes served up for himself, that no-

body else shared off. Their children approached them with awe, and never spoke with any degree of freedom before them.[27]

Mure paired the "feudle" with the religious, and she later remarked "that while that reverance and Awe remain on the minds of man for masters, Fathers, and heads of Clans, it was then that the Awe and dread of Deity was most powerful."[28] Her grandfather cast a long shadow, over both his tenants' households and his children's lives.

Landed families in the seventeenth century produced principled and violent people with far more regard for their honor and their "friends" than for wealth. Jacobite royalists forfeited their lands during the Commonwealth's occupation, and Lowland Protestants changed places with them during the Restoration. Later Jacobites would again forfeit their lands as a result of the uprisings in 1715 and 1745. To talk about agriculture in the seventeenth or eighteenth centuries without acknowledging that land was still the support of a political elite, as well as a point of production, is to create an illusory rural world.[29] While a few landlords concentrated on profit, many others used their land to generate loyal followers, even men at arms, along with less important rents.

One among the landed elite who did watch over the land with an accountant's eye in the seventeenth century was a woman, which tells us that the serious interests of landed men still lay elsewhere. Lady Anne Hamilton learned her trade by riding out with her grandmother to visit tenants, inspect livestock, and supervise work, and then coming home to watch the older woman, the Marchioness of Hamilton, meet her "constant stream of callers—tenants bringing their rents, local farmers complaining that their neighbors were encroaching on their land, poor people seeking financial assistance." And then her grandmother kept accounts, and supervised the eight chamberlains required to manage the enormous Hamilton estates. Lady Anne learned well, because when she inherited the enormous but heavily indebted estates after the deaths of her father and uncle, she quickly had them paying handsomely. By 1695, she was one of the few Scots with any sizable capital to contribute, and lose, in the Darien Scheme to trade in Panama.[30]

Grizel Hume, later Lady Baillie, was one of many Protestant refugees forced to spend the last years of the Restoration in the Netherlands. She lived in Utrecht, learned to do the work of an urban bourgeoise, never forgot the experience, and never lost her taste for management. While in exile the family lived on her mother's jointure, but it was managed by Grizel, the eldest daughter. That she should, at the age of twenty or so, have care of what little income the family had is hardly surprising, for the physical work of maintaining the household had already devolved upon her, and on the "little girl" who did washing: "She went to market, went to the mill to have their corn ground, which it seems is the way with good managers there, dressed the linen, cleaned the house, made ready the dinner, mended the children's stockings and other clothes, made what she could for them, and, in short, did everything."[31] Her labor stretched their income until it included a small measure of gentility for the rest of the family, and her father's attention could be given to politics, her mother's to the younger children. According to Grizel "they had no want, but plenty of everything they desired."[32]

They did not live badly in Utrecht, and in later years Grizel Hume's daughter could recall that her mother had hundreds of times "declared it the most pleasant part of her life." At her death in 1746, these words were carved on her tombstone, halfway down the list of her virtues: "At different times she managed the affairs of her father, her husband, her family, her relations, with unwearied application, with happy economy, as distant from avarice as from prodigality." That "happy economy" that balanced between avarice and prodigality was bourgeois, and Grizel Hume Baillie learned it in the streets of Utrecht.[33] She too, like the Duchess of Hamilton, would use her managerial skills throughout her life.

That taste for mastery was not confined to great landowners, because in 1729 we can see two small farmers in Ross physically fighting each other for control of the local source of lime. In late August Margaret Cuthbert, with seven other women and two boys, most of them holding harvesters' hooks, stood on a highway and blocked the passage of three men who were leading a horse-drawn cart full of seashells north to the estate of Alexander Ross of Ankervile. Cuthbert stepped forward and cut through the "horse graith," or harness, with a small knife. When two of the men attempted to use bits of it to keep one of the horses harnessed, she "Cut the remainder of the horse Graith." Others from the "Croud of women & two boys" pulled the body of the

cart off its wheels, and one of the men saw one of Cuthbert's daughters
hit his partner, James Vans, over the head with a hook, after which
Vans was pulled into the midst of the crowd by his hair.[34]

Several young men with business—or no business—on the highway
that morning watched the proceedings with some care. Hector Henry,
the sixteen-year-old brother of a tacksman, or landlord's agent, testified in court next spring that he had seen the cart standing on the
highway, and that he saw Cuthbert cut the graith, and that she had
"also in her hand afterwards ane ax." Whatever the others were doing
to the unfortunate James Vans, Henry's gaze was held by Margaret
Cuthbert, for he went on to say that

> he did not observe [her] do anything with [the ax] further than
> beat with it upon the Cart thereafter he observed one of her ten-
> nents servants take the ax out of her hand, and Said that he
> Could manage it to better purpose upon which the said servants
> wife desired her husband to go away, But [Cuthbert] said to the
> servant that She would stand betwixt him and a Stroke Thereaf-
> ter he observed the Said Servant with the ax beat out some of
> the boards out of the bottom of the Cart but depones that his
> So doing was after the horse Graith was Cutt and Ankervile's
> Servant[s] were Gone. (65–66)

Whether he was there by accident, or had heard rumors, Henry was
right to keep his eye on Margaret Cuthbert. The quarrel that was being
resolved on the highway was not between the crowd of women and the
men with the cart, but between Cuthbert and her neighbor, Ross of
Ankervile—generally referred to as "Ankervile" by the villagers who
testified—the man who owned the cart and claimed to own the shells.
The ground they were standing on was her husband's estate of Damm,
and the women and boys she led against the carters were drawn from
her servants, tenants, and cottagers, as well as her two daughters,
Marjory and Jean Gair. Until she led them down to the highway, they
had, perhaps all, been harvesting in one of the fields of Damm. Without
Ankervile there to protect his property—he rode with pistols and a
sword—the cart suffered, not to mention James Vans. The man who
came back the next morning to retrieve it found the "cart, bottom, and
wheels and the Iron of the wheels all lying on the Ground and broke in
pieces" (63–66).[35]

The argument was not over Ankervile's right to cart the shells across Damm, for his cart was on the public highway; the argument was over the shells, and was finally settled in court. Cuthbert's lawyer explained in his opening statement that the "Fishers of Ballintrait agreed to pay a toll to [Cuthbert and her daughters], for the use of the ground where the shells were placed And that the Pannells had reason to hinder the taking away of the shells till the toll was payed." Presumably, this meant that the fishers in Ballintrait, who were tenants, had no convenient ground to spare in their village and had to rent a bit on which they could store their shells (56).

In mid-August, Ross of Ankervile had concluded "some bargain" with the fishers about their shells. Two weeks later, during the harvest, Ankervile began sending servants with a cart and shovels to fetch the shells, which would be used to lime his fields after the harvest. The servants carting the first load had no trouble, other than the trouble of perhaps being called away from their own harvest work to do their

Carting near Inverary Castle in Argyll, on Scotland's west coast. In a similar scene on the east coast, two men were carting sea shells to the estate of Ross of Ankervile.

landlord's carting, probably as a labor service owed to him. Two of the men were referred to as Ankervile's servants, while the third, Robert Ross, was a cottager who seems to have hired himself out to Ankervile whenever possible.

Two days later, three men, including Robert Ross and Vans, one of the servants, returned to the shells and proceeded to load the cart. Margaret Cuthbert and one of her daughters accosted them, but Ankervile was also there. Perhaps he had heard rumors of trouble, or perhaps he merely intended to supervise, but he had ridden the four or five miles south from his estate, and was well armed. He found that Cuthbert had "Stopt their filling," but they resumed, whereupon she climbed into the cart and threw the shells out as fast as the three men shoveled them into the cart. Robert Ross claimed that the reason she gave for doing this was "that She had a letter from a Gentleman in Caithness to keep the shells for his use." Ankervile responded, saying, "Dame, if you will not Come out of the Cart I'll beat you," while slapping a switch against his hand; Cuthbert then "Gave ill names to the said Ankervile Such as Dog," and Ross concluded by saying that they then pulled a pin on the cart and tipped Cuthbert out, "but without any manner of hurt" (61).

Ankervile was clearly in control. Even though Ross preferred to recall the verbal confrontation between Ankervile and Cuthbert, he admitted hearing Ankervile threaten to beat Cuthbert, and "observed him moving a Switsh in his hand." He also "observed the arm of the sd pannel [Cuthbert] Red and blue," but insisted that he was too busy with the shells to have seen Ankervile strike, and speculated that perhaps her arm was bruised "by her turning the Shells out of the Cart" (60–61).

What Ross would not say Donald McCurchie would. He was one of Cuthbert's, or technically, her husband's, tenants, and he was also there, probably attracted by the sight of Ankervile riding up, and by his mistress, bare-armed, sitting in a cart full of shells. Donald McCurchie, like many of the tenants and servants who testified, spoke only Gaelic and required an interpreter. McCurchie recalled that he saw Ankervile "ride up to the Cart, with pistols before him and a sword about him," and said he heard Ankervile "order his servants to loose the pin of the Cart" and turn Cuthbert out. Cuthbert, not so easily disposed of, "fastened the heell of her shoe in the Sand," keeping her balance with one foot still in the cart, so that Ankervile had to grab her by the shoulder to pull her out. Despite the advice of a servant, she tried to get back in the cart. Ankervile "did with his whip switch her about her neck and shoulders," threatening "that if any of her Servants Came up to oppose him he would cut them to the eyes." At this point in McCurchie's testimony Ankervile, who was in court as plaintiff, questioned him, and McCurchie replied that Ankervile "uttered the foresaid threat in Such Irish as he Could speak but so as the deponent understood it" (69).

No doubt Cuthbert's people understood what they had just seen: Margaret Cuthbert turned out of a cart, shoved to the ground, and whipped about her shoulders, in front of one of her daughters, her tenant, and at least one more servant, perhaps a subtenant of McCurchie's. And she was obviously unable to protect her people from Ankervile at that moment. It was this struggle, as McCurchie called it, that set the stage for the next morning's confrontation on the highway. But that afternoon Cuthbert, probably still in a rage, ordered her servants to take her carts and carry the remaining shells to her fields and scatter them.[36]

Clearly the shells initially belonged to the fishers in Ballintrait. But the next question must be, to whom did the fishers belong, and what claims upon their goods might that dependency entail? This was not a free world, but a network of dependencies and displayed authority. Margaret Cuthbert was married to a landowner, accustomed to directing tenants, subtenants, and servants, and the fishers were almost certainly someone's tenants. It seems clear that whatever her agreement with them over using a bit of Damm, she tried to appropriate to herself control over the shells, and act as broker, if not owner. She never mentioned the toll, according to court testimony, but did insist that she had a letter from a gentleman in Caithness, north of Ross, who wanted the shells. She would not have had such a letter unless she had tried to act as broker, or unless others had treated her as such. Her claim to that role may have rested on the simple fact that the shells were kept on her husband's ground, and that she had arrived at some arrangement with the fishers, by which she was guaranteed a toll of some sort— probably payment in kind—for the use of the ground. That they were thus bound to her did not give her control of the shells, unless she could establish herself in that role, using all the means at her disposal: the toll, her status, her dependents, whatever connection she had with the gentleman in Caithness. That seems to be what she tried to do, although we cannot rule out the simple possibility that she feared that their deal with Ankervile meant that she was about to be cheated out of her tolls, through his bullying, perhaps of the fishers as well as herself.

In 1730, a jury decided in favor of Cuthbert and her daughters, even though Ankervile had brought the case, charging her with riot and oppression. The jury of eight lairds, two baillies, one merchant from Fortrose, and four tenants ordered Ankervile held, to ensure the safety of the defendants. It is hard to know whether that decision was meant to uphold Cuthbert's control over the shells, and the fishers, which might have depended on the inability of the fishers to pay the toll; or whether the decision was meant to control a violent laird who would whip another landowner; or whether the jury's judgment was directed against a man who would whip a woman. To modern sensibility, the members of the jury were choosing between upholding one or another illegitimate power, either Cuthbert's or Ankervile's raw power to determine the working out of so small, or large, a matter as the distribution of the local supply of shells.

Margaret Cuthbert's struggle over the shells illustrates how the smallest ripple of change, in this case a market for shell lime as fertilizer, might offer some opportunity to a woman, particularly if she could be spared from agricultural labor at times, and did not owe her labor elsewhere. In Cuthbert's case her resolve may have been strengthened by a sickly husband, since Alexander Gair was too ill to attend her trial. But women did what they could. Cuthbert probably worked in the fields when necessary, and her daughters certainly did. She was used to physical work, and the evidence is her willingness to climb into the cart and shovel the shells out with her bare arms. And it is worth remembering that one of the first prizes offered for livestock in Scotland went to Ann Wade, described as "tenant in Yester," for selling the largest number of calves to the butcher in 1756. While women had far fewer chances to run farms than did men, and perhaps neither Cuthbert nor Wade was entirely responsible for the farm, women were exposed to the same economic pressures, the same pleasures of innovation, and the same habits of exploitation that shaped men's lives, and would act on them when the chance came.[37]

Nigg, the parish in which Cuthbert struggled with Ankervile over the shells, was a pocket of early development. The highway was exceptional, as was the cart that Cuthbert and her servant destroyed. The

Carting in Strathpeffer, Ross, not far from the parish of Nigg, where the battle over sea shells was fought.

iron-rimmed wheels, the pin that allowed the body of the cart to be tipped without unhitching the animals, the fact that it was pulled by two horses rather than one are all marks of advanced design, all meant to save time and eliminate human labor. And Nigg sat on the coast, just north of the smaller and even more fertile Black Isle. From 1750 on, the area attracted well-known improving landlords, mostly lawyers, who presumably used the law and capital, rather than the whip and labor dues. When Ankervile passed into the hands of David Ross of Inverchasely in 1759, it had been just thirty years since Alexander Ross rode out to supervise his servants, armed with a switch, a sword, and a pair of pistols. However Nigg was improved in the second half of the century, less worldly proprietors had been exploiting both natural resources and their servants in the first half of the century. It was not the second serfdom of eastern Europe, but Scotland was hard up for capital, and Grant's labor dues and Ankervile's whip, as well as the loyalty of Cuthbert's servants, could provide labor that those landlords could not afford to buy.[38]

Christian Shaw and the Beginnings
of the Textile Industry

More difficult to comprehend in the annals of propertied women is the case of Christian Shaw of Bargarran, in Renfrew. She was eleven when she caught a housemaid drinking a glass of milk, and reported the theft to her mother. We know about this milk only because it resulted in the last large witch hunt in Scotland, in 1697, and because members of Shaw's community, the parish of Erskine, produced an account of her "sufferings and relief" which began with the root of all the trouble, the glass of milk:

> Christian Shaw . . . a smart, lively girl, and of good inclinations, about eleven years of age, perceiving one of the maids of the house, named Katherine Campbell, to steal and drink some milk, she told her mother of it; whereupon the maid Campbell (being a young woman of a proud and revengeful temper, and much addicted to cursing and swearing upon any like occasion, and otherwise given to purloining) did, in a most hideous rage, thrice imprecate the curse of God upon the child; and at the same time did thrice imprecate these horrid words, "The devil harle [drag] your soul through hell."[39]

To the great relief of her subsequent chroniclers, Shaw went on to found the linen thread industry of Paisley. She became adept at the fine spinning and bleaching of thread as a young woman, and devoted herself entirely to the business after her husband's death in 1725. The report for Erskine in the Old Statistical Account, written by Erskine's minister in 1792, described her efforts in thread manufacture within her parents' household:

> Having acquired a remarkable dexterity in spinning fine yarn, she conceived the idea of manufacturing it into thread. Her first attempts in this way were necessarily on a small scale. She executed almost every part of the process with her own hands, and bleached her materials on a large slate placed in one of the windows of the house. She succeeded, however, so well in these essays as to have sufficient encouragement to go on, and to take the assistance of her younger sisters and neighbors. The then Lady Blantyre carried a parcel of her thread to Bath, and dis-

posed of it advantageously to some manufacturers of lace; and this was, probably, the first thread made in Scotland that had crossed the Tweed. About this time, a person who was connected with the family, happening to be in Holland, found means to learn the secrets of the thread manufacture, which was then carried on to great extent in that country. . . . The young women in the neighborhood were taught to spin fine yarn, twining mills were erected, correspondencies were established, and a profitable business was carried on.[40]

This parable of Shaw's life is more than the story of a bright, industrious little girl. By 1697, in the midst of that last great famine, witch hunting had begun to look extraordinary, and the burning of the Bar-

Bargarran House, which may have been the family home of Christian Shaw, the witch-hunter and thread spinner.

garren witches was to be lamented as barbarous. Nonetheless, Shaw believed in witches, and she believed herself quite capable of producing the best linen thread in Scotland, and she did both before reaching adulthood. If she was not two people, we must reconcile what would otherwise seem an unnerving combination of old and new beliefs in one person. The tale of the glass of milk shows us a child, exercising the authority she had seen her parents use, perhaps for the first time. She asserted her right, or at least her obligation, to correct a servant, and then was soundly cursed by that adult woman, and it was apparently devastating.

Certainly Shaw responded as if her world had been turned upside down, by acting out, through the language of witchcraft and the malefice, her own exaggerated abuse at the hands of Campbell and other witches. And this tells us that she expected to be in control, much as Cuthbert expected her tenants to back her up, sickles in hand, and Grant of Monymusk counted on services provided in increasing quantity by his lesser tenants. Her "enthusiasm for the new spirit of inquiry and experiment" was not incompatible with an older view of social relations.[41] Loyalty and devotion may not have buttered any parsnips, but when loyalty could be turned into service, it could become an important economic tool, substituting for capital in a country rich in dependents, and poor in cash. And when that loyalty failed, as it did for Selbie, and for the eleven-year-old Shaw, the results could be disastrous for master and servants. As a result of that glass of milk, twenty-four people were accused of witchcraft, and at least five died.

Shaw's success with linen thread shows us a general trend, not a unique experiment, for linen manufacturing was to flourish in the eighteenth century. No doubt prompted by the British Linen Bank in 1746, Archibald Grant of Monymusk noted in his journal, "Get tennents' wifes to tea or punch etc about spinning plann, in which boyes may be used as well as girls" (xxix). A few pages later, he noted that he had hired two women in Aberbrothock to spin, and recorded how much yarn they should spin every day, and that "They are also to teach others; therefore if I have none fixed for to be taught before I goe you'll . . . get 4 of the children of tennents or crofters of largest families who are most in debt" (180–82). When he recorded that a shipment of wool was due, he noted that it was to be given to "the most needy and those that are in debt . . . and if they'll knit good tollerable ribbed stockings, I'll take payment in stockings."[42] By 1748, his standard lease, probably for tenants of his multiple-tenancy farms, specified that they should have no subtenants, "and no person whatever to live under them or have a house unless they keep two constant spinners in the house" (45). This demand for the labor of women and children would separate poorer tenants and landless cottars from those holding larger farms. Just as Grant had hired his two women from Aberbrothock to teach spinning, the British Linen Bank, both a bank and a putting-out system, began to send spinning mistresses into the north of Scotland after 1746. There was a great push to increase production of coarse linens for the colonies in the 1740s, and while the use of a wheel instead of a distaff helped, increasing the number of spinners would be the eighteenth-century solution.[43]

For those women who would not be doing the improving, running the farms, or selling calves, the greatest impact of rural reorganization probably lay in textile production. Elizabeth Mure, writing on changes she had seen in her life, discussed domestic linen in detail, recalling patterns, prices, and a ball in 1731 at which everyone wore clothes made of Scots linen. Spinning would come to the cottage door first, then pull families toward the textile towns. Shearing sheep, swingling lint, and spinning linen and wool often figure in the testimony of women accused of infanticide, but they are typically mixed with other kinds of work. Villagers wanting to talk to Katharine McKinnel found her at the door of her master's house, "spinning on a rock," in 1758. In 1749, Margaret Gillespie reported that she rose out of bed and went directly to her spinning, but she had also been to a fair, looking for work in the harvest. Janet Thomson harvested for a widow in 1761, then spun "at the Mickle Wheel" in a house nearby. A year later, Agnes Walker would swingle lint for her sister on a Tuesday, bake for a christening on Wednesday, cook the christening dinner Thursday, swingle lint on Friday and Saturday, watch her sister's child on Sunday, and spin with two daughters in yet another household on Monday. Margaret Comrie reported leading a horse and cart, loaded with wool, while a witness at her trial had been shearing sheep.[44]

Stealing Yarn and Clothes

With more swingling, spinning, bleaching, and weaving came more theft. While one or two women had been dismissed from the New Mills factory in the late seventeenth century for pocketing yarn, Parliament passed an act in 1745 aimed at preventing the theft of cotton, fustian, and linen from buildings and fields. In 1766 Grizzel Buchanan was caught sneaking out of a bleachfield in Paisley by the bleacher and his friends. When questioned, she admitted that she had been tempted by two other women, both of whom also stole from the same bleachfield. In all, her profits amounted to three and one-half spindles of linen yarn, and a silk kerchief, for which she was banished. So was Margaret Cusine, caught stealing from a bleachfield in Dunfermline in 1784. Both women were well on their way into the subculture of petty crime, which for women often meant stealing yarn or clothing.[45]

In 1782, Margaret Denoon, a dealer in old clothes in Aberdeen, in her early thirties and married to a blacksmith, bought two bits of clothing from a woman she met at the house of yet a third person. In October a young woman would visit her stand near the market cross, and claim "a Tartan plaid and a check apron." The young country woman claiming the clothes had fought off robbers in her parents' house a week or two earlier, and by diligently visiting Aberdeen, was able to reclaim what clothing of hers had been stolen. Denoon proved her innocence, but the woman from whom she bought the clothes, Margaret Elder, was hanged.

Elder, together with Jean Craig, had broken into a house at Whitemyres, in the parish of Newhills, where Frances Thomson, the older daughter, awoke, called out, and heard one woman yell to the other, "God damn you bring that pistol or else I will take your life." Undaunted, Frances opened the door and saw "a woman with a mutch on," who turned on her, saying, "I will take your life." Frances "laid hold of the woman and turned her to the door," where she saw another woman "holding a pice [sic] of Iron about the length of ones arm." The first robber then told the second to use the iron on Frances, but Frances "wrested the said Iron, out of the woman's hand."[46]

The robbers ran off, and Frances, victorious, noticed that a chest was missing. In it were all the clothes she owned, which probably explains the alacrity with which she walked the forty or fifty miles into Aberdeen to find her belongings. Unfortunately for Margaret Elder and Jean Craig, Frances was also worldly enough to find her goods, and offer testimony that would get Elder hanged. Nothing was found proven against Jean Craig, who found a new partner, continued to steal, and was hanged in 1784. Such was the underworld, in this case female, with which many small traders must have sometimes dealt, or struggled to avoid.[47]

Other New Opportunities in a Changing Economy

Women transported more than old clothes into cities, for late eighteenth-century Edinburgh was making new demands on outlying parishes. In 1792 Alexander Carlyle described the impact of Edinburgh's growth on women in his parish, Inveresk. Noting particularly that "the demand for vegetables has increased ten-fold within these fifty years," he described the heavy work done by village women in supplying the city. "The whole produce of the gardens, together with salt and sand for washing floors, and other articles, till of late that carts have been introduced, were carried in baskets or creels on the backs of women, to be sold in Edinburgh, where, after they made their market, it was usual for them to return loaded with goods, or parcels of various sorts, for the inhabitants here, or with dirty linens to be washed in the pure water of Esk." He pointed out that the women who carried sand had the worst of it, for each woman carried at least two hundred pounds into Edinburgh each morning, and then spent the afternoon and evening in the quarry, "digging the stones, and beating them into sand" for five pence a day.[48]

Far preferable to carry salt, or fish, or greens, which must have been a good deal lighter, Carlyle pointed out; yet all these women shared in a unique moment in the growth of the early modern economy, one which Carlyle caught faithfully, and with respect: "This employment of women, which has certainly prevailed ever since Edinburgh became a considerable city, when joined to that of the fish-wives in Fisherrow, has occasioned a reversal of the state of the sexes in this parish, and has formed a character and manners in the female sex, which seems peculiar to them, at least in this country (294). With true Enlightenment spirit, he gave in a footnote a traveler's account of women in Bilbao, where women unloaded ships, and generally worked as porters, "carrying burdens on their heads, which require two men to lift up." He concluded his footnote with the pronouncement that it was a "very exact picture of the fish-wives here, so similar are the manners of human creatures in similar circumstances" (295).

In this John Kay portrait of two Edinburgh gentlemen, engraved in 1792, an Edinburgh fishwife makes her way along the same street.

Carlyle admired these Scots women, "generally the wives of weavers, shoemakers, tailors, or sievemakers, who, being confined by their employments within doors, take charge of the children and family, while the females trudge to Edinburgh about their several branches of business." While he pointed out that their daily profits, leaving aside the sand carriers, ranged from eight pence to one shilling three pence, more than they could make for their families by any other work, it was his description of that working life—"free, social, and disengaged"— that betrays the cause of his admiration. If indeed "circumstances" created "manners," as his footnote implied, their work created them new, hard-working, healthy, free, social, disengaged. "[T]he wife yields not," Carlyle wrote, "in strength to the husband" (294–95).

Carlyle is remarkable for recognizing this strength, and not turning away in horror when he saw it in that particular female form. Then again, perhaps what he saw was not what those women experienced, but merely Alexander Carlyle decking himself out as a fishwife; but it is still remarkable. Consider what he had to say about the fishwives of Fisherrow, who earned at least one shilling a day, and sometimes two or three. These women were born into the coastal fishing business, daughters of fishermen "who generally marry into their own cast, or tribe" (297). Earlier, the fishwives had spent part of their week gathering bait and baiting lines for their husbands, but by the 1780s the coastal waters were fished out, and their husbands began to transport fish caught near Fife. While Carlyle knew a great deal about the fishing industry, it was chiefly the character of these women which impressed him. Writing more particularly about the fishwives, it is clear that Carlyle recognized differences between people of this class and his own. Yet he was not in the least troubled by the fishwives' work outside the house, indeed outside the village, nor by their resulting social position and worldliness: "Having no small share in the maintenance of the family, they have no small sway in it, as may be inferred from a saying not unusual among them. When speaking of a young woman, reported to be on the point of marriage, "Hout!" say they, "How can she keep a man, who can hardly maintain herself?" (297). He could not resist describing them as masculine, writing, "[a]s they do the work of men, their manners are masculine . . . Their amusements are of the masculine kind." On holidays they played golf, except on Shrove Tuesdays, when they played soccer (297).

Carlyle admitted that they were, like all "small traffickers," and market women across Europe, "very dexterous in bargain making" (297). But he admired their obvious comfort with the spoken word, a skill which he did not label masculine: "They have likewise a species of rude eloquence, an extreme facility in expressing their feelings by word or gestures, which is very imposing, and enables them to carry their points even against the most wary; and they are too well acquainted with the world, to be abashed when they are detected in any of their arts" (297).

These women took advantage of a wrinkle in the developing early

modern economy, and they disappeared, or persisted only as street
peddlers, once the deficiency in transportation was filled by carts, and
then the railroad.[49] If the traditions of market women were old, these
women were new at this business, pressed into service by Edinburgh's
growing demand for goods of all kinds. They made the best of their
brief advantage, just as Cuthbert or Shaw would have. But without
capital, they were limited, even though they remained their own
bosses, and were not shy in making their way.

But for other women, losing their footing on the land, what salvation
there was must have come from the demand for thread, and yarn, and
finally cloth. Initially, spinning would have helped cottars and small
tenants pay their rents, and hang on for a little longer. Between 1742
and 1753, the production of linen cloth in Scotland nearly doubled.[50]
Later, with the great cotton mills at New Lanark, another door would
open. There were always more women than men there, and work for
children as well. In 1793, there were 805 women, and 714 men. Most
were married, but among the single persons there were 56 women and
19 men. By 1811, the sex ratio was far more unbalanced, with 1313
women and 864 men, and by the early 1820s, some 10 percent to 16.9
percent of births at New Lanark were illegitimate. Although employment, the nursery, and housing should have made marriage easier, the
skewed sex ratio probably made it impossible for many women. But
there were no reports of infanticide at New Lanark. By 1885, the pattern would be repeated in the jute industry of Dundee, where women
outnumbered men by three to one, and constituted the labor aristocracy of the town.[51]

Women with property, and even those with little, if they were luckily
positioned in a vital trade, would act much like men in taking what
advantage they could. Others could take up textile work, which would
slowly pull them toward the cities. But what of all the others, hoping
to remain on the land, but finding that increasingly difficult? Many
women managed to marry, and to hang on to a familiar rural life, as
small tenants, skilled married servants, and cottagers; others, unmarried, clung desperately to the countryside as agricultural servants and
rural day laborers. Women who appeared in infanticide proceedings
often came from this middle ground, and if some spun for a day, they
also milked cows and threshed grain, sheared sheep, dug peats, baked,
and of course, spun. Whether they married or not, most of them proba-

bly believed that they would marry and live on a farm, if only because the great weight of quite literally centuries of past experience set that expectation before them. For those with their eyes open, the success of new farmers who were visibly doing well, and buttering their parsnips, must have made them all the more determined to stay, and cash in on the land's profitability. There must have been little incentive for many rural women to accept that their future lay in textile labor, or domestic service, during a century when the countryside produced so much, from grain and cattle to new stone two-story houses for the best farmers. Those who bent with the storm and moved to textile towns may have survived the changes more easily than those who stubbornly clung to an older vision of rural courtship, and a new vision of rural wealth.[52]

5

Making the Legal Machinery to Prosecute Infanticide, 1662–1719

In 1690, when the Scots parliament passed the Act Anent Child Murder, most Scots hoping or fearing change would have been watching the political drama of the times, the sudden flight of James II and the collapse of the Stuart monarchy followed by the careful integration of the new monarchs William and Mary into English and Scottish political life. Along with William and Mary came returning Scots nobles, Protestant exiles who had sought refuge in the Netherlands during the years of Stuart persecution, and with them came a moment of renewal for the Kirk. These grand changes obscured lesser shifts and adjustments in the social order, such as the trials of nine women for infanticide between 1661 and 1663, an enclosure riot of sorts in Peebles in 1681, and the growth of grain exports in the years before the great famine of the mid-1690s. With the Kirk restored, it has been easy to interpret the act as evidence of the Kirk's renewed desire to police its people, but the act had its roots in the Stuart years, and owed more to Stuart authority than to the Kirk.

Loosely based on the English statute of 1623, the Scots statute was far more exactly written, and described three conditions— concealing pregnancy, giving birth alone, and having no living child to show one's neighbors—which were to be taken as proof that the mother had murdered and had planned to murder her child. It stated

> [T]hat if any woman shall conceale her being with child dureing the whole space and shall not call for and make use of help and assistance in the birth, the child being found dead or amissing the mother shall be holden and reputed the murderer of her own childe, and ordaines all criminall Judges to sustain such pro- cesses, and the lybell being remitted to the knowledge of an in- queist, it shall be sufficient ground for them to return their verdict finding the lybell proven and the mother guiltee of mur- der tho there is no appearance of wound or bruise upon the body of the childe . . .[1]

The act's authors ordered juries to presume guilt, placed the burden of proof on the woman accused, and, most important, presumed that women could kill their own children, and indeed would do so if out of sight of their friends and neighbors, even for a few minutes. It is easy to see the statute as the Kirk's triumph over Restoration licentious- ness, and that may in part be true. The General Assembly of the Kirk apparently "pressed Parliament on the subject of the murder of bas- tards by their mothers" shortly before the 1690 act was passed, accord- ing to historian William Ferguson. In what is still the classic survey of modern Scotland, Ferguson claimed that the crime "stemmed from religious fanaticism," and characterized the law as having "no other effect than to butcher demented females," thus giving away his own dislike of the Kirk, as well as casting the accused as "demented fe- males."[2]

Ferguson's response was typical of an older historiography whose practitioners abhorred the Kirk, finding it intolerant, vicious, dog- matic, and capable of driving poor young women to kill their children rather than face the elders' wrath. That made a good argument, and many a minister would play his part in prosecuting women for the crime. But the statute had developed out of Restoration legal practice, in the 1660s, and might be better understood as a Stuart imposition, with an English precedent. Rather than signaling the rebirth of the Kirk's authority after James II's sudden departure, the Scots statute merely ratified legal practice developed in the courtroom thirty years earlier, under a prosecutor the exiled Protestants had called the Bloody Mackenzie.

That courtroom was still virtually a medieval one in 1661. Only in 1672 was the ancient figure of the justice general replaced by the High Court of Justiciary, with its lord justice clerk and five ordinary lords of session. This Stuart reform of the Scots criminal courts had begun in 1628, when Charles I had reclaimed the office of justice general from the hereditary control of the earls of Argyll. The eighth earl resigned the office to the king's control in 1628, but kept for himself and his heirs the administration of law in Argyll until 1747. Yet the advent of the High Court in 1672 brought no great change, because it was embedded in a system of ostensibly lesser courts, all competing for jurisdiction in criminal matters. Not only did the shire of Argyll have its own mirror-image High Court, but sheriff courts could pronounce doom if murderers were taken "red hand," and courts of barony and regality had perhaps even greater criminal jurisdiction, and the Privy Council still issued "commissiones of justiciary," allowing local worthies to try cases themselves.[3]

After 1708, the law lords of the High Court consolidated their control over local cases, by riding the north, west, and south circuits twice a year. But this modern, centralized system belied numerous abuses. Accused persons were held in prison for years before coming to trial, and judges could select jurors.[4] The king's advocate, or prosecutor, was the king's man in every sense, except in those moments when his own purse came first. Sir George Mackenzie, the king's advocate during the Restoration, is reputed to have claimed that "No King's Advocate has ever screwed the prerogative higher than I have. I deserve to have my statue placed riding behind Charles the Second in the Parliament Close."[5] Law was still very much a tool of monarchy, and in these years, when it was still a rough tool at best, gave birth to the infanticide statute.[6]

If the act was partially intended as a sop to the godly in 1690, it was one that served the monarch and the state as well, making the king's law a palpable presence in many villages, reinforcing the authority of the minister and elders, but leaving real power in the hands of judges, lawyers, and the landowners who sat on juries. And the evidence is there, in the records of the Restoration court, to show us that the future statute's presumptions had coalesced into a set indictment by 1663, hot on the heels of Charles II's vengeful restoration of his friends to political office. In other words, the presumptions that would later become the statute were being used in court to demonstrate the power of the king's law in the 1660s, at the very same moment that the Kirk was profoundly out of power.

The unidentified Scots jurist, possibly Sir George Mackenzie himself, who annotated the records of the High Court of Justiciary late in the seventeenth century made it clear that the presumptions of the English law were already in use by 1662, in the trial of Margaret Ramsay. Indicted for murdering her child and throwing it in Edinburgh's North Loch in 1661, Ramsay was "cleansed by the Assise for want of probation [proof]." Regardless of the verdict, the justice-deputes felt obliged to prescribe an arbitrary punishment for Ramsay. She was "whipt thro' the high street of Edinbro and banisht."[7] The justices could not hang her, because the jury had acquitted her of murder, but they could exercise their right to inflict arbitrary punishment (29 n. 1). That Ramsay was whipped through the streets and banished meant that the justice-deputes recognized the need for some remedy beyond that of common law, because the direct evidence required to convict at common law was nearly impossible to obtain in infanticide cases. As the annotator put it, or perhaps the court clerk: "but yet considering that she confest that she was with child and concealed her being therewith, and that she brought out the said Child privately without the help of Women, and did prevaricate anent the casting thereof in the North Loch of Edinbr, Therefore they decerned and adjudged her upon the 7 March instant to be whipt . . . (29)."

Some intelligence was at work here, however, because by 1663 the annotator found an example of a "sure way" to obtain a conviction, and he was careful to explain how the pursuer, or prosecutor, had conducted his case:

> Observe here a sure way to prevein scruples that might arise before an Assize for want of a positive Probation of the murder. The Pursuer lybells all the Presumptions and the extrajudiciall Confession, whereupon he founds, which did put the Justice to give their Interloqr upon the Relevancy of the probation as it

was circumstanciate, and the Justice Deputes having found it
so, the Assize had nothing ado but to consider whether these
circumstances and presumptions were proven, and all of them
being proven and joined together was a very sufficient Probation, so both the Interloqr and the Verdict were just. (62)

Mimicking later prosecutions under the statute, the pursuer did not
charge Margaret Taylor with murder, but with the presumptions of
the English law: concealment of pregnancy, giving birth alone, and
having no living child. The judges, in their interlocutor of relevancy,
then found these sufficient grounds to infer that murder was the crime
in question, if the jury should find the presumptions proven. Hence the
annotator's glee at seeing a clever pursuer steer the jury around their
own scruples about finding a woman guilty of murder when they were
not shown "positive probation." But the proof of this method lay not in
its success, but in the way Bessie Brebner, indicted and found guilty
in the same fashion slightly later, in the summer of 1663, acted at her
trial. The court clerk recorded that "This pannell confesses the Dittay
[indictment] judiciallie with tears, and craves God pardon, and is found
Guilty and sentenced to be hanged" (64). That Brebner wept justified
all the pursuer's presumptions, for her tears made her guilt visible in
court.

But the statute, so quickly passed in 1690, when the Stuart regime
had fallen, and the Protestant monarchs William and Mary had been
installed on the throne, was never the absolute arbiter of any accused
woman's fate, although occasionally it was followed to the letter, and
even beyond. In a fit of exuberance in 1695, the judges refused to accept
the fact that Christian Park had revealed her pregnancy to another
woman as relevant to her defense, thus presuming evil intent beyond
the letter of the law, and the jurors obediently convicted.[8] Such harshness, as well as such obedience, was typical of erratic early responses
to the statute. In 1709 another jury, having been allowed to consider
such a defense relevant, found that Isobel Taylor had told one other
person, and on that verdict the court simply freed her. And the court
exercised its power to impose arbitrary punishments until at least
1715. Both Elizabeth Arrock and Elizabeth Johnstoun, tried on two
consecutive days in March of 1715, escaped hanging but were scourged
before being set free.[9]

In the summer of 1692, Edinburgh juries returned two ineptly written verdicts. Jannot Greig was found guilty of not revealing her pregnancy, and not calling for help, but "not guilty of death"; the verdict for Cirill Beaton was essentially the same, with the jurors finding "murder not proven."[10] It is hard to say whether the jurors were acting out of stubbornness, sympathy, or ignorance, but clearly the statute initially met with rough handling and possibly resistance from juries. The presumption of murder was always a difficult one to make, especially for jurors used to seeing direct evidence in common law murder cases; and the presumption, linked as it was to the Kirk's strict morality, suffered as many of the godly became more moderate and urbane.

In a case before the Argyll Justiciary in 1719, Mary McIver's lawyer argued that she was ignorant of the law, and that the constant troubles taken to acquaint the people with this among other laws proved that the subjects needed constant reminding before they could be held to have broken such extraordinary "correctory law." Reminders had been read from the pulpits. Queen Anne proclaimed against "prophaness and immorality" in 1708, and George I ordered another in 1719, to be read by every parish minister at least four times a year. These proclamations leave little doubt as to the Kirk's visible role in discouraging infanticide, and suggest that the law was an unexpected imposition in some corners of Scotland. Mary McIver did not hang.[11]

Signs of change abounded during the late seventeenth century, but whether these economic innovations, along with the growth in grain production, and in the number of market towns, had anything to do with illegitimate births is utter speculation. A paper mill was erected outside Edinburgh in 1675, apparently with the help of French workmen. (It burned in 1679, was rebuilt, and seems to have failed, for want of sufficient rags.) In 1678 three men petitioned for the right to run a regular stagecoach between Edinburgh and Haddington. Shortly thereafter, an Edinburgh merchant set up another, between Edinburgh and Glasgow.[12] If the road to London was in appallingly poor repair in 1680, Scotland's first elephant nevertheless was delivered, and shown about the countryside.[13] And in Peebles, the town officials attempted to rent a piece of the "commonty," or communal land, in 1681, complaining that it was "a pretext for incomers to the said burgh, and the poor people, to eat up their neighbours' corns." A mob of at least thirty-seven irate burgesses broke into their meeting, threatening to assassinate them. Two of the burgesses were thrown in prison, but the next day a mob of women—seven were named, and some three hundred were estimated to have participated—forcibly liberated them, took them to the town cross, and there drank their health, "as protectors of the liberties of the poor."[14] Such protests suggest that the various experimental economic innovations of the period must usually have disturbed the traditional economy, to someone's disadvantage. Forty-three years later, in 1724, it would be mostly men who turned out for the Galloway levelers' riot.[15]

By 1705 one prosecutor had apparently mastered the skills needed to use the statute successfully. In that year, the Argyll Justiciary heard the case against Margaret Campbell, alias Guinich, as it was prepared by William Inglis "for her Majesties interest." While her crime was initially mentioned as murder, with reference to divine law, laws of all nations, and finally to the "Lawes and acts of parliament of this Kingdom," Inglis carefully specified that this was all the more "wicked and atrocious when committed by parents upon their own children especially infants." This exhortation would eventually become the first line of infanticide indictments, as the older stricture against simple murder slipped away and prosecutors learned to go straight to the point.[16]

The point, of course, was to establish that the indictment was based on the 1690 act, which Inglis reiterated, with some embellishment. What he chose to emphasize was the instruction to the jury contained in the statute, to find the mother guilty of murder whether or not there were marks of violence on the child's body. He also specified that the act had been publicly displayed and read out in churches; he must have known that in previous cases in Argyll, defending lawyers had argued that villagers had never heard of the law, presumably because Argyll's coastal and highland territory was not easily accessible and parish churches served vast areas. The bulk of the indictment then specified the evidence that Inglis had in hand to prove that Campbell was vulnerable to the act: she had concealed her pregnancy, moving many times, denying it to many people; she gave birth alone, and buried the child in a lonely place, which she confessed to the kirk session of Killmichell, and again to the Argyll Justiciary four days before her trial.

In conclusion, Inglis returned to the language of the statute, almost as if he were delivering instructions to the jury:

> . . . by all which it appears that she hath stiffled her said new born chyld or left it exposed in the condition it came to the world

that he soon died or have murdered him some other way at leist her concealing her being with chyld during the whole space and not calling for or making use of help in the birth her said chyld not only being found dead but also obscurely and shamefully buried or hidd by her self alone in manner above written conform to the tenor of the act of parliament. . . .[17]

The first thing to notice is that he was drawing the attention of his audience back to the crime at the center of all the statutory language: "by all which it appears that" he was stifled, or exposed, or murdered in some other fashion. The problem is the repeated use of the word *or*, for with each new proposal it becomes more obvious that there is no direct evidence of murder here. Campbell never confessed to murder; she confessed to concealing her pregnancy, to giving birth in a desolate place, and to burying the child there. When it was dug up, she confessed further that it was her child. But then, under the act, the point was not the direct evidence, but the degree to which the accused woman's behavior matched the outline set forth in the statute: "conform to the tenor of the act." As Inglis wrote "at leist," he was pulling the jury back to what the statute prescribed as the points upon which they were to judge: concealing, not calling for help, the child found dead. It was a brilliant conclusion, cutting right to the core of the act's great strength and greatest weakness, demanding that the jurors judge the degree of fit between what the woman did and what the act called murder, not what these men thought of as murder in their world.

The jury, consisting of ten men from the town of Inverary, one farmer, and four tenant farmers, found Campbell "guilty of the foresaid murder by her own judiciall confession and the foresaid Act of Parliament as above cited."[18] There is little question that they were impressed by the careful language of the indictment. The case stands as something of a model of the congenial handling of such cases by all. There was not even a recorded word spoken in defense, perhaps because in light of her confessions, the conclusion was hardly open to debate. The women of the village suspected her and she was caught by servants of her previous master. The initial investigation was made by the kirk session with the help of local midwives, and then her confessions were carefully repeated before the civil authorities. The jury simply accepted the direction given by the statute, leaving Inglis with a prize example of how smoothly such a case might be handled.

But the statute did not rule supreme, and lawyers began to work harder to find ways around it. In the spring of 1713, Margaret Anderson, one of the servants of the laird and lady of Kilbrachmont, was tried for child murder. Her lawyer, James Hamilton, advanced an extraordinary argument in her defense. He insisted that the lords take up the power of the old, now defunct, Privy Council to intervene in the case while it was in progress, on behalf of Anderson, because the one witness she had for her defense could not save her. But, he argued, she should not be allowed to hang simply because she had told only one person that she was with child.[19]

It was a bizarre appeal, in which he urged that Anderson be saved from hanging, not because she was by right not liable to prosecution, but because her defense, and she herself, was weak. And her proper protectors, he argued, were no longer close at hand, sitting on the Privy Council. Hamilton was indulging in a bit of fond reminiscence, hardly rare in 1713, for the old, direct powers of the Privy Council, which had represented royal authority in Scotland, and often used that authority with a free hand. Hamilton emphasized the Council's power, and Anderson's neediness, by referring to her repeatedly as "this poor pannel," especially in his closing statement:

> Tis very certain the remedy was easy when it was at hand, But this poor pannel and others of her rank and Condition who could have gote their cases represented to the privy Council, neither have moyen nor means to get such minute matters laid before her Majestie, And seeing that its a part of your Lordships power, which must belong to your Lordships Jurisdiction . . . The poor pannel hops [sic] your Lordships will see it no extension that her revealling be sustained as a Defence to mitigate her punishment. . . . Especially seeing the punishment is death, the Crime a presumption, And the pannel may still be punished sufficiently at your Lordships arbitriement [sic] for her negligence.[20]

Having described her as the "poor pannel," he also invited their lordships to take for themselves a rather grand, arbitrary power to intervene in the courtroom, as if he wished to restore an older relationship between poor pannels and great lords, and perhaps to reclaim some of the immediate power that had left Edinburgh, and gone to London, when the Act of Union had dissolved the old Parliament and Privy Council in 1707.

His argument did not persuade their lordships. Margaret Anderson's case went to the jury, under the statute, and the jury sent her to the gallows. The witness of whom Hamilton had made much turned out to be a seventeen-year-old servant, also at Kilbrachmont, who testified that Anderson had told him that she might be pregnant. Possibly suspecting that he was the father of the child, probably refusing to accept "might be" as a true disclosure, the jurors found it not proven that she had revealed her pregnancy. No doubt the weakness of this evidence had prompted Hamilton to attempt to save Anderson before the case came to trial, thus leaving us a record of where he thought the power to save Anderson lay.

Eighteenth-century Scots lawyers and judges are often spoken of as rising to fill "the void in Scottish public life" left when the Union drew Scots to the British Parliament in London, and dissolved the Privy Council and the Committee of Articles. But although the law lords of the High Court had been members of the Privy Council, and the powerful Committee of Articles, they did not simply or mystically rise to fill that void.[21] Instead, the dukes of Argyll dominated Scots politics from 1725 until 1761, because they were powerful, and wealthy, and the English relied on them to keep order in the north. After the Jacobite rebels were destroyed in 1746, the road was clear for the Dundas family, civil servants and distinguished lawyers for many generations. They built an empire out of patronage politics, with Henry Dundas rising to be Home Secretary at the end of the century.[22] Both Argyll and the Dundases figure later in this book. A fictional John Campbell, Duke of Argyll, was to secure Effie Deans's pardon in Walter Scott's novel about infanticide, *The Heart of Mid-Lothian*, while Robert Dundas, as lord advocate, was to lose, on appeal, one of the last infanticide trials conducted under the statute of 1690.

Before moving on to Robert Dundas's defeat in the next chapter, there is one more lesson to be learned from the early cases, and that stemmed from the impossibility of convicting married women. In 1701, Katharine Smith was tried before the High Court in Edinburgh. Her husband, who was in hiding because of debt, had visited clandestinely, and left her pregnant. She concealed the pregnancy to protect him, and fled when suspicious neighbors wanted to examine her. She was caught

Kilchurn Castle, Argyll. Argyll was home to the dukes who controlled Scots politics in the difficult early decades of the union with England in 1707. Hence Scott cast a Duke of Argyll as Jeanie Deans's protector in *The Heart of Mid-Lothian.*

and brought to trial, even though the child's body, which she claimed was "a shapeless decayed abortive thing," was never found.[23]

Her lawyers, typically for 1701, began by attacking the statute itself, insisting that an indictment ought to be "founded upon the very cryme and facts which positively inferr it." This was pointless, given that the statute created a wholly presumptive crime. Then they argued that the statute was never meant to apply to married women; and third, they quite reasonably argued that she concealed her pregnancy only to protect her husband. They won, with a plurality of the jury finding the prosecutor's case not proven, and Katharine Smith was free to return to Rutherglen.[24]

Because she was married, and because in 1701 the statute was still new and disputed, Smith was set free on evidence that would have sent an unmarried servant to the gallows. Her lawyers quickly gave up disputing the statute's existence, and shifted ground to an argument that would not be made for unmarried women until late in the century. Smith was protected from the statute's presumptions because hers was a case "where naturally ther aryses ground of more powerful Contrair presumptiones, Viz the affection that Mothers are presumed to have for their Children."

This "powerfull presumptione of the naturall affectione toward her Child for preserving it" did not apply to all women, however, for in their next paragraph they offered the case of the unmarried mother as antithetical: "The said act of parliament, As the narrative thcrof manifestly proports was made with relatione to murders that were or might have been committed upon infants by mothers unmarried who therfor conceall their being with Child and call not for help at the birth wherthrew the Child came easily to be destroyed[.] Whylle as the pannall [accused] is nottourly [notoriously] knowen to be ane married woman . . ." Natural affection applied to wives but not daughters. To twentieth-century readers, it is as if a wedge had been driven into our notions of maternal behavior, which are now far more deeply gender-specific, and minus any such blatant admission of the ways in which gendered behavior is shaped by one's place in the social relations of one's community. The line between married and unmarried women, marked in Scotland as in other countries by differences in clothing and hairdressing, still mattered at the beginning of the eighteenth century, even though it would be eroded by biological determinism much later. But maternal sentiment never struck lawyers as a sufficient defense in itself, and as they attacked the statute in the second half of the eighteenth century, they would learn to combine a Whiggish, liberal vocabulary of natural rights with the language of maternal nature.

6

The Demise of the Act Anent Child Murder

[T]he Lives of the Leiges [*sic*] cannot be taken away, nor their Liberty
or fortunes hurt upon the Implied meanings of words, But certain
Evidence & the clear Expression of it is in all cases necessary[.]
                    —Andrew Crosbie, in defense, for Agnes Walker
                                                    Dumfries, 1762

When Agnes Walker, many months pregnant, dragged herself from
Crossmichael to her sister's house in Terregles in 1762, only to leave
an infant in a small hole where it was found by the local minister,
she could not have known that her trial would set a significant legal
precedent. Her stay in Terregles (discussed in Chapter 3) was brief,
but the defense organized on her behalf was exhaustive, probably ex-
pensive, and possibly influenced by her sister's landlord, Maxwell of
Terraughtie. Many witnesses were called, and a recognized lawyer,
Andrew Crosbie, took up her defense.

   If life and liberty ring out in Andrew Crosbie's defense of Agnes
Walker, we must remember that in 1701 Katharine Smith's lawyers
had made much the same point, arguing that the statute flew in the
face of common law, creating a crime defined by presumptions rather

than direct evidence. But in 1701, her lawyers had quickly moved on to a more particular defense, based on her status as a married mother. While they were willing to say that the statute was, in effect, illegal in the eyes of common law and god's law, they were not willing to base their defense on an indictment of the statute. Sixty-one years later, Andrew Crosbie, in a last-minute appeal, was willing to risk Agnes Walker's life on just that argument, and if we consider Agnes Walker's trial from the perspective of the gentlemen of the court, rather than the villagers of Terregles, we can begin to piece together the legal history of the statute's demise.[1]

In 1762, at the October sitting of the South Circuit in Dumfries, Andrew Crosbie tried to move heaven and earth in defense of Agnes Walker. Crosbie was a well-known lawyer, whose reputation suggests that a great effort was being made to save Walker. Having called an extraordinary number of witnesses for the defense, including a midwife, a surgeon, a physician, and women who had borne children, he got an awkwardly written verdict from the jury, apparently favoring the prosecution.[2] By a plurality, they found her

> Guilty of having brought forth a Child without Discovering her Pregnancy or calling assistance during her Labour, according to the Act of parliament. . . . They are sorry to observe that this Law is not so well published & generally understood as it ought to be, And they therefore presume humbly to recommend the misfortunate Pannel to the Compassion of the Judge & to such Exertion thereof as to his Wisdom shall seem meet.[3]

The case was heard by the justice clerk (or senior judge) himself, Charles Erskine, and he assumed, along with the prosecuting advocate depute, that such a verdict was sufficient to condemn Walker, because the court clerk actually copied the formulaic sentence of hanging into the daybook, only to cross it out and scribble underneath, "Mr Andrew Crosbie for the Pannel Craved he might be heard upon the Import of the foregoing Verdict before pronouncing sentence thereon." There followed a short, sharp exchange between Crosbie and the prosecuting advocate depute, after which the latter gave up his case, and agreed to banish Agnes Walker.

John Maxwell, foreman of the jury, was the landlord of Walker's elder sister, a sister comfortably placed on a single-tenancy farm, and

The lawyer Andrew Crosbie, who defended Agnes Walker in her 1762 infanticide trial. From an illustration to Scott's novel *Guy Mannering*. Scott modeled a lawyer in *Guy Mannering* on Crosbie.

he may have authored the recommendation to mercy. If he was very smart, he may have carefully botched the verdict. He may also have been responsible for persuading Crosbie to take up Walker's case. But it was Crosbie, responding quickly when the trial was in its last minutes, who saved Walker. He insisted that the verdict was insufficient to convict Walker because the usual form, invoking the exact terms of the indictment, and three conditions of the statute, had not been followed. The jury had not, he said, found her guilty of "Actual Murder," or murder at common law, and what they had found her guilty of, concealing her pregnancy and labor, was not a crime in itself, nor could it stand as proof that the three conditions of the act of 1690 had been met.

The advocate depute replied that Crosbie was "too critical," and that "from the whole of it, it appears past a doubt, that the Jury have found her Guilty upon the Statute." He explained that "in the plain meaning of the words, the Jury has certainly said, that she never revealed her Pregnancy, & that she had no Assistance at the Birth." Ignoring what the jurors had forgotten to mention, namely that the child was dead or missing, and that the concealment lasted throughout the pregnancy, he relied on the implication of the jury's recommendation of mercy: "Besides the Recommendation to mercy plainly demonstrates, that the Jury themselves understand, that they have found her Guilty."

But "the plain meanings of the words" did not strike Crosbie as being quite so plain. He snapped back,

> That the Lives of the Leiges [*sic*] cannot be taken away, nor their Liberty or fortunes hurt upon the Implied meanings of words, But certain Evidence & the clear Expression of it is in all cases necessary to found a Sentence Condemnatory in matters Criminal. That the Jury in so far as they have not found the Pannel Guilty in terms of the Statute have not found the Lybel proven; And if they have not found the Lybel Proven, the Presumtion of Law is for Innocence, . . . That the Jury are Judges of the fact, not of the Law, And as they found only certain Circumstances proven, without finding all that was required by the Statute 1690, it is the Court that must apply these facts to the Statute & not the Jury. That the Recommendation to Mercy in the end of the Verdict is no argument that the Jury Intended to find any more than they have found: It only Shows that they have Erred in point of Law, and mistook what the Consequence of their Verdict might be.

This is the language of natural rights, of life and liberty, and it is the language of common law: "certain Evidence & the clear Expression of it." Crosbie drew both together to oppose "the implied meanings of words," which was a way of opposing the long arm of the king's statutory law.[4] And it is worth remembering that the jury struggled with the formula required in their verdict, perhaps intentionally got it wrong, and ended by recommending the accused to mercy, which suggests that they were not comfortable with the concept of statutory murder.[5]

But it was Crosbie who spelled out what the verdict meant, not only for Walker, but for all lieges, or persons subject to the king's law. He began by invoking powerful words—life, liberty, fortune—precisely because those words, representing important rights of the individual, could stand against the power of statutory law, especially a law so all-inclusive as to presume guilt as the old Act Anent Child Murder did. Having begun with the thunder and lightning of individual rights, he proceeded to the more particular problem of the verdict in Walker's case, that of "clear Expression." By demanding "certain evidence & the clear Expression of it," he meant that if the statute laid out three conditions—telling no one, not calling for help at the birth, and having no living child to show—that would constitute infanticide, then the verdict must indeed show that the jury found that all three conditions had been met. Walker's verdict mentioned only two, and Crosbie insisted that the court could not accept that the third was indeed implied, just because the jury recommended Walker to mercy. As he bluntly put it, their recommendation that Walker be treated mercifully by the judge only meant "that they have erred in point of Law, and mistook what the Consequence of their Verdict might be." In other words, Walker would escape hanging by what we would now call a technicality, but it was an important technicality, because it meant that prosecutors as well as women would be held to the letter of the statute. It also meant that Walker's case would exist as a precedent where the language of life and liberty had been used to oppose a prosecution that was locally popular, and a statute that should have had the power to hang her.

The great irony in Crosbie's enlightened defense lies in knowing that Agnes Walker almost undoubtedly killed her child, leaving it in a hole outside her sister's yard, even though the jurors were unwilling to see her hang. In saving Agnes from the hangman, Crosbie took the opportunity to hammer away at an old problem, the distance between the observed world, reflected in common-law standards of evidence and proof, and the world that existed by presumption, in the statute. The case ended in a draw, because the justice clerk did not find for Crosbie, and as a compromise, he hastily handed in a petition from Agnes Walker, craving banishment, and the advocate depute, having had enough, accepted it.

Dr. Hunter Challenges the Statute

Crosbie's challenge to the statute was not the only one. William Hunter was a Scottish anatomist, surgeon, and midwife with a substantial

London practice in obstetrics.[6] In his 1783 essay "On the Uncertainty of the Signs of Murder, in the Case of Bastard Children," Hunter challenged the medical proof that a child had been born alive, and then murdered, by discussing all the difficulties of childbirth that he had seen or could imagine. Not all doctors would agree with him over the coming years, but he shaped one side of a medical debate that continued for decades. By speaking out, he was offering to mediate between society and women accused of infanticide, substituting his voice and intimate knowledge of women for the presumptions of the statute.[7]

Hunter began his essay with an anecdote demonstrating how he, with a single letter, had successfully intervened in the trial of a woman accused of infanticide. He recounted being approached by a gentleman, "distinguished by rank, fortune, and science," on behalf of a young woman accused of infanticide. This person believed her innocent, "from the circumstances," and feared "she might fall a victim to prejudice and blind zeal," as "the minds of the people in that part of the country were much exasperated against her." In pursuing "an unprejudiced enquiry," the gentleman had been referred to Hunter, as one who had "made some remarks upon it which were not perhaps sufficiently known." Or so Hunter described it: "I told him what I had commonly said upon that question. He thought some of the observations so material, that he imagined they might sometimes be the means of saving an innocent life." He asked Hunter to put them in writing. Hunter com-

Crosbie was appealing to the Enlightenment sensibilities of gentlemen such as those shown here: Adam Smith, David Hume, John Home, Lord Kaimes, Dr. Hutton, Dr. Ferguson, and Dr. Black. From an illustration prepared for a nineteenth-century edition of Scott's *Guy Mannering*.

plied, the young woman was acquitted, and Hunter could report that the gentleman said "he had reason to believe that my letter had been instrumental" (266–68).[8]

In Hunter's account, the important role of the prominent gentleman slips from view, and so Hunter intervenes, via the letter, in a situation he knows without seeing. And Hunter's description of the letter as "instrumental" is telling, because it recalls his relationship to his instruments, his anatomical knowledge, and the bodies of pregnant women.

But what he was intervening in was not a woman's body, it was the courtroom, and the presumptions the statute created as a means of penetrating into the mystery of the unknowable time each accused woman spent alone in childbirth. The law claimed that these women could be known by their public behavior, in other words, by their relations with others. Hunter claimed to know them by their often hidden, unique relationships with him:

> The world will give me credit, surely, for having had sufficient opportunities of knowing a good deal of female characters. I have seen the private as well as the public virtues, the private as well as the more public frailties of women in all ranks of life. I have been in their secrets, their counsellor and adviser in the moments of their greatest distress in body and mind. I have been a witness to their private conduct, when they were preparing themselves to meet danger, and have heard their last and most serious reflections, when they were certain they had but a few hours to live. (269)

Having established himself so intimately, he insisted that women "who are pregnant without daring to avow their situation . . . are generally less criminal that the world imagine" (269). It is, Hunter insisted, the father who is criminal, while "the mother is weak, credulous, and deluded" (269). And so he began to establish his special perspective. When he spoke from the bedside of a woman in labor, he displaced the father of the child, both at that moment and by dismissing fathers of illegitimate infants as criminal. He is the only male allowed to speak from this experience, and his is the controlling consciousness, for those women who spoke to him in secret and in fear of death were rapidly replaced, in his narrative, by women unable to speak, who were weak, deluded, unconscious, fainting, or rigid with fear. In childbirth, Hunter argued, women ceased to be actors. It was at just that moment that the law had claimed they were most active, and most dangerous (268).

Hunter claimed that infanticide was rare, even when a woman felt shame, because it was opposed by "that powerful instinctive passion, which, for a wise and important purpose, the Author of our nature has planted in the breast of every female creature, a wonderful eagerness about the preservation of its young" (272). The power of that instinct was such that Hunter could only explain what he believed to be the rare intentional child murder by the impenetrable intentions of "temporary insanity" (272). Hunter seems to have understood women as shaped by two great forces, that "powerful instinctive passion" for the preserving of her young that was "planted in the breast of every female creature," and the purely social need to achieve respect and avoid shame. If the former was basic, the latter was still powerful.

If women were driven by such passions, or needs, why should they not be capable of murder, when those two forces were called into conflict by an illegitimate pregnancy? Because, as Hunter would argue, childbirth was an all-consuming physical experience, which erased reason and learned, social behavior. Women, in other words, were helpless in the face of nature, and even if they thought of murder, were incapable of committing it. Hunter was quick to say that "as well as I can judge, the greatest number of what are called murders of bastard children, are of a very different kind" (272). By "different kind," he meant they were not murders. Instead, women fumbled inconclusively with "difficulties on all sides, putting the evil hour off, and trusting too much to chance and fortune" (272).

"In that state," he continued, "often they are overtaken sooner than they expected; their schemes are frustrated; their distress of body and mind deprives them of all judgment, and rational conduct; they are delivered by themselves, wherever they happen to retire in their fright and confusion; sometimes dying in the agonies of childbirth, and sometimes being quite exhausted they faint away, and become insensible of what is passing; and when they recover a little strength, find that the child, whether still-born or not, is completely lifeless" (273–74). With the phrase, "they faint away," Hunter solved the problem he had set himself, reconciling statutory appearances, not to mention dead infants, with the biological instinct to preserve young. Nothing less than unconsciousness would do to block the maternal workings of instinct, and little else could contribute as much to emphasize the importance of the attending male midwife.

Here we have the secret divulged, but by Hunter, not by the woman. The woman fainted, the unattended child died. In that loss of consciousness we have one solution to the threat that infanticide posed to one man's belief in the maternal nature of women, not to mention the threat the will and competence of a murderous—or caring—mother posed to Hunter's professional stature. And so Hunter offered his audience a new archetypal situation, built around the woman's loss of consciousness.

This was a hypothetical offering on Hunter's part, and he was quick to provide the example of two dead bodies, both adult women who had died in secret childbirth. His point was that women concealed their pregnancies out of a terrible shame, not out of malice, and that they were so distraught by their situation that they were pitiful, and not dangerous (274–75). The dead bodies surely represent a deeply felt, masochistic shame, but they are also exaggerated representations of that moment of unconsciousness, when "being exhausted, they faint away":

> Among other instances which might be mentioned, I opened the bodies of two unmarried women, both of them of irreproachable and unsuspected characters with all who knew them. Being consulted about their healths, both of them deceived me. One of them I suspected, and took pains to prevail with her to let me into the secret, if it was so; promising that I would do her the best offices in my power to help her out of the difficulties that might be hanging over her: but it was to no purpose. They both died of racking pains in their bowels, and of convulsions. Upon laying out the dead bodies, in one of the cases a dead child, not come to its full time, was found lying between the unhappy mother's limbs; and, in the other, a very large dead child was discovered, only half born. (274–75).

What Hunter offered his readers was not proof of women's disorderly ways of meeting childbirth, their penchant for fainting, or even their determination to deny it—it was proof of his ability to see into their secrets, rendered in a bluntly physical way. What he saw into were not their secrets, however, but their bodies. As bodies, dissected, they

demonstrated his skill, and they represented an accomplished transformation, on which, deeply buried, Hunter's argument rested: How
was the overpowering will to deny her pregnancy changed into the qui-
escence of the fainting woman, the dead victim, the woman physically
incapable of harming her child, that Hunter repeatedly put before his
audience? With these bodies, Hunter let death mold that fierce determination into the utter passivity of the dead. It was an illusionist's
masterpiece, but a commonplace demonstration for an anatomist, who
saw all the ravages of life, over and over, come to rest in the body on
his table, harmless. By their deaths, they unwittingly made him their
spokesman, and by telling what he had seen, he made it clear that the
mediator, the man who could make these secrets public, was no longer
the lawyer, but the male midwife.

Having repeatedly removed the woman from center stage, it remained only for Hunter to install himself in her place. He did so by
listing the hardships of midwifery, the children born alive who died
despite his efforts. The common thread in all the stories is that "if this
may happen where the best assistance is at hand, it is still more likely
to happen when there is none; that is, where the woman is delivered
by herself." It is a plaintive argument, for clearly Hunter had seen
"children die in spite of all our attention," and had no choice but to
assume that worse awaited women giving birth alone. And his closing
anecdote, which was his most important revelation, and his best self-
advertisement, detailed his entry into a room just after a woman had
given birth:

> Her labour proved hasty, and the child was born before my ar-
> rival. The child cried instantly, and she felt it moving strongly.
> Expecting every moment to see me come into her bedchamber,
> and being afraid that the child might be someway injured, if an
> unskillful person should take upon her the office of a midwife
> upon the occasion, she would not permit the nurse to touch the
> child, but kept herself in a very fatiguing posture, that the child
> might not be pressed upon, or smothered. I found it lying on its
> face, in a pool which was made by the discharges; and so com-
> pletely dead, that all my endeavors to rouze it to life proved vain.
> (289)

The story is literally about his absence, and implicitly about the importance of his presence at the birth, where the mother can be present

only physically. He is expected at any moment; the mother's "fatiguing posture" serves to remind us of the painful passage of time. In his absence, all activity is frozen; the mother has not the presence of mind to rescue her child, nor to let the nurse touch it. She is concentrated in a physical gesture, and her refusal to let the nurse act merely extends her physical rigidity to another, and magnifies it. With both women immobilized to signify the mother's response, the child dies, faceless, in the pool of discharges. One might argue that the pool is itself an emblem of female nature, always present at that moment when a woman is not in control. But more important, especially in court, was the triad Hunter described, the woman, the pool, and the face-down child, for this could stand as visible representation of that moment that the law had claimed to know, but which only Hunter, as midwife, could claim to have entered. By establishing his professional competence, in this anecdote by holding out the promise that the child would have lived, had he been there, he also established that a woman giving birth alone should not be expected to produce a living child.[9]

Hunter was not writing to rob women of their souls. He wrote in good faith, intent on sharing what he had seen in those closed rooms where women gave birth, no doubt convinced that empirical observation could save innocent women from a dismal statute. What he had seen in those rooms was shaped by his own preoccupation with his indispensability, his centrality, and his importance. And also by his innocence, his failure to imagine how his presence as midwife changed the experience of childbirth for the women he delivered, no doubt with growing confidence, over the years. Whatever simple improvements the male midwife offered, his presence made childbirth different, and eventually safer, at the cost of marking women as incompetent to deliver each other, or themselves. Had he lived a generation later, he might have glimpsed himself in Mary Shelley's Frankenstein, attempting to command life and death. But in his own lifetime, as a younger son intended for the poor boy's career of the Kirk, he had every reason to take pride in his career, and even exaggerate his importance (270).

Hunter performed in two places, at childbed, and as a lecturer. Women were his subjects, and his audience, even at childbed, was ultimately male, and consisted of those men to whom he explained, justified, and displayed his skills. His position in society depended on both men and women—he was midwife to his Queen for many years—but it was with men that he actively negotiated his status, and saw his authority acknowledged. And yet he probably had learned something from women in all those years, namely that they did not wish to kill their children. But what he did not understand was that that did not mean that they could not do so.

If Hunter was careful to present his views on infanticide late in his life, and then at the invitation of another, he also expected to speak authoritatively. That he chose to leave his essay to be published posthumously may have been accident, wisdom, or the complex diffidence of an unenfranchised Scot living in London.[10] Hunter undoubtedly found women useful in coming to see himself as necessary and important. In return, he sketched in a bluntly empirical picture of good women struggling with the rigors of labor, but never wishing to harm the child. This stood in rather stark contrast to the picture created by the statute of 1690, which forced jurors to assume that single women out of sight would maliciously destroy their children. Both were powerful archetypes, and important precisely because the statute forced jurors to presume they knew what a woman had done while hidden from public view. In the end, the unwillingness of the jurors to presume so much would matter more than what they were asked to presume, but the spread of views like Hunter's no doubt helped men to hem and haw, and return doubtful verdicts, like the one that allowed Andrew Crosbie to save Agnes Walker.

The Final Legal Assault

The statute's demise would depend upon the gap between statutory and actual murder that had been recognized earlier, by the Restoration jurist who celebrated it, and by Katharine Smith's lawyer, who denounced it in 1701. But recognizing that the common law demanded one sort of proof of actual murder and the statute a more circumstantial proof did not seriously undermine the statute's existence until quite late in the century. In 1734 Robert Craigie, defending Janet Black, claimed that no "actual murder" could be proved, and in reply the prosecuting advocate depute, Hugh Forbes, cited the Act and said he could prove that its three conditions had been met. The result was a verdict in which the jury found "her presumptive Murder proven," but not the "actuall Murder," and the court had no qualms about sentencing her to hang in Perth on the fifth of July.[11] A similar verdict in 1798 would stop the court in its tracks, leading to a lengthy appeal.

In the spring of 1798, Janet Gray was tried for infanticide on the South Circuit, and the jury returned a troubling verdict, finding her guilty under the statute, but not guilty of "actual murder." The two law lords riding the South Circuit, Swinton and Dunsinnan, referred the case back to the High Court. When the appeal was heard in Edinburgh that summer, the prosecution's case was prepared by His Majesty's Advocate Robert Dundas of Arniston, and Gray's defense undertaken by Henry Erskine. It was an appeal on which the future of the statute depended, and it was a battle between Erskine and Dundas, in which Janet Gray was a pawn.[12]

Henry Erskine and Robert Dundas knew each other well. Erskine was a Whig leader in Edinburgh, while Dundas was a Tory, representing his uncle's political empire in Scotland.[13] That uncle, Henry Dundas, had been home secretary since 1791, and Robert was also his son-in-law and representative in Parliament. As lord advocate, Robert also represented government opinion and the extensive Dundas patronage network in Scotland, and as member of parliament for Midlothian, he acted as the Scots' whip in the House of Commons.[14] Called to the bar at twenty, made solicitor-general at twenty-five, and lord advocate at thirty-two, Robert Dundas more or less replicated the distinguished careers of his father and his uncle, but with far less talent. As Henry Cockburn put it, "his abilities and acquirements were moderate; and owing to the accident of his birth, which placed him above all risk of failure in life, he was never in a situation where he was compelled to improve either."[15] Writing as a staunch Whig, as well as Dundas's childhood friend and distant relative, Cockburn respected Dundas's moderation, for he well remembered that Dundas was "Lord Advocate in the most alarming times, and at a period when extravagant powers were ascribed to that office." Dundas, along with his powerful uncle, became the focus for antigovernment feeling in Scotland during the French Revolution, and in the summer of 1792 both had their windows broken during the King's Birthday Riot.[16]

In contrast, Henry Erskine was perhaps the best lawyer at the Scottish bar at the end of the eighteenth century. He was also a leading Scots Whig, and albeit a moderate, he paid heavily for his principles, which separated him from the great majority of his colleagues, and from what has been called the Dundas gravy train. He and Robert

Robert Dundas of Arniston,
His Majesty's Advocate, who
prosecuted the 1798 appeal
of an infanticide case against
Janet Gray in Edinburgh.
From a celebratory
nineteenth-century history
of the Dundas family.

Dundas would play musical chairs with the office of lord advocate, with
Erskine holding it twice, briefly, when the Tories were out of power.
His younger brother, Thomas, defended Thomas Paine, and his older
brother, David, Earl of Buchan, probably joined the Society of the
Friends of the People in 1792. But Henry, ever moderate, regarded
such associations, as he wrote to a friend, as endangering "that rational degree of reform, of which I have already said I think our Constitu-
tion would admit."[17]

Both Dundas and Erskine were gentlemen, committed to moderation
and reason, despite the high stakes and high emotional pitch of the
times. But they served different masters in the 1790s, although Erskine seemed slow in grasping the depth of the division. When he chose
to speak at the public meeting called in Edinburgh late in 1795 to protest the war against France, Erskine may not have understood the risk
he was taking. Within weeks he had been deposed as dean by the Faculty of Advocates, the equivalent of a Scottish bar association, in favor

of Robert Dundas. The message was unmistakable, and Erskine must have been shocked, for he destroyed all his correspondence from 1795, save for one letter from the Earl of Lauderdale. That one, written when the faculty was about to eject him, reassured Erskine of "the propriety and manly energy of your conduct," and condemned the "subservient adulation" of the faculty. Two and one-half years later Dundas and Erskine argued the Gray case in 1798.[18]

The verdict that forced the South Circuit judges to send the case back to the High Court was much like the one Andrew Crosbie had taken advantage of thirty-six years earlier. But this verdict was clearly not the simple result of a kindly, inept, or calculating landlord sitting on the jury. The jurors, "all in one voice," found Janet Gray guilty under the statute "but, by a plurality of voices, find, that the actual murder mentioned in the Indictment is not proven against the said Janet Gray" (6).[19] Some of those jurors chose to respond to both kinds of murder mentioned in Janet Gray's indictment, the statutory and the "actual," or common-law murder, as if they were separate crimes. Of course they found her guilty of statutory murder, yet found the common-law murder not proven, for that was precisely the statute's purpose: to convict women who could never have been found guilty at common law, with its demand for direct evidence.

In the past juries usually had returned single verdicts, and even when the phrase "no actual murder" had been used, as in the trial of Janet Black, judges had felt no qualms about sentencing on the statutory conviction alone. But in the spring of 1798, Dunsinnan and Swinton balked at sentencing Janet Gray to hang, even though Gray was "guilty of the Crime charged in the Indictment, in so far as it is founded upon the 21st Act of the Second Session of the First Parliament of King William and Queen Mary." And then, with great simplicity, a plurality of the assizers found "that the actual murder mentioned in the Indictment is not proven against the said Janet Gray." In 1734 that had meant nothing, but in 1798 the power of the contradiction was stunning (6).

The weight of the phrase "actual murder" should not be underestimated in assessing the law lords' discomfiture, for at first glance it appears that no murder was committed, but that, nonsensically, Janet Gray was guilty under the statute. The problem Dundas and Erskine addressed was the great difference in the kinds of evidence needed to convict Gray by statute on the one hand, and at common law on the other. The common law demanded direct evidence, preferably witnesses to the murder, but at least witnesses who could establish that the child had been born alive, and connect the woman with the child, or with the place where the body had been found. The statute required none of this, merely specifying three circumstances which, if met, required the jury to find the woman guilty of murder: concealment of the whole pregnancy, giving birth alone, and the child found to be dead or missing. Erskine attacked the infanticide statute because the statute denied a basic principle of the common law, the demand for direct evidence. In doing so, Erskine was judging the statute, and he was doing it at a time when Parliament was cranking out statutes that presumed much about men of his Whiggish bent. He was a lawyer wise enough to be afraid of the law.

In practice, few women had been hanged solely by the statute's presumptions, if only because prosecuting lawyers were used to bringing such direct proof as they could, and understood that juries preferred compelling evidence, especially when they were being asked to hang a woman. Hence, marks of violence on the child's body, suggesting willful murder, and testimony from midwives, surgeons, or physicians, claiming that the child had been born alive, became usual. This was not necessary under the statute, which did not differentiate between murdered, stillborn, or missing children, but trials in which the child's body had not been recovered were extremely rare. Statute or no statute, the demand for direct evidence remained fairly constant in the court room. Most women had been tried by prosecutors using a combination of direct and statutory evidence, and most women, especially after mid-century, were banished without ever coming to trial, probably for a lack of that evidence.

It became difficult to convict a woman of infanticide after 1740. Anne Mackie, or Mather, widow of the surveyor David Mather, was hanged in Midlothian in 1776, and Jean Bisset, the wife of a laborer, was hanged in Ross in 1793.[20] Apart from these two women, another fifteen, at least, would hang between 1740 and 1790. That was roughly half the number hanged between 1690 and 1739. At least 111 more were banished after 1740, which shows that the court was virtually always struggling to find the right way to deal with these women.[21] Both Mather and Bisset had been married, and had raised children, and they probably were hanged because, as adult, married members of the community, they were being held to a high standard of behavior. In the face of the prosecuting lawyers' developing preference for banishing women without going to the trouble of a trial, the High Court of Justiciary's final struggle with the statute seems almost irrelevant, for the statute's power to convict had already ebbed. Much as the coming of the statute ratified presumptions that were already in practice in the courtroom, the statute's demise in 1809 marked the end of a slow erosion of its power. But it was still law in 1798, and Gray might have hanged.

Confronted with the Dumfries jurors' decision, Dundas had to argue that Janet Gray's conviction, founded only on the statute, was quite sufficient to hang her. Dundas took a hard line, insisting that "this Crime may be committed in two different ways," and went on to describe how Janet Gray's verdict made perfect sense as it stood:

> If the finding of the actual murder not proven, is applied to the charge at common law . . . the verdict seems natural and proper, and the two findings are in no respect contradictory or inconsistent; whereas if the words actual murder are made to extend to the Statutory case, the most gross absurdity would follow, as the Jury would be made to pronounce the Pannell guilty and innocent in the same breath; and in the same Sentence in which the Pannell is declared guilty of the Statutory murder, they must be held to have found that no murder whatever was committed by her. (10–11)[22]

Dundas was right about the ludicrous verdict, but he failed to see the larger principle at work here.[23]

The jurors meant something by their verdict, quite beyond finding Janet Gray guilty under the statute, for they troubled to take a second vote on the "actual murder." They were probably not awed by the circuit court, for their chair was a vice admiral, and they had a writer, the equivalent of an English solicitor, for a clerk. Of the other thirteen, four were landowners, four were tenants, two were merchants, and the remaining three were listed as tobacconist, nurseryman, and seedsman.[24] It is possible that the vice admiral was officious, and the writer a small-town pedant, and that they were merely taking pains to appear wise in the ways of the law. But on balance, the verdict seems too clear, and too clearly a challenge, and officiousness and pedantry could have taken so many less pointed forms. As it stood, a plurality of the jurors

forced Dunsinnan and Swinton to sentence on the basis of a bare, statutory conviction, and whatever the jurors' intentions, the lords balked
at such a hanging in 1798.

Henry Erskine made the most of that doubt by arguing for the primacy of the common law, and describing the statute as a subordinate
clause. Erskine was a smarter man than Dundas. He argued in principle, set the statute in a larger perspective that damned it, and spoke
of "the fundamental maxim of the criminal law," the "feelings of humanity," and a number of English authorities who had seemingly baffled Dundas (36–37). When he finished, the statute had, as Scots
statutes were liable to do, fallen into desuetude. But what had changed
in Scots society was not the incidence of infanticide, but the willingness
of Erskine, Crosbie, and the jurors to challenge the statute, using the
language of natural rights, and a newly exclusive definition of women
as maternal.[25]

This is not to imply that Erskine had an easy time of it. He had to
hammer away at the statute, insisting on its subsidiary nature. The
statute, of course, as Dundas believed, looked like much more than a
specification of evidence, and Erskine lamely argued that "to have
made a provision that omissions, which may proceed from various
causes consistent with innocence, shall necessarily, and of themselves,
constitute a capital crime, would have been a degree of rigour which
the Legislature of this country would not probably assume, and is contrary to the fundamental maxim of the criminal law" (37). Pushing
further, he claimed "that the statute is expressed in terms so doubtful
as to render the precise object of the Legislature uncertain" (39). The
statute was, however, terribly clear, no matter what Erskine said, and
Parliament had no doubt meant to assume that "degree of rigour"
toward "common" women in 1690.[26] Erskine was quite right to point
out that such a statute was exceptional, but he chose not to mention
how that statute had once expressed his society's belief that women
were dangerous. But then he chose to argue partly from Crosbie, and
largely from English jurisprudence.[27] He quoted from Lord Chief Justice Hale, writing late in the seventeenth century, who had commented
on the similar, but less severe, English infanticide statute. According
to Erskine, Hale had remarked then that "the Statute only directs the
evidence where the case is within it, but created not a new crime" (42).
Then he turned to the fourth volume of Sir William Blackstone's *Commentaries,* where the great jurist and lecturer collegially mentioned

that "I apprehend it has, of late years, been usual with us in England, upon trials for this offence, to require some sort of presumptive evidence that the child was born alive, before the other constraining presumption [that the child whose death is concealed was therefore killed by its parent] is admitted to convict the Prisoner" (44).[28]

Erskine saved for last a lengthy excerpt from the English scholar Daines Barrington on mothers:

> This hath by many been considered as a law of severity, because it substitutes presumption of guilt in the room of actual proof against the Criminal. I should conceive that it arose from the difficulty of proving the offence against the mother, rather than an intention to make the bare concealment, arising from a mistaken shame, amount to a capital felony. I conclude, that it must have frequently happened in these prosecutions, that the child being found dead, (perhaps in the mother's room), she insisted on its having been born in that state, of which no witness being able to prove the contrary, she was of course acquitted. If the dead child, however, was discovered with any apparent marks of violence upon it, I should apprehend that this, with other circumstances, might have proved the guilt even at common law, without the intervention of this Statute; and I rather mention this, as I think no Execution should be permitted, unless the Criminal, convicted under this act, would have been guilty of the murder by the common law, as she is otherwise to suffer, merely from the presumption arising from the circumstance of concealment, of which it is believed there is no instance in the English law. (44–46)[29]

Only Barrington attempted to enter the concealed birth scene, and set before his reader a simple and compelling picture of all those mothers' rooms, stretching back in time, replete with "mistaken shame," then adding the easily visualized argument that only if marks of violence were found on the child should the mother be found guilty. For Barrington visible evidence took precedence over the statute's presumptions. Between 1690 and 1766, when Barrington wrote his *Observations on the Statutes,* the weight of presumption was shifting from murder to affection,[30] and Erskine used Barrington's words to good ad-

vantage, for Barrington was engaged in hammering out that new presumption of a mother's affection for her child.

> If this inference of conjecture is, by the Statute, made the offence
> itself, should it not be encountered by another natural and most
> strong presumption in favour of the criminal? Is it not extraordi-
> nary therefore to suppose, that the mother, at once forgetting
> every sensation of parental fondness, should be the wilful au-
> thor of the death of her new born child, which, by its cries, en-
> treats her protection; and the father of which she probably hath
> as great affection for as if she had a right to call him by the
> name of husband? And are not children born dead every day? Or
> may not the mother, in the agonies of childbirth, be the involun-
> tary occasion of the infant's death? As for the circumstance of
> hiding the body in places proper for its concealment, if the death
> is not received from the hands of the mother, it is but a natural
> consequence of endeavouring to continue to bear a good charac-
> ter in her neighborhood. (46)

Barrington's genius lay in the use of the word *nature,* for the natural
could only be revealed, not constructed, and the word was perfectly
suited to Erskine's uses, for all of the statute's evils could be labeled
constructions, or presumptions, about maternal behavior.[31] Erskine
could hardly refuse to turn loose the force of Barrington's picture of
female nature. Barrington wrote in 1766, and Hunter's paper appeared
in 1784. Like the work of Jean-Jacques Rousseau, or Dr. Gregory, their
writing was simply early bourgeois realism at its best: confirmed, be-
lievable, about to harden into ideology, still fresh for Barrington, an
empirical discovery for Hunter, and perhaps new to Erskine in 1798.[32]
Barrington's rhetorical questions were brilliant, for they converted the
possible into the probable, as the reader affirms each—"Are not children born dead every day?"—until that affirmation included the whole
of Barrington's scene, and not just its separate propositions.

Barrington's words rang true in 1798, but by 1826 an English surgeon would complain that a newborn infant, obviously battered and
then drowned while still living, was found by an English jury to have
been stillborn, and its mother acquitted of murder. His outrage over
this slight to his reality, as well as over "the increasing frequency of
the crime of child-murder" spilled out as he wrote that "prosecutors

take no pains to convict, and judges and juries are determined not to believe that a child has been murdered, unless they find it with its throat cut, or its brains dashed out upon the pavement."[33] But living with benign motherhood was easier. The argument between Dundas and Erskine, over the importance of direct evidence, was not only an argument over the primacy of the common law, but also over just what that direct evidence would show women to have done. The great irony was that Janet Gray had probably killed her child, as Agnes Walker had before her, and the authors of the statute had been right all along, in their presumptions if not in the harshness of the penalty. The world that Crosbie, Hunter, and Erskine claimed to reveal was indeed a better one, but it too was a presumption.

The more important point is that Janet Gray did not hang, and that Erskine had played an important card by quoting liberally from Crosbie, a respected Scots lawyer, as well as Barrington and other English authorities. In what must have been a small victory for Erskine, Dundas agreed to banish Gray. With that, the infanticide statute was virtually dead, and its death was a Whig victory which showed that Tories like Dundas, who could have their way in most things in Britain in 1798, could not compel men to presume guilt when there was little direct evidence.[34]

But we must remember that Erskine's victory relied, in part, on the difficulty Dundas and all lesser prosecutors faced in compelling men to see women as killers of their own children. In 1762 Crosbie had argued only against presumption, and for the "Lives of the Leiges," and even though Agnes Walker escaped the gallows, infanticide prosecutions continued. But in 1798, when the arguments about rights and direct evidence were joined by presumptions of maternal affection, trials virtually stopped. From 1799 until 1809, twenty-six women were accused of infanticide, most before the circuit courts. There were no convictions. Nineteen women were banished without coming to trial, four cases were dismissed before trial began, one woman ran off and was outlawed, another seems to have left no record, and the one woman who stood trial in 1799 was found not guilty. In 1809, the statute was repealed, and another took its place, making the same circumstantial crime a rather small one, for which conviction meant no more than two years in a local jail.[35] In the wake of the new law, convictions again became possible, and four women were sent to prison in 1809 and 1810. But the village society that had once made suspicion, accusation, and

Tranent churchyard, where Mrs. Anne Mather was probably buried in 1776.
Mather was the last woman condemned and hanged for infanticide by the High
Court of Justiciary in Edinburgh. Another woman, tried by the North Circuit
in 1793, was probably the last to hang for infanticide in all of Scotland.

conviction easy was unraveling, making even these lesser convictions
difficult. Those villagers had given the old Act Anent Child Murder
much of its backbone. But by 1809, fewer villagers would exercise that
kind of authority, working with or without their ministers. And perhaps more important, there were virtually no gentlemen of the court,
lawyers or jurors, who wished to inquire very closely into the lives of
young women, urban or rural. If the old act had been the product of
men more than willing to make assumptions about what women did
when they were alone and pregnant, by 1809 very few people cared.

7

Confessing to Child Murder

The law came, and the law went, and the new statute of 1809 took its place. Through all these years, as neighbors accused, and relented, the women who bore the brunt of these accusations, and who must have often killed their children, got to say very little. While the survival of the ballad *Mary Hamilton* suggests that some villagers were prepared to acknowledge that a woman could kill, and that she would wish to speak out, we know very little about what these women thought. What we can know comes from their confessions, which were sometimes verbal, and sometimes implicit in their behavior. Few women confessed to killing their children with the bluntness and self-possession of Mary Hamilton. More often, women tied identifiable scraps of their clothing to infants before abandoning them, or left such violence written on the child's body that death could not have been their only intention.

Those who confessed were no longer estranged from their community, and their own identity, but confession often cost them their lives. But once the facades came down and their stories spilled out, they could, like Mary Hamilton, face the gallows with some equanimity. Most continued to deny that anything had happened, which tells us that they now saw themselves as permanently at odds with their communities, or bereft of community, struggling alone for their survival. What each woman confronted was a new sort of individualism, probably seeming all the more unfair because most of these women had thought they were dallying and courting and carrying on in ways that were ordinary and even traditional. Much of that courtship was probably old hat in rural communities where young people traditionally worked as servants before marriage.

In the summer of 1689, two old men fishing in Haystoun Burn in the south of Scotland discovered the body of an infant in the water.[1] They found that the child had a string about its neck that "was yet so hard that it made a furrowe." The culprit, Margaret Craigie, had wandered south into Peebles a short time before, and had been seen with her child, "begging," in the kitchen of the farm at Haystoun, and wearing the plaid in which the child's body was found. She was easily caught at Potterfield, a mile and a half away. When confronted, Craigie said that her friends "hade tempted her to murder the child, because it would be troublesome and fashous [troubling] to her." But her wandering suggests that she could not make up her mind, and in the end both blamed others and claimed the child as she killed it, by wrapping that infant in her own plaid. In that mute gesture, she confessed not only to the murder, but to the devastating twoness of her experience, by killing the child and offering it the protection of her plaid.

Elizabeth Brown, tried in 1710, was equally indecisive but far more willing to talk. She left blue marks on her child's throat, but without quite killing it, for an old woman heard Brown say "that the Child weept after it was in the holl and that She satt down above it." Apparently unable to kill the child with her own hands, she contrived to kill it by burying it alive. But she could not bring herself to leave it, and sat down on top of the child until she believed it to be dead. When the child was dug up, Brown "owned it and fell aweeping," and after she was jailed she talked about how it had "weept" in the hole. She could not stop telling her neighbors about it, and she, like Margaret Craigie, hanged.[2]

Katharine Comrie, tried in 1693, fell into "a great rourement" when made to handle her recently exhumed infant. Her distress convinced the minister that she was guilty; Jannot fford, a tenant's wife, added that the child bled when Comrie handled it, a magical sign of the murderer's presence. But Comrie herself then "ack[nowledged] that she hade cutted her child's throat and the divile hade given her a kniff to doe it with." Comrie's devil is enough like Craigie's friends to suggest that these women were not exactly shifting blame, for they were already on their way to the gallows, but genuinely saw themselves living in a network of neighbors and relatives, where their wills were always subject to others' needs and advice. If they wept while recalling friends and devils putting knives in their hands, their feelings of guilt were probably less acute than those of women who had acted alone.[3]

Ministers and elders of the kirk had a sturdy reputation for pressing their noses to local windows. But villagers were likely to find infant murder objectionable, without the kirk's help. And the kirk's power dwindled in the eighteenth century, caught between the new intellectual authority of the Enlightenment, and the new economic interests of landowners. Nonetheless, the pressure sometimes applied by kirk sessions, urging suspected pregnant women to confess and repent, probably saved many women, especially those who valued their place in the community, and recognized that community as their own. But those the kirk didn't save were driven into solitude, and taught to lie.

In 1704 Grissel Tullo, who lived with her parents in a small village in Fife, came to be suspected by the elders of the kirk, who ordered some women to examine Tullo in her father's house. The women found an infant at the foot of her bed with its neck broken and they drew her breast, and "milk came springing out on her apron." One of the women testified that Grissel Tullo then "cryed out the Lord have mercy what will word [fate] of me I am undone." Her thoughts were clearly focused on herself in her moment of despair, and not on her child. Somewhere in those months of concealment, she had, perhaps, turned into a somewhat more wary individual, in a more modern sense of the word. She did not weep for the child, but for herself.[4]

The kirk, despite its reputation, could not control much. Illegitimacy was far from rare in the late seventeenth and eighteenth centuries, and irregular marriages became common after 1707. When Mary Pearson's neighbors entered her tenant cottage in 1748, fearing she had done away with a child, they found the infant strangled in its umbilical cord. Pearson, a widow with a young son, holding the farm herself, readily confessed. The infant's father was Adam Hunter, a widowed neighbor, and their relationship may have been prompted by Pearson's need for help with her land. As a man by the name of Lamb put it she "frequently lamented her condition and said Oh that Adam Hunter he has been the occasion of two lives." Lamb then asked "whether she had any previous intention of murdering the Child," to which Pearson is reported to have replied, "it is too true She need not deny it."[5]

Pearson was a villager, a widow working a tenant farm in the parish of Old Cumnock, in Ayrshire, and was caught by neighbors and elders in an entangling alliance with Adam Hunter. The comparative equanimity with which she confessed to her neighbors suggests that her relationship with Hunter was not unusual, even if her decision to murder the child was; and it further suggests that as an older woman, with firmer ties to the community, and land, she found it much easier to speak. Younger women found it much harder, especially later in the century when community had eroded, and elders and midwives no longer pried. Janet Ramsay, a servant on a large farm, declared in 1798 "that she had no sooner committed the cruel act than she repented of it & has been miserable ever since & was very much relieved last night when the discoverie was made . . . [and] wished that some person had said to her that she was with child that she might have an opportunity to confess her situation, that she twice went to the door to go make her confession to the Minister but her heart failed her & she did not go."[6] Telling the jury that she had wished to speak earlier was very effective, and they refused to find her guilty, even though she had confessed.

The nature of confession changed after mid-century because the courts preferred to banish women sensible enough not to leave marks of violence on their babies' bodies, and women on trial ceased to be surrounded by men who believed they had murdered their infants. Verbal confession, along with hangings, virtually disappeared. One exception was Anne Morison, an Edinburgh office cleaner in 1757, who was gotten pregnant by "one of the Lads," at the law office and left work, to reappear in the spring of 1758 as a servant to Mr. Stewart, a lawyer with a small estate outside Edinburgh. By July, she had given birth, murdered the child, and hidden it in a "corn-field." She almost immediately confessed this to several baillies, and led them to the body. "When the child was taken up and she saw it, she was in great confusion and concern, pulled her gown over her head and fell back upon the wall." The condition of the child's body explains why Morison pulled her dress over her head, for it had been beaten, strangled, and stabbed in the head, arms, and legs. The anger that emerged here was probably directly related to Morison's loneliness. Thoroughly alone, she was reduced to expressing herself within so small a compass as that of the child's body, and then coming back to it, precisely because the child was her only companion.[7] For Morison, confession could not gain her readmission to her community, for she no longer had one.

Women's need to make known, to come to terms with, the lived experience of concealing and then killing their children remained. Many women undoubtedly learned the hard lesson of living with what they knew, as the price they paid for their lives. What knowledge those women had was driven inside them, and if they had any companion it was the child, and if they left any message for their neighbors, the child's body became the slate on which they wrote.

The Inscrutable Behavior of Euphemia Hunter and Jean McKay (after 1809)

After the trials of Janet Ramsay and Janet Gray in 1798, a definite silence fell. Women were left to their own devices, and were relatively safe from prosecution, or at least from serious punishment, if they did not force others to watch them murder their children. But silence was not an acceptable solution, at least not to those women who sang *Mary Hamilton, The Twa Sisters,* and *Sheath and Knife,* and not to those women who found killing their infants to be a great tragedy, albeit an unrecognized one after 1809. After that date, two women, Euphemia Hunter and Jean McKay, left very public records of their infants' deaths, while ensuring their own escapes. On Monday, 10 February 1812, a boy in Haddington picked up something he had seen a crow drop.[8] He recognized it as the arm of an infant, and buried it where he had found it, in a field called Broomylees. That evening two boys who had watched him bury the arm dug it up and took it to a substantial local man, a brewer in Belhaven, who wrapped it in a piece of paper and sent it to his brother, a surgeon in Dunbar. The surgeon threw it in a bucket of water, and went to bed. That same day Andrew Denham, an agricultural servant at a farm called Eweford, found a child's leg in Broomylees. He brought it to his parents' cottage, and they buried it in their garden that night.

On Tuesday morning the surgeon, Alexander Johnston, examined the arm and, no longer preoccupied, hurriedly wrote to the provost of Dunbar, declaring that he had "the Right Arm of a full foetus separated from the body at the Shoulder to which was attached the Shoulder Blade." It had, his apprentice later noted in testimony, been both torn and cut with a knife. Back in Belhaven, two more boys returned to the brewer's house, and led the brewer's clerk, Alexander Cockburn, to a field a little south of Belhaven, to show him some bones they had seen there. Cockburn, not knowing whether the bones were human, had the boys carry them to Mary Williamson, a widow in Belhaven, who identified them as the ribs and backbone of a child. Cockburn did not want them back. Mary Williamson buried them in her yard, then dug them up late that night and buried them in Dunbar churchyard.

On Wednesday evening, a young agricultural servant at Eweford, Euphemia Hunter, left the farmhouse with her fellow servant, Alison Burnet. Hunter, known to everyone as Effy, walked south to her parents' cottage, spoke with them briefly, and then disappeared into England. Alison Burnet later told two justices of the peace that Effy's "Father sat down before his Daughter took her by the hand and mentioned the impropriety of her conduct in putting away her Child." Burnet said that Effy's only response was "that she could not help it."

If Effy Hunter was less than forthcoming with her father, she seems to have said little to anyone. Andrew Denham, who was the father of her child, accosted her in the kitchen at Eweford, shortly after finding the child's leg. He claimed to have said to her, "will you not confess now," and that Hunter replied, "if you will not hold your tongue you will have me in my linen Cloths." Effy Hunter never said much more than this. She did, probably rather formally, admit giving birth to a child to her mistress—her bedclothes betrayed as much—but insisted that she had thrown her child into a nearby stream. With that, and her brief conversations with her lover and her father, she broke a long period of denial, of refusing to admit that she was pregnant to people in her community. But when she spoke, it was not to reveal or reclaim, but to ease herself out of that community, revealing as little as possible. She had successfully put the child from her, parceling it out so that it was no longer a child. She may have cut up the child to destroy evidence, out of an older fear of the child's ghost, or out of anger. Other women did show an interest in protecting themselves from the corpse's testimony, by filling the mouths of their infants with earth. A Scots ballad in circulation in 1825, *The Cruel Mother,* features the ghosts of two murdered infants, who haunt their mother at every turn, repeating their story.[9]

But any calculation on her part seems to have been overridden by anger. Euphemia Hunter so clearly made visible a deep anger that it stood as a confession, and while other women left marks of battering on their children, they stopped well before the child had been dismembered. Cutting and tearing the child into pieces might well have been a task avoided by the most calculating and remorseless of women, and we have no evidence that Hunter was a new Caligula, only an utterly determined young woman. The effort required to dismember and distribute the remains could have been better spent on a quick and secure burial. What seemed at first sight careful concealment, at second glance betrays an impulse to advertise the anger and frustration of a predicament now unspeakable. Hunter risked her life to cut up the child, because in 1814 a calculating woman could have left an unmarked child exposed, wept copiously, and risked no more than a few months in a local prison. But Hunter, by violently attacking the child, and risking observation, risked prosecution for ordinary murder.

Hunter displayed the child in a way that made manifest her urge to destroy someone—the child, herself, Andrew Denham, others. There would be no other public resolution of her tragedy, for her community, like her child, was so fragmented in its responses to her that she had disappeared over the border into England before anyone acted to take her into custody. The Kirk was invisible in this case, and no midwives pried. She and her parents had a secure living on the large farm of Eweford, but it must have come at a price. Most probably the price was patience, and a willingness to postpone marriage until a cottage for married servants became available. She acted alone, and, except for her response to the child, showed formidable constraint in her dealings with others, saying no more than necessary, and betraying no emotion. It would be easy to say that she acted to please herself, without regard to others, especially since Denham's parents had offered to raise the child. But it is hard to see the pleasure in it, and probably more accurate to see her acting out of some great compulsion to take care of herself. Out of that compulsion or necessity came Hunter's violent form of female individualism. By mastering herself, she mastered her situation. Two years later, a young woman from the Highlands, then a servant in a doctor's house in Glasgow, would find an even more bizarre way to make her child's death public, without risking prosecution herself.

Early on a Friday morning, the twenty-first of January, 1814, a night nurse named Janet Mulloch was making her way home from the Royal Infirmary in Glasgow. Mulloch, at the end of her shift, left the wards by a side door that opened into a walled yard. As she came out of the door, "she saw something lying on the ground," clearly outlined against old snow. It was a newborn infant. Mulloch testified later that she was "in great alarm [and] did not touch the child, but cried out to the cook Margaret Clark."[10] Clark came, and told Mulloch to pick up the frozen body, while she went back for a towel in which the child could be wrapped. Mulloch refused to touch the child, however, and so the cook, returning with a bit of cloth, "lifted the body and carried it into the house"(54).

Margaret Clark not only picked up the body, she looked at it, and was able to describe it for the magistrates several days later. What she described was a naked male infant, "lying on its left side in the snow" (19). She thought the child had been thrown to the ground, probably from one of the windows in the wards, for it was flattened against the ground. She also examined the place where the child had lain, for she could say that the snow was white, and icy, and retained the impression of the child's body, from which she "concluded that the snow had been melted by the warmth of the Infant" (20).

The discovery of the child's body triggered an investigation, and pushed members of the infirmary staff and the patients in ward six to see Jean McKay, a young woman whose swollen belly was being treated as dropsical, in a rather new light. After Mulloch and Clark carried the body in, depositing it on a stool in a lobby leading to the kitchen, word of their discovery spread rapidly. Margaret Clark, the cook, seems to have had more presence of mind because unlike Mulloch she was beginning her work day rather than ending it, and it was probably Clark who informed Mrs. Stewart, the matron, and also spoke with another of the night nurses, Janet Lamont. With the child's body as a clue, Lamont was able to talk about Jean McKay with suspicion, suddenly making sense of events that she had previously preferred to treat as discrete medical phenomena beyond her comprehension. Armed with Lamont's suspicion, the matron informed Andrew Wilson, the apprentice physician who visited the patients, that a child had been found, and she told the day nurse of ward six, Nelly Christie, to inspect Jean McKay's bed.

Janet Lamont, the wife of a weaver, had spent much of the previous Wednesday night warming a borrowed flannel jacket and wrapping it around McKay's belly. She stopped doing this at daybreak, at McKay's request, and went off to tend other patients. On her return another patient, Mrs. Sutherland, told Lamont "that McKay had continued very ill in the morning, and that she Mrs. Sutherland had never seen anything liker a Woman in labour" (17). Sutherland, the wife of a coal carrier, soon to be released in improved health, clearly kept an eye on McKay. She was later able to testify in some detail about McKay's cries, vomiting, and trips to the water closet, and she had probably already told both nurses. But Lamont, officially at least, discounted Sutherland's observations all day Thursday. Instead, she told the bail-lie "[t]hat Jean McKay was reported to have a dropsy and it never en-tered the Declarant's mind that she was with Child, till after that Infant's body was found, when a suspicion struck the Declarant, which she mentioned to the Cook" (18). By Monday, the twenty-fourth of Jan-uary, Lamont was openly accusing McKay of having borne the child. On Monday evening, "there was some talk at the fire side about the child having been found," and Lamont "observed to McKay, that there was not a swamper woman in the house" than McKay. *Swamper* is a northern English and Scots term meaning thinner in the belly, espe-cially applicable to a sudden shrinking in physical bulk. It is no wonder that after several days of physical examinations and Lamont's pro-nouncement, McKay disappeared from the infirmary on Tuesday morning. She did not simply leave, she fled, first stopping at her moth-er's, nearby in the Drygate, and then traveling across town to stay with an aunt, her mother's sister, on the other side of Glasgow.

Lamont's initial disinclination to suspect a woman who was seven or eight months' pregnant was probably not a pose, nor a disingenuous ploy tactfully signaling her subordination to a medical hierarchy of clerks, physicians, and surgeons. She seems to have genuinely ac-cepted that the doctors knew more than she did. The day nurse on ward six, Nelly Christie, said at the beginning of her statement that

McKay was admitted with "a swelling in her belly, but what was the particular description of the case *the Declarant had not access to know*" (7; emphasis added). The distances among physicians, surgeons, their respective clerks, and the untrained nurses was no doubt greatly reinforced both by the earnest professionalism of medical men early in the century, and by class distinctions.[11] Could both Lamont and Christie look at a woman nearing the end of a pregnancy, without ever thinking she looked pregnant? We can know only what they told the baillie. No doubt their experience in the infirmary had shown them many unfamiliar diseases, and they became used to the doctors' expertise. Nonetheless, Nelly Christie, who was not forthcoming in her statement, did admit asking "Jean McKay in a jocular way whether she was with Child, which she denied but in the same way" (12).

The joke suggests that McKay's resemblance to a pregnant woman was obvious, and still could be discounted within the walls of the infirmary, where doctors knew what was unknowable to ordinary humans who saw only the outside of the body. Yet her physician, Robert Graham, and his clerk, Andrew Wilson, saw her only a few times while she was in the Royal Infirmary, Graham two or three times, and Wilson briefly on mornings when he made his rounds of the wards. Those who saw her constantly were the other female patients in ward six, and the two ward nurses, Christie and Lamont. It was from the nurses that information about the child, and then about McKay, moved up to the males, as the housekeeper, Mrs. Stewart, told Wilson about the child, and then Christie told him that McKay's bedclothes were suspiciously dirtied.

Mrs. Sutherland's testimony filled ten pages of the lord advocate's records, more than any of the other witnesses called, and she was eager to talk. She remembered that "the said Jean McKay mentioned to the Patients that her disorder was an obstruction which had continued for eleven months" (22), recalling the conversations that must have gone on in wards containing ten to twenty beds.[12] By five in the morning of the Thursday on which the child was born, Sutherland said that McKay "got up and passed to the fire side, and told the Declarant that she was very ill and believed she would die" (23). Sutherland told her to warm some beer and drink it, along with some of the gruel kept warm for the patients. McKay did this, and promptly threw up, which caused some argument with another woman, who objected to McKay's using the dishwashing basin to clean up. McKay returned the boyne, or basin, to the water closet, cleaned up with a rag, and went "directly from this to her bed" (25). At seven Sutherland was awake again, and saw McKay sit up with bedclothes wrapped around her, and she "exclaimed that the pain was returned" (25). By seven-thirty she was holding on to the sides of her bed, saying "there it was again. That she added that she could not stand it:—that it was death" (26).

It may be worth noting that Sutherland records McKay volubly complaining between seven and eight in the morning, just when the nurses' shifts changed, and no nurse was on the ward. It was Sutherland herself who got up at this time, and went to McKay, spoke to her, "made her rise, that she might put her bed in order," and looked at McKay's "night clothes." By now, Sutherland and the woman in the bed next to Jean McKay were quite sure that some change had taken place in her body, but Sutherland insisted that, even after the child was found, "The Declarant for one, never suspected McKay of being the Mother" (29), even though she also said that when she first saw McKay, "she was very big, and the bulk had the appearance that a Woman with Child has, being full at the back as well as before" (30–31). Could the image of the pregnant woman, and of the woman in labor have come to these women, without some suspicion that that was what they were seeing? It would seem that the sight of her virtually forced the words for pregnancy out of her observers' mouths, yet those expressions were partially if not wholly understood as metaphors within the infirmary, where doctors had chosen to read her physical shape as a sign of something other than pregnancy.

In other words, Nelly Christie might jokingly ask if McKay were pregnant—perhaps could not avoid the question—and Margaret Sutherland could tell Janet Lamont that she had never seen anything that looked "liker" a woman in labor, but not one of the people initially connected with McKay from the date of her admission was willing to say that she was pregnant, was in labor, was the mother of the child found in the courtyard. Even Lamont, who clearly suspected her, was sitting by the fire with Jean McKay on Monday night, doing no more than implying that McKay's sudden thinness might mean something.

The powerful empirical triad of McKay's pains, the appearance of the infant's body, and McKay's rapidly shrinking belly would have brought her to the gallows one hundred years earlier, but in 1814, in the Glasgow Royal Infirmary, such material observation ran head-on into the doctors' authority, and dissolved into no more than a suspicion. But there is more here than the emergence of doctors' authority to label a big belly as dropsical. There is also the question of their willingness, or at least Dr. Graham's willingness, to believe that Jean McKay was not pregnant, and McKay's choice of the infirmary as a suitable place to give birth. On the whole, it seems best to assume that Jean McKay, probably acting with her mother, understood that she was pregnant when she applied for admission to the infirmary in January, and that they were villagers who learned fast in the city. Jean McKay had been born in the northern Highlands, in Sutherland, in 1796, and had lived in Glasgow for the last ten years. In 1813, at the age of seventeen, she had gone as servant "to the Family of Doctor MacNeish of this city." She left MacNeish in July "on account of illness," but presumably knowing that she was pregnant, for she said that her belly began to swell before she left service.[13] She was lucky; she could return to her parents' house, in the same city, and she lived with them from July until she entered the infirmary on 5 January 1814.

Two or three days before being admitted to the infirmary, she went there "merely to get advice as to her case." At that time she first saw Dr. Graham and his clerk, Andrew Wilson. Graham remembered this visit with difficulty, or perhaps embarrassment, for he began his declaration by bending over backward to explain his failure to recognize a pregnancy: "That she had a very big belly, but Mr. Wilson the Declarant's Clerk, having mentioned to him that she denied being with Child, the Declarant conceived from all the circumstances that it was a dropsical case" (33). He then reconsidered and declared "upon recollection that he thinks it was subsequent to this, that Mr. Wilson mentioned that she denied being pregnant, but as the Girl's Mother was along with her at the beginning, the Declarant entertained no suspicion that she was with Child, *or if he did it was momentary*" (34; emphasis added). Conceiving of the case as dropsical, Graham prescribed a mercuric ointment. McKay took her prescription, which Wilson had written out in Latin, to a surgeon's shop, where she received "some of the blue ointment." She showed the stuff to "her Mother's Neighbors, they said it was Mercury, and unsafe for her to take in her Mother's house." As a result, her mother applied to a Mr. MacIntosh, who apparently had the necessary influence to provide "a recommendation to the Infirmary" (2), which must have been granted on the spot, for she was admitted within a day or two of having seen Graham.

At this point we know something of Jean McKay, and can reasonably assume even more. She initially spoke of returning to her father's from MacNeish's service, and later referred to living in "her Mother's house." This may well mean that her father died between July and January, and that his death ended any hope she had of her parents' taking the child. Second, her mother's ability to quickly procure a recommendation to the infirmary suggests that the family had a reputation as respectable working people, confirmed by McKay's finding a place in a doctor's household. It is of course also possible that the recommendation was the result of that physician's influence, prompted by guilt over a child most probably forcibly fathered on McKay in his house. But in either case the recommendation testifies to McKay's respectable connections. And third, McKay was well aware that the "blue ointment" prescribed for her was a dangerous drug. If she knew she was pregnant, she may have looked upon the mercury as an abortifacient. And Dr. Graham was all too ready to prescribe that mercury, without even asking her if she was pregnant.

Jean McKay's own description of her "illness" sounds rehearsed. She was not describing, but explaining, as if she had constructed her experience of "illness" defensively, always in relation to unasked questions. She claimed ignorance, and articulated her ignorance by speaking about her own body as if from a great distance.[14] As the magistrate's clerk recorded, "she never well understood the nature of her complaint, but sometimes before she left her service her belly began to swell, and the swelling increased till she went to the Infirmary." She then implied that once at the infirmary, and under treatment, the illness subsided: "That after this however it gradually became less, and on the morning of Thursday last the twentieth instant it fell almost entirely. That on the said morning the declarant altered, which had not happened for thirteen months before, and to this she ascribes the diminution of the size of her belly" (2–3).

This is a simple narrative of illness and its cure, shaped by her contact with the doctors. Once under treatment she gradually became completely well. Presumably what she meant by "altered" was menstruation, which fits with Margaret Sutherland remembering that she said "that her disorder was an obstruction which had continued for eleven months" (22). The obstruction, if not alimentary, must have been menstrual, and this was a narrative used before by women suspected of pregnancy, who claimed labor to have been a particularly

painful fit of menstrual cramping, after a long absence of menstruation. Having developed the tale of obstruction, it was easy for her to
cite an eleven months' absence, later lengthened to thirteen in her declaration. This meant that her mysterious condition was too long to re-
semble a pregnancy, and predated her entry into the MacNeish
household.

It was a workable story, more workable than dropsy. It could encom-
pass abdominal pain, dirtied bedclothes, even a good dose of recalci-
trance and feminine shame, with the effects of mercury thrown in for
good measure. On Thursday morning, after great agony, McKay
avoided speaking to the physician's clerk, Wilson, on his rounds, claiming later that she "did not mention to him her particular situation
being ashamed"(5). Some time after midnight, the night nurse saw her
go to the water closet, wrapped in a blanket. The afterbirth was never
found, but the child was found in the courtyard, more or less in line
with the windows of the water closets on that wing. On Friday the
child was discovered, and word spread that a woman in ward six was
suspected of having been in labor. After the child's body was discovered, McKay continued to play on that shame, and keep everyone at a
polite distance from herself. Describing Friday, she was sure that her
bed had been made by the day nurse, but then could only say that she
"believes the nurse measured her body" (6). On Saturday, when she
was examined in great detail by several physicians and surgeons, and
Nelly Christie, McKay recalled that "the nurse aforesaid tried the Declarant's breasts, to see if there was any milk, *but the Declarant cannot
say whether they found any*" (7–8; emphasis added).

McKay probably did know. She insisted that she left the infirmary
on the twenty-fifth, "being tired with being constantly harassed by the
inspection of her person, and measurements taken" (8). But she could
not say what she knew; at least she would not say to the magistrate
even as much as she said to her companions in the ward. Nelly Christie
asserted that McKay knew she was suspected of bearing the child after
her breasts were tried, and that "she told [Nelly Christie] that she was
not the Mother of it, and suppose she was cut to pieces would never
own it, but she could not tell how milk came to be in her breast" (13–
14).

McKay was examined by Wilson on Friday evening, who not only
measured her belly, "he likewise felt a hard swelling at the lower part
of the belly like what occurs from the contraction of the womb after

delivery. That he also slightly examined the Patient's Womb, and found the parts more relaxed than their natural state, but the Declarant could not procure any milk from her breast that night" (39–40). On Saturday, she went through a far more elaborate examination, external and internal, by men who had just previously dissected the infant found outside the ward. She was probably lucky not to have been infected, for at least two men reported feeling her cervix that day. In the presence of five other men, and the nurse Nelly Christie, a surgeon named Miller took over for the possibly less than competent Dr. Graham. As an outsider to the entire fiasco, he recorded bluntly what he found—that "her breasts to the feeling seemed to contain milk, but upon applying the most powerful and even painful suction none could be drawn from her" (42–43). He also listed marks on each breast, "a brownish mucous discharge from the vagina," a separation of the perineum from the vagina, and ulceration and callousing (his words) on the vulva (43). He was less than forthcoming about his internal examination, saying that "the parts within seemed to the Declarant's feeling to be much in the state which he would have expected . . . after the birth of a Child" (43–44).

On Sunday they were back, and Nelly Christie "with a nipple pipe" drew about an ounce of fluid from one breast, the appearance of which "was not like any human milk which the Declarant had ever seen; And on tasting it, it gave a different sensation to his mouth and throat from any human milk he had ever tasted" (44–45). This foray into absolute empiricism may have been enough to lead Mr. Miller to a difficult conclusion. When asked if Jean McKay had had the child, or any child, recently, he answered at length: "That there are many circumstances in the case which would induce the Declarant to suppose that she was lately delivered; but there are also other circumstances which he cannot reconcile with this opinion, and therefore declines giving a decided answer to the question" (46).

No doubt this indecision was partly an act of deference to Graham, who had initially diagnosed dropsy, and whose blind spot had to be defended. Perhaps the reputation of the infirmary and its medical men required that nothing so obvious as a pregnancy be allowed to muddle its claim to special scientific vision. Miller never did enumerate those "other circumstances," that led him to indecision, but he could claim to have seen them. It is clear that until the child appeared, staff and patients in the infirmary were willing to accept Graham's diagnosis, and whether they laughed to themselves we will never know, but McKay's condition was probably subsumed within the infirmary's collection of horrors and diseases.

There is also something pathetic, as well as masterful, in the medical men's response to Jean McKay. It becomes clear that in 1814 physicians and surgeons did not understand the female body. Miller's indecision, and Graham's diagnosis, if not willfully wrong, reek of empirical puzzlement, and call to mind the story of Mary Toft, who in 1726 convinced two leading English surgeons that they had just delivered her of fifteen rabbits. It was probably easy for Toft to fool them, as at least one commentator has argued, because they did not really want to look too closely, even when medical practice forced them to do just that. The outside of McKay's body might be seen, but the inside was felt, the milk tasted, and even though Miller gave a blunt report of what he saw, he was unwilling to come to any conclusion.[15]

The battleground had shifted between 1726 and 1814, for Jean McKay did not want to be known as the notorious mother of anything, rabbit or human. But like Toft, she was wagering on the incompetence of medical men when faced with a problematic female body, and she too won, for much the same reason. When the object of male empirical gaze was female, the empiricism of that gaze was very fragile. Unfortunately for Dr. Graham, medicine's claim to authority in the workings of the female body, coupled with still inadequate knowledge, made the consulting room a better place than most to conceal a pregnancy. It is hard to imagine a midwife a century earlier being so easily duped or baffled. Jean McKay and her mother understood two things in 1814. One was that the best way of having oneself poisoned sufficiently to abort was to consult a physician. The other was that the best place in Glasgow to conceal the birth of an illegitimate, and, they hoped, stillborn, infant was not in a boarding house in some overcrowded close, but in the Royal Infirmary. What the community had demanded of Craigie, Comrie, and Pearson in the first half of the century was that each tell a hard and damning truth. What McKay and her mother took advantage of in 1814 was a community that preferred not to see that truth, and whose institutions abetted that desire.

The doctors fumbled while the women on the ward were quick, but in charge of nothing. The lawyers were not taken in, but they were wise enough to know when they had been outsmarted. The prosecutor for Glasgow, John Bennet, earnestly pursued the case, and prepared an information stating that McKay had given birth, and thrown the child out in the snow. The city magistrates sent it on to the lord advocate's office, where H. Home Drummond had the last word, written on a scrap of paper.

> I scarcely think there is such evidence of *concealment* or of *calling no assistance* as a Jury could be fairly asked to convict upon. She complained & shewed her belly and asked assistance she did not say for what; but the Doctors & nurses might have discovered the disease and the sort of assistance wanted. I sh^d have been inclined even to believe she did not think herself with child, had she admitted the production afterwards. I suspect the child to have been killed by the mercury. She may be liberated.[16]

Smart enough to see that the law had been outwitted, and that McKay knew what she was doing, Drummond nonetheless chose to cling to the mercury as the agent of the child's death. It may well have been so, but omitting to recall that someone carried the child to a window and threw him out must have made it easier for Drummond to order her release.

The difference between the confessions of Craigie, Brown, Comrie, Tullo, Pearson, and even Morison, and the extraordinary performances of Hunter and McKay is enormous, and telling. Those few women, who left some record of their confessions, made between 1689 and 1758, spoke not only because they were questioned, but because they had an audience. They were part of a community, sufficiently embedded in their places to share their neighbors' horror of what they had done. Even Morison, who was learning to move between city and country in search of work, still had to confess, although it was to strangers. Their confessions were small gestures, pathetic, tragic, grim, painful, and difficult, and they show us women who could not, finally, conceal their lives from their neighbors. To have successfully concealed their pregnancies would have separated them so completely from their communities that it might have seemed a social death more frightening than the gallows. But by 1812, and then 1814, Hunter and McKay had learned that trick of concealment so well that we cannot begin to know who they were. The only clue lies in Hunter's display of the child's body, which suggests that she wished to say something she would not put into words. But from McKay we have only a performance. In what must have seemed to them a modern world, on that comfortable farm at Eweford, and in the heart of Glasgow, they learned to be inscrutable. For them, that would be survival, and individualism.

8

The Bourgeois Novel of Infanticide

Walter Scott's *The Heart of Mid-Lothian*

Nothing is more free than the imagination of man, and though it cannot exceed that original stock of ideas furnished by the internal and external senses, it has unlimited power of mixing, compounding, separating, and dividing these ideas in all the varieties of fiction and vision. It can feign a train of events with all the appearance of reality, ascribe to them a particular time and place, conceive them as existent, and paint them out to itself with every circumstance that belongs to any historical fact which it believes with the greatest certainty. Wherein, therefore, consists the difference between such a fiction and belief?

—David Hume, 1748

Particularly because statutory infanticide was a presumptive crime, coming to grips with it entailed a certain use of imagination for all concerned. Women who killed their children learned to "feign a train of events" while also expressing some of their anger and, for Jean McKay, their contempt for those around them. Judges, jurors, and prosecuting and defending lawyers had to wrestle with what they and others thought a woman could do when alone with her newborn child. And then the poet, novelist, antiquarian, lawyer, and ballad collector Walter Scott pitched in, writing a novel about infanticide, in which no crime had been committed. Everyone had simply misunderstood, and the law imagined, as it were, a crime where only innocence and passion existed.

The "heart of Mid-Lothian" to which Walter Scott referred his readers in 1818 was the Tolbooth, or jail, which had stood in the center of Edinburgh's Old Town. An early fifteenth-century public building with slit windows and heavy doors, it was surrounded by the old city: St. Giles Kirk, Parliament Hall, the Royal Bank, and the Royal Exchange—all these were the buildings of Kirk and court and modest wealth. The Tolbooth was taken down in 1817 to make way for traffic and trade in the street, and Scott wrote his novel while it was being dismantled. In fact, he hoped to get several lintels and niches from the old building for use in his hodgepodge baronial farmhouse, Abbotsford.[1] But he wrote about the Tolbooth itself with ambivalance, as an antiquarian flushed with the heady joy of having outlived the past. And despite its venerable nickname, "the heart of Mid-Lothian," the real heart of his novel was its heroine, Jeanie Deans, and not the Tolbooth.

Isobell Walker, the Source of Scott's Story

The story Scott was telling, with great license, was that of Isobell Walker, tried for infanticide in 1738 in Dumfries. But Scott had two sources for Isobell Walker's story, the court record, and the reminiscences of Helen Walker, a very old woman who claimed to be Isobell's older sister. Her story reached Scott in the 1790s through a Mrs. Goldie, who sometimes bought eggs from her. And after Helen Walker's death, Scott reported talking with the old woman who had shared Walker's cottage. She told Scott that "Helen was a wily body, and whene'er ony o' the neebors asked anything about it, she aye turned the conversation."[2] If Scott ever read the court record, he ignored it, preferring Helen Walker's more admirable story, ignoring any suggestion that she might have been "a wily body." While it is true that Isobell Walker was pardoned, and possible that she had a sister who got that pardon, everything else that Scott wrote was a carefully constructed fiction about the lives of village women and tenant farmers. His version of Isobell Walker, Effie Deans (Jeanie Deans's younger half-sister), would look nothing like Isobell, or Euphemia Hunter; and she would not kill her child. The changes he made would not have served Isobell Walker or her society half so well as they must have calmed the fears of his own era, and the magnitude of the changes can only be seen if we first confront what remains in the court record.

The old Tolbooth of Edinburgh, before it was dismantled in 1817 to make way for traffic and trade. Although Walter Scott acknowledged the Tolbooth as the "heart of Mid-Lothian," the real heart of his novel was Jeanie Deans.

On a Thursday late in October 1736, William Johnston left his mill in Nether Cluden to walk along the bank of the Water of Cluden, a small stream still noted for its trout. He was walking southeast along the Water "a little below the town" when he discovered a dead child lying at the stream's edge on a sandbank.[3] Without touching it, something he particularly noted in his testimony, he "called some of his neighbors" to come see the child. The child found by these neighboring villagers was a male, and had been strangled and trussed up in a peculiar fashion. He had one arm tied to his head, and the same scrap of cloth also covered his mouth and nose. Whether of practical or magical value, the intention to silence and stifle the child, living or dead, is still clear, and was perhaps even more so to those who saw him on the

The town of Dumfries, the market center near the parishes from which Isobell
Walker and, later, Agnes Walker were taken for trial. Walter Scott drew upon
the story of Isobell Walker when fashioning his heroine, Jeanie Deans.

sandbank. Johnston noted the "Old Blew and white napkin [kerchief]
tyed about the Child's neck with severall knotts," but seemed more
impressed with the "peice of a Clout tyed over the Child's mouth and
nose." Johnston must have studied this carefully, for when he testified,
about eighteen months later, he had forgotten which day it was and
which neighbors came, but dwelt on how "this Cloath was so strait tyed
that the Child's nose was turned aside." Apart from his urge to blurt
out immediately that this was a male, and in his estimation a ripe
child, this was his only direct recollection of the child's condition: "that
the Child's nose was turned aside."

   William Crockat, a much older man, remembered the date, but he
seemed not to have peered so closely at the child, for he described the
scene as if he had stood back and watched the others. He recalled the
child's "lyeing dead on a sand bank at the side of the water and which
seemed to have been thrown out there by the water while it was
Great." The child, he told the court, was "Quite naked," excepting the
strip of linen tied around its face, and the napkin "tyed about the neck
and which the women in the Company did take off." We should probably assume that Crockat and Johnston stood back while the women in

the group handled the child. But we will never know whether, when Johnston said "they took up the child," using "they" rather than "we," he was excluding himself from a group of women, from poor villagers, or from the community. Johnston was the proprietor of a mill in Nether Cluden, and there were four Johnstons chosen for the jury in this case, all large local landowners. The others at the riverbank, William Crockat, his wife, Agnes Baxter, John Crockat younger, and his wife, Mary Haining, were probably tenants of some sort in Nether Cluden. But Johnston was also a tenant in a cloth-finishing mill, or "waulk miln," and Johnston, Crockat, and Haining were all able to sign their testimony in the court minute books, suggesting that Johnston was not the only literate person in the village.

Mary Haining, the woman Crockat thought had "loosed" the kerchief from around the child's neck, spoke precisely. The child was on a sandbank, but close to the water, leading her to assume that the child "had been thrown out of the water while it was in flood the day before." She referred to the scrap of cloth tied around its face as "a Bit of Harden ragg," but was even more exact about the kerchief, which she particularly must have recognized as the cause of death. She said that the child was naked, except for the rag, "and a napkin Striped blew and white tyed about its neck with three or four knotts which had been tyed so ticht that the Childs neck was Drawn in to the Ordinary bigness of a Childs arm of six years old." This was undoubtedly what His Majesty's prosecutor wanted, and only Haining could have told this, for she had immediately untied the napkin and wrapped it loosely around the child's neck. "In that manner it was carried away to the Church" of Holywood about a mile distant, which was the parish church for Nether Cluden.

The child lay in the church for an hour and a half. On that same day, Thursday, at "about the same time," Isobell Walker was repeatedly confronted by earnest villagers in Cluden, just south of the Water. She lived with her mother in a two-room cottage in the town. Her father, William Walker, had been a day laborer before he died. On that Thursday, she called at a neighbor's house, either to visit with the woman there, or to do some work. There she was confronted by Emelia Walker, perhaps of no relation to her, and several other women. Emelia Walker had planned the meeting, and it was not sudden anger that led her to confront, and later, in the company of other women, physically to attack Isobell Walker.

Emelia Walker testified that for some time before Hallowmas, she and others in the town of Cluden "Suspected the pannel's being with Child but the pannel still denied it." To understand what happened on Thursday, we must take into account several months of rumor and chiding, slowly building to a climax. John Stott, who was sixty-five and the only deponent from Cluden who could sign his name, recalled telling his neighbors in July "that he would wager a guinea of Gold She was with Child But the pannel threatening to call him before the Session for scandal denying she was with child" he relented and "there was no more talk of it neither by [himself] nor others for some time." But on the Monday or Tuesday of that last week in October, "upon seeing her look pale and sickly and small and lank in the Body [he] did then suspect she had bore a Child."

Whatever Isobell Walker looked like, she was no doubt judged by her neighbors in light of local rumors of courtships and illicit sexuality. Like John Stott, Emelia Walker began her testimony about Thursday by referring back "a Considerable time before Hallowmass" to what must have been a confrontation, when Isobell "Still denied it." Emelia was not convinced, and said that "the suspition still Continuing the deponent in Conversation with one of her neighbors Said that if they allowed her to go on She would beguile them all and deny her ever being with Child." Accordingly, Emelia persuaded her neighbor to send for her the next time Isobell "should come to her house."

On that Thursday just before Hallowmas Emelia was summoned by her unidentified neighbor, and "remonstrated" with Isobell about her position in the community. "She again remonstrated to the pannel the Suspition She lay under And that therefore for her own vindication she should allow the deponent and the other women to Inspect her and if she was not with Child they might Justify her." Isobell, she said, "asserted She had never been with Child, but said she would not allow them to Inspect her that day but would allow them on another." At that point in the conversation, Emelia and her silent partner "Griped her and after a good dale of Resistance and Struling and some other women Comeing in to their Assistance they drew the pannel's breasts & found that she had as full Breasts of Milk as any woman that has born a Child." Isobell still "persisted" that she had never given birth, and was allowed to go, apparently back to her mother's house.

Word of the dead infant lying in the Holywood kirk, or church, must have reached the women who inspected Isobell quite quickly, because

Emelia Walker was able to say "that about the same time . . . as afore-said a Dead Child had been found." It was Emelia who crossed the stream and "fetched the Child from the Church and Brought it where the pannel then was in her mothers house." It was a walk of about a mile and a half from Cluden, at the edge of the parish of Kirkpatrick-Irongray, to the church in Holywood, the bordering parish just across the stream. Surely after this second procession, this time with Emelia Walker carrying the child's body back to Cluden, to confront its mother, few villagers were ignorant of Isobell Walker's misfortunes, or of Eme-lia Walker's claim to village authority.

With the dead child on her knee, examined again by a midwife and another woman, and surrounded by neighbors, Isobell admitted that she "had brought furth her Child" the Sunday before, and had thrown it into the Water of Cluden, but it was a girl, she said, and premature, being "only of the Bigness of her two fists." Emelia Walker, unrelent-ing, complained that Isobell "did prevaricate" because she first admit-ted that she had been pregnant since Lammas, or August first, and then "acknowledged she had been with Child from the preceeding Whit[sun]," which would fall in May or June.[4]

No simple narrative emerges from the villagers' testimony about what they heard and saw as they converged on Isobell Walker at her mother's house. Walker and her mother, who never testified, lived in a small cottage, the interior divided into two rooms by a thin wattle wall. There were probably seven people in one room, not counting the dead infant. Asked to recall events in that room, their testimony is dis-jointed and fragmented, as if each had no comprehensive point of view, except for Emelia Walker, or were not being encouraged to present it. These people, all women except for John Stott, spoke only about Isobell and the child's body, and not each other, and so chronological narrative fails us, in a deluge of loosely ordered conclusions and observations. This failure may be due to the confusion, which we will never be able to penetrate, that so impressed Jean Johnson. A widow of sixty, John-son said she did not know whether the child "was come to full time" because "there was such Confusion in the Room." No doubt the court, as audience, can be blamed as well, for teaching the villagers to frac-ture the narrative to extract the particulars of evidence, and that at a distance of eighteen months from the event.

The results can be summarized easily enough. A group of at least three women, one of whom was a midwife sent by an elder of the kirk,

came to examine Isobell, and Emelia Walker, possibly accompanied by
John Stott, arrived from Nether Cluden with the child's body and deposited it in Isobell's lap. Walker and Stott were seeing through long-
standing allegations as they argued with Isobell in that room, while
Ferguson and Johnson, the midwife and her assistant, were there formally and spoke reluctantly. Narrative sequence was dissolved by the
court's privileging of certain information, and all that remains is the
order in which the villagers testified. Isobell, clearly tougher than
many women who broke down and confessed in great detail under similar circumstances, finally admitted to giving birth to a child on the
previous Sunday, but insisted, while holding this one, that it was not
hers.

Elspeth Ferguson, a professional midwife, widowed and about sixty
at the time, testified first, and immediately said that she was sent to
Isobell by one of the elders of that parish, to make a "proper Inspection
and Examination." She "found her in such a condition as women lately
Brought to Bed and particularly that she milked her Breast and found
that she had fair milk . . . and Likewise by other simptoms She Judged
that she had born a Child to the full time." She went on to say "that at
the same time She Saw a Dead Child lyeing upon the pannel's Knee
which had been brought from Holywood That the said Child appeared
to be a ripe Child and come to the full time both by its Size Colour and
that it had nails." Midwives had a vocabulary of their own for such
occasions, which is formulaic yet concrete. Ferguson seems to have relied on this language, perhaps to reinforce her sense of herself as an
expert witness, but perhaps also simply to distance herself, living in
that same small town. One clear example persists. All five testifying
adults heard Isobell deny that the child on her knees "was any of hers,"
to use Ferguson's phrase. But when we come to the express terms of
that denial, four recalled Isobell saying that her child was no bigger
than her two fists, while Ferguson translated this to its point, "that it
was not a ripe Child." Ferguson probably chose the technical phrase to
reinforce her professional identity, and it also allowed her to avoid the
more painfully literal description of a child that Isobell Walker had
used.

Jean Johnson, a married woman of sixty-six, accompanied Ferguson.
She was "not a midwife by trade yet she sometimes assists in bringing
women to bed." But Johnson, who tried to confirm Ferguson's findings,

could not. She spoke plainly enough about Isobell's signs and symptoms, but said "there was such Confusion in the Room" that she had no opinion about the dead child she saw on Isobell's lap. She stumbled over her testimony at this point, or was stopped, and fourteen words were deleted, after which she began again, saying that the child on the pannel's knee was naked and "Seemed to be Comed to the full time." Her memory of confusion, which she seems to have reenacted in her testimony, gives us our only glimpse of the tenor of negotiations inside that room. And the contrast with Ferguson's dispassionate phrases was so sharp that Johnson's last comment, probably in response to a question, was "that Elspeth Ferguson the preceeding witness was present at the same time."

The remaining three witnesses knew Isobell rather more intimately. John Stott and Emelia Walker had challenged her months before, and their suspicions would have been well known in the community. Emelia had sufficient concentration in the room to be able to provide a detailed account of Isobell's questioning, still the only thing that interested her. When she said, "But at last the pannel acknowledged tht She had Brought furth a Child" we should hear the resolution of months', and not minutes', worth of waiting on Emelia's part. She had had months to think about Isobell, and hence was able to complain about how Isobell "did prevaricate" about the length of her pregnancy. But Emelia's interest in uncovering the truth of the matter was just that; she did not lie when she might have, and when it might have guaranteed Isobell's hanging. Apparently asked about the child she had carried back from Nether Cluden, she said it was naked except for the kerchief, now loosely tied, and "remembers She has seen napkins of the same Collour about the pannel's neck before but cannot say that they were the same."

Her restraint is admirable, because two other witnesses would swear that it was Isobell's kerchief tied around the child's neck, and because she probably believed that Isobell was guilty. When she described how she and others had pressed Isobell about the time of conception, reminding her of their months of suspicion, forcing Isobell to fall back from Lammas [August] to Whitsun [May], Emelia described Isobell's wavering as "another Difference wherein she did prevaricate." The length of her pregnancy was important, because her claim that the child was very small and stillborn rested on its early, premature birth.

If Isobell's claims were prevarication, Emelia must have believed that the ripe male child was Isobell's, and that she still intended to "beguile them all," as Emelia had originally feared.

The last words of Emelia Walker's testimony reiterated what she remembered of Isobell's confession: "That the pannel said that she had brought furth her Child upon the Sunday preceeding her being searched as above And said She had thrown it in to the Water of Cluden and that it was only of the Bigness of her two fists." That phrase, the bigness of her two fists, was recalled by four of the five people in that room. It is not a commonplace in these trials, recurring from case to case like "ripe child." The image speaks, if we assume that Isobell killed her child, to a wish that the child be smaller—a striking phrase, perhaps the visual remnant of her attempt to make the child smaller, knotting the kerchief, constricting its throat to the size of an arm, flattening its nose—the image of her two hands working over the child as she killed it. If this is true, the experience left her referring to her two fists as if they were, or had become, her child; as if she could put it from her, and hold on to it.

The only person to testify who seemed truly interested in hanging Isobell was Jean Alexander, who was twenty-two and lived with her widowed mother in Cluden. Most like Isobell in age and position, her words bring us closer to Isobell's life than anyone else's; they are tightly focused, carefully narrative, and intentionally damning. And, in the words of detective fiction, they place her at the scene of the crime, although she insisted on her ignorance, while she exerted herself to make Isobell look guilty. But she was not a pillar of the community, and her damning evidence was unlike Emelia's, because Jean Alexander had no history of confronting Isobell, or of voicing suspicion, or even of using her knowledge of Isobell's life to prompt her confession. So we are left to consider why she took sides when it came time to testify. As a twenty-two-year-old unmarried woman living with a widowed mother, half orphaned, she would have been an unlikely pillar of her community, or moral voice, especially as unmarried women were not expected to speak with authority on childbirth.

What she said was more detailed than what anyone else remembered, even Emelia Walker. While others referred back to Hallowmas or Martinmas, Alexander began with a precise date, "upon a Sabath day about eight days before Hallowmass." On that Sunday, the day that Isobell finally named as the time of birth, Jean had gone to Isobell's mother's house and found them both in it. Shortly thereafter, she said, Isobell had taken herself off "to the other end of the house which was separated from the place where her mother and the deponent was by a Thin wattle wall." Jean stayed there for another hour, until "near sun setting," during which time she "heard a person moaning in the other end of tye house which she knew to be the pannel." She claimed to have "no Suspicion" of Isobell's pregnancy, and implied that during that hour neither she nor Isobell's mother went to inquire into the moaning. It is hard to believe that she and Isobell's mother chatted in one end of the house while Isobell gave birth in the other, but not impossible. What is impossible is to believe that she had "no Suspicion," for the village was rife with rumor.

It makes more sense to assume that Jean Alexander helped in the delivery and perhaps disposal of the child's body, probably at night and in the rain that temporarily flooded the Water of Cluden on Wednesday. Fear, if not guilt, would have provided her with the energy to both structure and remember her story. After carefully noting that had she suspected a delivery, "She would have called for assistance," Alexander described joining the women who questioned Isobell on Thursday. "[T]he two preceding witnesses and some others went to Inspect the pannel and the Deponent went at the same time and upon the Inspection the Deponent as well as the other women present were of the opinion by the milk they drew from the pannels Breast and other symptoms that the pannel had lately brought furth a Child." Within that sentence Jean Alexander worked her way back into membership in her community, for she began alone, going to the house, but not in company with either Elspeth Ferguson's or Emelia Walker's group, and ended by speaking for herself "as well as the other women present" about the milk "they" drew, as well as their conclusions.

But nowhere is there any suggestion that Alexander used her knowledge against Isobell Walker that day, in that room. So, she heard Isobell admit to having given birth, but never said what she must have known by then, innocent or not, that the child was delivered that Sunday night when she heard Isobell moaning. And she heard Isobell insist that the child was not hers, but does not seem to have said then what she said later in court:

> the Child was naked But had a ragg of a napkin Stryped Blew & white tyed very strait about its neck with three seale knots That

the deponent though[t] she knew the napkine and could [go] far
to be positive that about a moneth before she had seen the very
same napkin about the pannels neck and she knew the napkin
the Better not only for the Collour but Likewise because a ragg
had been tore off from it.

As Isobell's acquaintance she had that one damning piece of information to offer. Her last words to the court, "the pannel own'd that she
had told nobody of her being with Child," recalled a significant statement that no one else had remembered, and one that clearly exoner-
ated Jean Alexander. If indeed she were an indictable accomplice, her
motives may nonetheless have been more complex than simply saving
her own neck. In offering her few small bits of intimate knowledge
about Isobell, she may have been relieving guilt, protecting her place
in the community, and revealing her unspeakable knowledge, that she
was that close to Isobell. And so she knew that the kerchief was Isobell's, and even as she condemned Isobell, she implied that Isobell
wanted to acknowledge the child as her own.

By Friday the twenty-ninth of October, five days after giving birth,
Isobell Walker faced a different audience, swearing before Hugh, Samuel, John, Edward, and Thomas Walker, her minister, Mr. James
Guthrie, David Ogilvie, William Neilson, and Thomas Kirkpatrick, a
tailor in Dumfries, that she had given birth but that the child was
stillborn.[5] She named David Stott, a tenant farmer in Barncleugh, as
father of her child. Stott, who apparently never testified, made a statement on Saturday, the thirtieth. He had admitted his "carnal dealings"
to a landowner, John Neilson of Chappell, and said they took place on
Candlemas last, or February second. He had heard that Isobell was
"with child to him," although not from her, and when he had asked
her, she had denied it.

On the first of May, 1738, the jury of fifteen male property owners
found Isobell Walker guilty of child murder, and the court sentenced
her to be hanged on the fourteenth of June, between three and four in
the afternoon, in Dumfries. On the twelfth of June, a great seal warrant arrived from George II, postponing execution for two months. On
the twelfth of July, a great seal warrant of remission arrived. Isobell
was pardoned, but banished from "the Kingdoms of Brittain and Ireland." Emelia Walker and other villagers in Cluden could hardly have
regarded George's benevolence as an integral part of village justice,

although they may not have been appalled at the thought that Isobell would not hang. But the last word came in 1818, when all the villagers were dead, and it came from the last of the great Scots pretenders, Sir Walter Scott, knighted for writing novels, if not for his pretense of being an ancient Lowland laird. An uninspired lawyer at best, he held a sinecure as clerk to the civil court as his novels paid his way to a country estate, and in 1818 he gave the world his version of Isobell's story.

Walter Scott and the Making of *The Heart of Mid-Lothian*

Walter Scott was the product of an urbane, bourgeois home. Born to Whig parents in 1776, his father was a lawyer, and his mother was considered an accomplished woman. He was himself a lawyer of indifferent ability, but by choice he was, anonymously, a poet and novelist, and ostentatiously, a self-made Lowland laird with "yearnings for a feudal past."[6] The great income generated by his writing went to build his estate at Abbotsford. Scott also spent money on land, often before it was earned. To the original modest farm of Abbotsford, he added Kaeside, and then Toftfield. He denounced reform, towns, and manufacturers,[7] instead acknowledging the Duke of Buccleuch as his "chief," and preferred a vision of the agricultural old order as a series of hierarchical relationships, among tenants, lairds, and clan chiefs.[8]

What he expected from female Scots villagers is evident from his description of what he required in a housemaid, taken from a letter of 1817 to his friend and overseer, William Laidlaw. "For our housemaid (for housekeeper we must not call her), I should like much a hawk of a nest so good as that you mention: but would not such a place be rather beneath her views? Her duty would be to look to scrupulous cleanliness within doors, and employ her leisure in spinning, or plain-work, as wanted." That Scott, in his rather grand establishment, still wanted a maid who could spin, in other words, that he maintained a household with at least a vestige of productive work within, suggests that Abbotsford, for all its fripperies, had a bale or two of combed wool within. Few of Scott's Edinburgh neighbors, one imagines, would have thought of a hawk as the suitable image of a housemaid.[9]

Abbotsford, Walter Scott's estate. Scott, a self-made Lowland laird with
"yearnings for a feudal past," used the income from his writing to build
Abbotsford from a simple farmhouse.

Perhaps not surprisingly, Scott married the politically conservative
Mademoiselle Charpentier, the orphan of French royalist parents.
Scott became engaged to her in 1797, the same year that he was rejected by a woman he still wept over thirty years later. Biographers
have struggled for years to find anything good to say about Mrs. Scott,
the most positive coming from Scott, and sounding like faint praise:
"Whatever her failings, they hurt only herself and arose out of bodily
illness, and must be weighed against one of the most sincere loyal and
generous hearts that ever blood warmed." Other diarists left record of
her made-up air, unnatural curls, "artificial bloom," showy dress, for-
eign mannerisms, broken English, and variable temperament. Lady
Shelley called her "the greatest bore in Europe," and Mrs. Grant of
Laggan, one of the great inveterate Scots diarists, called her a snob.
One hopes that Scott was truly as taken with the *ancien régime* as he
claimed.[10]

For Scott to have dealt directly with Isobell Walker's life would have been extraordinary, and he did not. Isobell appeared in the novel as Effie Deans, but she was not the heroine, nor was her tragedy central. Her character became peripheral in Scott's hands, displaced by a competent older half-sister. As the perceptive Lady Louisa Stuart noted at the time, "Had this story been conducted by a common hand, Effie would have attracted all our concern and sympathy, Jeanie only cold approbation. Whereas, Jeanie, without youth, beauty, genius, warm passions, or any other novelistic perfection, is here our object from beginning to end" (vii). Jeanie was based on a person invisible in the court record, Helen Walker, a sister or, more likely, a half-sister to Isobell. The idea of using Helen as protagonist came to Scott in a letter from Mrs. Goldie, who lived near Dumfries and knew the local rumor that Helen, the "wily body," had somehow procured Isobell's pardon. Jeanie Deans, or Helen, is not merely the antidote to Effie; she is a model woman, and arguably a model of bourgeois womanhood. Scott took great care in her creation, but like Frankenstein's attentions to his monster, it did not guarantee that he would find her admirable. In *The Heart of Mid-Lothian,* Scott wrote a political novel in which the main characters were women, and the goal was to repair the political order by using relationships established between and among families. That he was so easily able to combine politics and women was a mark of his respect for the old order, in which the household had easily contained both.

The novel opens with a description of the Porteous Riot of 1736, the disorder of which Scott exaggerated by dressing the leader, a highwayman, in women's clothes. More to the point, George Staunton, the robber, borrows the clothing of Madge Wildfire, a hellion from the Edinburgh underworld, whom Staunton had gotten pregnant years before, when he, a minister's son, and she, a respectable servant, both lived in his father's household. Thus, from the beginning, Scott paired private sexual disorder with a very public political riot. The riot took its name from that of a captain of the guard who in 1736 had ordered his guardsmen to fire into an Edinburgh crowd at the hanging of a popular smuggler. A Scots court found Porteous culpable, but the queen, Caroline of Anspach, pardoned him in George II's absence. When this news reached the Edinburgh streets, a crowd pulled Porteous from the Tolbooth and carefully hanged him. London was outraged, but powerless against the unidentifiable crowd.

From the Porteous Riot in Edinburgh, Scott moved to the countryside, to the cottage of a respectable, godly tenant farmer, David Deans,

and his two daughters, raised for the most part by David alone. Jeanie
is a model of good sense, and the younger Effie willful, spirited, and
pregnant, by George Staunton. Sensing some liaison, Deans sends
Effie into service with respectable friends in Edinburgh. When Effie's
child is due, Staunton brings her to a boardinghouse, where Wildfire
and her besotted, vengeful mother will act as midwives. The child dis-
appears, Effie is charged with child murder, David Deans is left in
tears, and Jeanie emerges as the stable center of her household.

Jeanie, called by the defense at Effie's trial, cannot bring herself to
lie to save her sister. But as soon as Effie is condemned to hang, Jeanie
decides that she must, perhaps more out of duty than love, walk all the
way to London to ask the Duke of Argyll to intercede with George II
and Queen Caroline, to save Effie. In the course of her journey, Jeanie
becomes a model of Scots good sense and honesty to hundreds of gawk-
ing Englishmen, escapes from a gang that includes Madge Wildfire and
her mother, and unravels the mystery of George Staunton's quite respectable birth; she also persuades the Duke of Argyll that she is virtue
incarnate, and is introduced to Queen Caroline. The pardon ensues,
but better yet, she becomes, always in a way fitting to her station, an
acquaintance of the duke's. He sends her home, not only with a pardon,
but with a job for her father, managing the duke's progressive new
cattle-breeding farm, and a good living for her beloved, a sickly, unplaced minister of no perceptible character whatsoever.

The novel might have ended with the pardon, and the new jobs all
around. Jeanie had been created and displayed to great effect. But
Scott chose to elaborate on the creeping rot of illicit sexuality, as it
disfigured Effie and George. After Effie is pardoned, a reformed George
Staunton, once again his father's heir, reclaims her, and sends her to
a French convent, whence she emerges as Lady Staunton. She can no
longer admit to familiarity with her sister and father, and only occasionally writes to Jeanie, who finds her sister's elevation appalling.
The Stauntons, however, are doomed. They are unable to have children
after their marriage, and their lives subsequently become unbearable.
George is killed on a trip to the Highlands by their long-lost son, who
had been sold to gypsies by Madge Wildfire's mother. The son's reap-
pearance might have proved that Effie was no murderer, but Scott uses
the son, now a killer, to force the reader's attention to the evils of illegitimacy. After George's death, Effie proceeds to lose her mind, and
spends the remainder of her days in yet another French convent.

Meanwhile, Jeanie's family prospers, the duke sends gifts, always appropriate to their station, and her children all marry into the gentry. This Jeanie does not find appalling at all.

But Jeanie and Effie, opposite as they may be, are both modern to Scott's readers, and the true antiheroine is not Effie, but Madge Wildfire. When Jeanie is about to reenter Scotland, riding in one of Argyll's carriages, she sees a woman being hanged. It is Madge's mother, hanged by a mob as a witch. Madge tries to save her, only to be attacked herself. The duke's party are barely able to save Madge, and carry her to a hospital, where she dies with Jeanie by her side. Madge's death leaves Jeanie alone on center stage, replete with the spoils of her London triumph, although she is far too modest to act that part. Her reward is the stability that Madge could not have, her place in one of Argyll's parishes, her father's work, and her husband's ministry. Out of urban chaos, Scott created rural order, simply by bringing Jeanie face to face with the old hierarchy, from duke to queen, and then placing her on the land. The problem of the novel, disorder in Scotland, with the king and queen at such a distance, is resolved by Jeanie's journey, and the royal pardon of Effie neatly rights the initial wrong, the royal pardon of Captain Porteous.

Scott, in *The Heart of Mid-Lothian,* wrote about heroines. He shared that task with many other novelists, most of them women, but he wrote without much of the domestic vocabulary that they understood. He was a conservative for whom the historical romance was a means to a political order, and he was a romantic for whom the political novel was also the means to a personal, sentimental satisfaction. Scott grew up in, and continued to live through, a period of constant and violent change, with rioting in Britain, revolution in France, the industrial revolution, controversy over the poor, and the coming of the Reform Act in the year he died. He did not come by his identity as a Tory laird through birth; he constructed it as a response to the chaos of his times. His creation of character in the novels is much the same exercise in establishing stability, using a vocabulary of rural and quasi-feudal characters: tenants, lairds, a duke, and a queen.[11]

To understand how Jeanie Deans was both a model of bourgeois, or urban middle-class, womanhood, and as Scott's villager, a bulwark against the unraveling of old, face-to-face, yet hierarchical rural social relations by capital requires both a well-defined use of the word *bourgeois,* and a clear sense of the pragmatic modernity of Scott's Toryism.

The bourgeoisie included both men and women, and both used the language of natural rights.[12] Natural rights, that astonishingly "self-evident" idea that "all men are created equal," was a powerful solvent when it was fresh, and Scott knew that appeal to nature when it was new, when it was called Whiggery, and he knew it as a Scot who was watching the erosion of Scottish culture by hands that were urban, anglicized, and Whig. As much as he denounced Whiggery as the voice of the unlettered mob, he knew its face among his literary and legal colleagues as an urbane and educated one: the critic Francis Jeffrey, the canny and worldly lawyers Henry Erskine and Henry Cockburn.

If that bourgeois vocabulary had been chosen again and again by men and women using words not to dominate, but to stand up to aristocratic dominion, Scott was either simple enough or clever enough to imagine that it might also be used to defend the old order. In other words, he stumbled on the secret that one had only to present something as natural to make it right, and that there were few, if any, constraints on what might be so presented, especially for those with a nice prose style. The bourgeois conceit of naturalness was perhaps at its best when used by the bourgeoisie to oppose the aristocratic value of imposed, artificial order, as it was in numerous romantic prints of ruined castles nearly lost in new, healthy vegetation. But in *The Heart of Mid-Lothian* Scott reversed this, attributing naturalness to Jeanie, and through her to her relations with the duke, and the queen. To make it work, he had to work from the bottom up, and focus on Jeanie, which offended some conservative critics, and delighted some progressives. But his result was profoundly reactionary, for he restored grace and nature to the hierarchy of the old order, and cast the city and the English as evil and uncontrollable. And the great success of this and Scott's other novels suggests that he succeeded in pleasing many people with his command of antique props, ancient landmarks, and shiny, natural, appealing faces.

The natural, for women, was soon understood as the biological, with a resulting emphasis on biological relationships, preeminently with children. Initially nature had invaded the household through egalitarian, or companionate, marriage, both practiced and discussed. But in the nineteenth century the companionship of husbands and wives gave way to the new primary relationship of mother with children. The explanation was to be simple, as husbands and productive work left the household, and the house became a home, filled with women and children. But this would take many decades of economic change, and ideals of feminized domesticity were taught to novel readers many years before it became economic reality. If that domestic empire appealed to many women, we must remember that Scott's Jeanie also appealed, and she was not domestic. Kitchens and children did not interest Scott the warrior and political romantic, and he never put Jeanie in a kitchen, and only mentioned her children as an afterthought. She was never displayed as a mother, and that set her apart from the developing ideal.[13]

In *The Heart of Mid-Lothian,* Scott addressed contemporary problems of tradition and disorder, and he did it by using the language of the natural, and by taking up contemporary themes and characters made familiar by better, and worse, novelists than himself: Effie, the seduced, saved, and ruined; motherhood, if tangentially; and Jeanie, in her realm of competence and insight. What he accomplished was to sequester sentiment, and the reader's concern with motherhood, in Effie, leaving him free to develop a female heroine who is free of the taint of that sort of femininity.

As surely as he cast aside Effie, his interests stray from Jeanie after she has been to London to see the duke. It was her mobility that attracted him, her great journey to London to save her half-sister, her worldliness and not her domesticity; but much to his credit, he made the same virtues and skills serve her in both places. By doing so, he taught his readers to see the political and moral value of "domestic" skills, in a way that would have made Hannah More or Catherine Beecher proud.[14]

The distinction Scott made between Jeanie and Effie he drew quite literally, in terms of their occupations as well as preoccupations. Effie occasionally does her chores, but above all Effie sings, and teases, and runs wild.[15] The unobservant reader might remark that Jeanie keeps house for her father, who is a dairy farmer, or "cow-feeder," in the words of one of Scott's caustic critics. But that is wrong. Jeanie Deans lives on a working farm, in a productive household, where her work is inseparable from the work of the farm. She oversees a milkmaid, makes cheeses, and almost incidentally manages the cooking and laundry, but with no special sentiment apart from the care, earnest concentration, and moderated pride that informs all her work. Scott's great accomplishment was to fit out a village woman with the virtues of an earnest bourgeoise, thus offering bourgeois women the model of a working woman, while creating the illusion that these were the simple qualities of tenant farmers, qualities bred by the social relations of the old agricultural world. Yet Scott wrote many letters to his overseer, William Laidlaw, about work to be done on his estate, and just as many complaining about how work had been done. He railed against Tom, one of his laborers at Abbotsford, who had a "Scotch slovenliness which leads him to see things half-finished without pain or anxiety." The pain and anxiety were Scott's, not Tom's, just as Jeanie's pride in her scoured pans and perfect cheeses was Scott's pride in the thought of her as his ideal tenant, or housemaid. His fantasy of the Deans as perfect tenants must have been shared by other landlords, like Grant of Monymusk, as they berated their tenants for laziness.[16]

It may have been his own favorite delusion, yet Scott deserves credit for making a village woman the heroine of a novel. He drew criticism and disbelief as well as great approbation for this particular representation of womanhood. *Blackwood's,* a Tory journal, printed the complaint from a reviewer that "even with persons not very aristocratical, the attention may appear to be too long, and too diffusely called to the concerns of a cowfeeder and his daughter." Walter Bagehot said flatly that Jeanie was not feminine. But the great Whig critic of the *Edinburgh Review,* Francis Jeffrey, praised her: "She is never sentimental, nor refined, nor elegant; and though acting always, and in very difficult situations, with the greatest judgement and propriety, never seems to exert more than that downright and obvious good sense which is so often found to rule the conduct of persons of her condition." It is telling that the Tory critic disliked her, but the great Whig found her a model of good sense.[17] Scott differed from this reviewer in being a Tory who understood the necessity of establishing some connection between Jeanie and Argyll, and the necessity of not surrendering the vocabulary of work to the urban bourgeoisie.

Lady Louisa Stuart, on the other hand, was sure that Scott had recreated their mutual friend, Lady Douglas, in the character of Jeanie Deans. Insisting to Scott that Lady Douglas had been far more charming and dazzling, she listed the qualities she saw alike in both: rectitude, simplicity, singleness of heart, inward humility, forgetfulness of self, "the same strong, plain, straightforward understanding, always hitting exactly right."[18] It would be easy to argue that this is a catalogue of bourgeois virtues, and that Louisa Stuart could mistake Jeanie Deans for Lady Douglas precisely because those virtues had permeated the social hierarchy in 1818. Whether they had or not, it is instructive to note that so many people claimed or rejected Jeanie.

If Scott's friends and reviewers fought over Jeanie, no one wanted to claim Effie, and Scott himself made sure that she had little in common with Isobell Walker. Helen Walker, however, he was prepared to claim, and cite as a recent authority. But her name is not on any of the lists of witnesses that survive, and she probably never appeared in court. Yet she, as Scott's Jeanie, replaced Isobell as the heroine, and the novel became her story. As Louisa Stuart put it in 1818 in one of her long letters to Scott, "one may congratulate you upon having effected what many have tried to do and nobody yet succeeded in, making the perfectly good character the most interesting" (vii). One might add that probably no woman of means aspired to being quite that good, and hence Lady Louisa's delight, and one suspects, relief, at discovering the good woman to be a cow-feeder's daughter. Scott dealt Isobell Walker a great blow in choosing to understand her as a stock character from bourgeois romance, re-presenting her dilemma as the result of rash behavior and great passion, not hardship, necessity, and poor judgment. Effie is not a young agricultural laborer at risk until she marries, and Isobell was not, that we will ever know, passionate, carefree, and beautiful, and certainly not securely established on her father's prosperous farm. Scott distorted Isobell's story, if he ever consulted the court record, and it is hard to avoid the conclusion that infanticide and the problems of rural laborers did not concern him.

If Jeanie Deans triumphs, her family taking root in the rich Argyll soil, Effie is sent to the bleak hell of a contrived Gothic subplot reeking of illegitimacy and hysteria.[19] It is hard to imagine Isobell Walker in that place, if only because she did not break when harassed by Emelia Walker and other villagers. Effie Deans falls prey to guilt and bad conscience, quite without a mean word spoken. Effie, incapable of killing the child, is also incapable of life. Isobell, banished, most likely made her way in the world; perhaps that "wily body" who called herself Helen Walker was Isobell, disguised after a few years of hiding in England, living utterly on her own, and making up a story in which she is saved by a good sister, rather than betrayed by Jean Alexander.

Scott worked hard to convince his readers that Jeanie was capable of this triumph. He began with the land, specifying her exact surroundings, the work that stemmed from them, and her father's guiding hand as the shaping forces of her early life:

> Jeanie Deans, as a girl, could be only supposed to add to her
> father's burdens. But Douce Davie Deans knew better things,
> and so schooled and trained the young minion, as he called her,
> that from the time she could walk, upwards, she was daily em-
> ployed in some task or other suitable to her age and capacity; a
> circumstance which, added to her father's daily instructions and
> lectures, tended to give her mind, even when a child, a grave,
> serious, firm, and reflecting cast. An uncommonly strong and
> healthy temperament, free from all nervous affection and every
> other irregularity, which, attacking the body in its more noble
> functions, so often influences the mind, tended greatly to estab-
> lish this fortitude, simplicity, and decision of character. (96–97)

She was her father's daughter, schooled by him in tasks and lectures.
Scott led his reader to this passage by describing the land: "If I were to
choose a spot from which the rising or setting sun could be seen to the
greatest possible advantage, it would be that wild path winding around
the foot of the high belt of semicircular rocks, called Salisbury Crags,
and marking the verge of the steep descent which slopes down into the
glen on the south-eastern side of the city of Edinburgh" (87).

Scott was describing a world in which property became a school.
Jeanie's work is inseparable from her place in the family, and both are
inseparable from her relations with others. As Scott's narrative voice
put it, "her only peculiar charm was an air of inexpressible serenity,
which a good conscience, kind feelings, contented temper, and the regular discharge of all her duties, spread over her features" (101). Jeanie
is almost no more than a conduit through which the influence of her
station and workday flow, as if by capillary action. The result is that
she is shaped by her work, without being conscious of the degree to
which her tasks have entered her, until they come spilling out. Only
by making Jeanie leave the farm does Scott have occasion to demonstrate this:

> There was an ancient servant, or rather cottar, of her father's,
> who had lived under him for many years, and whose fidelity was
> worthy of her full confidence. She sent for this woman, and ex-
> plaining to her that the circumstances of her family required
> that she should undertake a journey, which would detain her for

some weeks from home, she gave her full instructions concerning the management of the domestic affairs in her absence. With a precision, which, upon reflection, she herself could not help wondering at, she described and detailed the most minute steps which were to be taken, and especially such as were necessary to her father's comfort. (269)

The one challenge to conceiving that the roots of Jeanie's character lie in the material world comes from Scott's choice of fathers for her: a Covenanter who remembers the Restoration with bitterness, and decries the moderating influences of his own day on the Kirk. Jeanie is possessed of religious principles, but she is untouched by her father's depth of learning, knowledge of doctrinal debate, and martyr's passion. Scott probably would not have known how to draw such a female figure; he resorted to seventeenth-century biography and memoir to fill Davie Deans's mouth with arguments.[20] But how to create a woman in Jeanie's circumstances with time to read as widely as her father? Betrothed to an unplaced minister, Jeanie is by contrast all the more obviously doctrinally illiterate, as young Reuben and her father argue for hours. Perhaps Scott could not imagine a woman lettered enough to participate in that highly politicized theological discourse; perhaps it was too political; perhaps he knew that her religious streak would seem sufficiently accounted for, to his readers, by an evangelically tinged selflessness, and a hard reading of the Ten Commandments. Dressed up as the religion of her father, Jeanie's comes from within, in a way that marks individual consciousness just as much as it does the divine will. "Nevertheless," she writes to her father from the London road, "it was borne in upon my mind that I should be an instrument to help my poor sister in this extremity of needcessity" (295). Her language is pious, but introverted, as when she assures Reuben that she will be able to speak to the great worthies in London, saying "But I have that within in me that will keep my heart from failing, and I am amaist sure that I will be strengthened to speak the errand I came for" (289–90).

Despite the pious resonance and implicit self-consciousness of "I should be an instrument," and "I will be strengthened," Jeanie's ability to impress her view upon others depends on her earnest appearance, not the facts of Effie's case, or Jeanie's ability to speak. When she tells Reuben that she must go to London, she argues that her presence will mean more than her words: "[B]ut writing winna do it—a letter canna look, and pray, and beg, and beseech as the human voice can do to the human heart. A letter's like the music that ladies have for their spinnets—naething but the black scores, compared to the same tune played or sung. It's word of mouth maun do it, or naething, Reuben" (290–91). Jeanie takes her words seriously because they are a reflection of her self. Effie's lawyer has told Jeanie that Effie can be saved if he can prove that she did not conceal her pregnancy; in other words, if Jeanie will say that Effie confessed the pregnancy to her, Effie will not hang. But Jeanie will not lie. In a prison interview with Effie, Jeanie recounted her conversation with the lawyer. " 'I told him,' replied Jeanie, who now trembled at the turn which her sister's reflections seemed about to take, 'that I daured na swear to an untruth. And what d'ye ca' an untruth,' said Effie, again showing a touch of her former spirit—'Ye are muckle to blame, lass, if ye think a mother would, or could, murder her ain bairn' " (226).

Jeanie cannot lie. But it is a curious problem, whether we are to understand her truthfulness to derive from her religious understanding, or from her earnest, clear self-knowledge. She did not know that Effie was pregnant, and therefore she cannot misrepresent herself as a person who did. But only as she weeps over Effie's fate, and hers, which is to tell the truth and see Effie hang, does Scott show a Jeanie Deans struggling with emotions that run contrary to her duty and her identity. But Jeanie is not sentimental. Sentiment got Effie into trouble in the first place, as she told Jeanie in that same prison interview. " 'Love him?' answered Effie—'If I hadna loved as woman seldom loves, I hadna been within these wa's this day; and trow ye, that love sic as mine is lightly forgotten?' " (224). It is love, or sentiment, or passion, that hangs over Effie like a Gothic curse, and order, duty, or simplicity that saves Jeanie. It should be no surprise to the reader that when, in the courtroom, Jeanie says what she must, to the consternation of all, it is Jeanie who must remind the judge to continue, for he is weeping, and she is quite in control of herself.

Jeanie is not a badly drawn one-dimensional character; she is internally and externally consistent for a purpose.[21] On the road to London, Jeanie finds refuge from kidnappers with a minister, George Staunton's father. " 'Young woman,' said he, 'there is something in your face and appearance that marks both sense and simplicity, and if I am not deceived, innocence also—Should it be otherwise, I can only say, you are the most accomplished hypocrite, I have ever seen' " (362). And again, when she first meets the Duke of Argyll, she is described in detail, and he briefly:

> She wore the tartan plaid of her country, adjusted so as partly to cover her head, and partly to fall back over her shoulders. A quantity of fair hair, disposed with great simplicity and neatness, appeared in front of her round and good-humoured face, to which the solemnity of her errand, and her sense of the Duke's rank and importance, gave an appearance of deep awe, but not of slavish fear or fluttered bashfulness. The rest of Jeanie's dress was in the style of Scottish maidens of her own class; but arranged with that scrupulous attention to neatness and cleanliness, which we often find united with that purity of mind, of which it is a natural emblem.
>
> She stopped near the entrance of the room, made her deepest reverence, and crossed her hands upon her bosom, without uttering a syllable. (373)

From the minute she sets foot on the London road, until she returns to Scotland, Jeanie's life consists of meetings with strangers, at which Jeanie must repeatedly impress upon them who she is, by appearance, and then by speech. As Scott frames it, the duke, "on his part, was not less, or less deservedly, struck with the quiet simplicity and modesty expressed in the dress, manners, and countenance of his humble countrywoman" (373). It is not a question of individuality, but of displaying the qualities that entitle her to a hearing, and in the long run, to win. It was merely the female manifestation of the modesty and propriety that would make men of her class feel fit to rule empires; what was admirable in her at the moment she faced the duke would seem less so when it matured, in her daughters, into the voice used with servants.[22]

Yet Scott raised Effie in the same family with Jeanie. He made Jeanie singularly skilled and disciplined by her father's widowed hand, but he has Effie's mother die when she is young, and their father spoils his youngest, letting her do as she likes. The result, "this untaught child of nature," presumably cannot avoid her painful, Whiggish end, believing "in her own conceit at least, to the right of independence and free agency." How she comes to this, after being treated by both father and older sister as a child until she is seventeen probably only reveals

Scott's perceptions of the evils of his time—spoiled children and Whigs—and his willingness to conflate them. Effie "seemed a child for some years after she had attained the years of womanhood, was still called the 'bit lassie' and 'little Effie,' and was permitted to run up and down uncontrolled" (111–12). But Scott, also in good Jacobin fashion, connected Effie and her dangerous passion to the aristocracy, making Effie and George end their days as Lord and Lady Staunton.

Scott's Toryism must always be understood as Scottish; it is the English aristocracy Scott incriminated, and the Duke of Argyll whom Scott presented as a good father, whose children are free to rough-house with him, and tease him like a playmate. It was not the old order Scott wished to incriminate, although in Staunton he certainly played on a radical discourse attributing licentious behavior to nobles of both sexes. Scott compared an irresponsible English heir who took up with the commoners of the underworld to a great Scottish lord who took his rights and his duties seriously. In connecting Effie's "independence" with aristocratic license, Scott was making a connection that had been made before by bourgeois men, but Scott used Effie's behavior as an excuse to elevate Jeanie and the Duke of Argyll as models.[23]

Jeanie's code of behavior is clearly the intended lesson, but we must remember that *The Heart of Mid-Lothian* is a political novel, about social order, minutely examined at the points at which it has broken down into anarchy. It opens with a serious riot that threatens the Act of Union, continuing to a criminal court case, as a result of which a village woman petitions the Duke of Argyll, who helps her to speak to the queen, who controls the king, all to free a seventeen-year-old girl in an Edinburgh still rumbling with discontent over the last person pardoned by the Crown. Scott constructed the story in such a way that a village woman could bring about a successful conclusion. To do so meant giving Jeanie Deans power in that world, but the price exacted was high. She would not be like Effie, and she could not be like Madge Wildfire. She could only be very, very good.

There is no corresponding set of male characters, and no male hero or villain. It is the value and the consequence of women's behavior that Scott has exaggerated, and that came to be *The Heart of Mid-Lothian*. By making women the bedrock, or quicksand, on which men's actions rest—even the pardon is procured through Queen Caroline, upon whom George II depends—Scott was giving them great influence. Given the predominance of women and the threat of infanticide, one might have expected a novel with at least one prominent mother in it, but Scott provided none, other than the slightest glimpse of Jeanie later in life, and Madge Wildfire's monstrous mother, occasionally the caricature of motherliness. Jeanie could not, although she tried, take a maternal attitude toward Effie and Madge, because they had borne children, when she had not. Scott probably did not depict Jeanie, or any of his female characters, as a mother, settled in full-blown domestic dominion, because he saw her, and Effie, and Madge, as daughters. Jeanie can be a political actor only as her father's daughter, acting as agent for the family honor. She moves from her father's house into the protection of the Duke of Argyll, all this seen through the proud paternal eye of Scott himself. Jeanie was the daughter he tried to choose, the good daughter he commissioned to act on behalf of the rural social order. She was a son he never had, and the Joan of Arc of Scotland.[24] But it was Madge Wildfire he loved.

In Madge Wildfire, Scott created his female antiheroine, his dangerous, proscribed creature on the verge of extinction, and he created her in his image. She is first shown to the reader when she is brought before the Edinburgh magistrates after the Porteous Riot:

> The officer retired, and introduced, upon his return, a tall, strapping wench of eighteen or twenty, dressed fantastically, in a sort of blue riding-jacket, and tarnished lace, her hair clubbed like that of a man, a Highland bonnet, and a bunch of broken feathers, a riding-skirt (or petticoat) of scarlet camlet, embroidered with tarnished flowers. Her features were coarse and masculine, yet at a little distance, by dint of very bright wild-looking black eyes, an aquiline nose, and a commanding profile, appeared rather handsome. She flourished the switch she held in her hand, dropped a courtesy as low as a lady at a birth-night introduction . . . (180)

At a little distance, he says, she appeared rather handsome. But the distance he created is not so much physical as temporal; the fantasy evoked is that of an aristocratic past. The distance is not only that between sanity and insanity, but between present and past. The lace is tarnished, the flowers tarnished, the feathers broken, and the masculine riding habit was used by Maria Edgeworth as well as Scott to mark the unfeminine woman. But the illusions of masculinity and aristocracy only serve to mark her, as does her fitful insanity, as distant, at the same time that they ground her in the past. Despite her youth, Scott set her up to stand as the last representative of an older society, one into which she would have fit, and one into which Scott would have preferred to fit. What is odd is that she would have fit in Edinburgh in 1736, and fit much less well in 1818, so that her aura of archaism depends very much on extending the sensibilities of Scott's present back nearly one hundred years.

Wildfire is delivered up to the reader direct from the bleak underside of aristocratic power, and aristocratic license. Seduced by a much younger Staunton, her child murdered by her mother, she is also probably illegitimate, perhaps half noble. Outlawed, she and her mother wander the underworld of north Britain, which is also its infrastructure, its highways and market towns. They have a mobility that would be new to most people in the early eighteenth century, but they are the waste of the old order, walking symbols of the illegitimacy of its power and its erotic license. If Effie has been pulled into George Staunton's world, Madge is at home nowhere else.

And Madge died in it, beaten to death in the street as her mother was hanged as a witch. Scott clearly intended to tie them to old rather than new models of womanhood. He described Wildfire a second time, walking on a Sunday:

> To her dress, which was a kind of riding habit she stitched, pinned, and otherwise secured, a large furbelow of artificial flowers, all crushed, wrinkled, and dirty, which had first bedecked a lady of quality, and then descended to her Abigail, and dazzled the inmates of the servants' hall. A tawdry scarf of yellow silk, trimmed with tinsel and spangles, which had seen as hard service, and boasted as honorable a transmission, was next flung over one shoulder, and fell across her person in the manner of a shoulder-belt, or baldric. Madge then stripped off the coarse ordinary shoes which she wore, and replaced them by a pair of dirty satin ones, spangled and embroidered to match the scarf, and furnished with very high heels. . . . They entered the hamlet without being observed, except by one old woman, who, being nearly "high-gravel blind," was only conscious that something very fine and glittering was passing by, and dropped as

deep a reverence to Madge as she would have done to a countess. (330)

Madge is the last bearer of these remains of noble trappings, inappropriate wherever she goes. Time passed can be measured in the accumulated dirt on her once-shiny tinsel. Her ability to dress up, to appear to be what she is not, is of course a great crime against Jeanie's self-evident goodness. Witchcraft is the classic expression of duality in female nature, of the threat that beneath the social surface lies another identity, and dressing up is another way of alluding to the same tension. It makes a mockery of the great bourgeois hope that the inner self, liberated from archaic constraint, was of course the most useful, perfectly social self, as with the monolithic Jeanie. Scott tried to believe in Jeanie. No doubt her straightforwardness and purpose struck him as manly, and Madge's dissimulation as feminine, her swashbuckling profile notwithstanding.

But Scott's sentimentality led him to cherish Madge, much as Davie Deans had spoiled Effie, and he gave her a switch and a riding habit and the ability to mimic fine ladies, and let her carouse like a tomboy, and speak in riddles. Wildfire is one more last minstrel for Scott, who saw his world, older, distinctly Scottish, disappearing before his eyes. She is a keeper of old secrets; her insanity excuses her knowing too much. She speaks in quotations, as Scott often wrote in them, and recites snatches of ballads, hymns, and *The Pilgrim's Progress*. Her language is canny, anarchic, poetic, and she has custody of the ballads, even though she has so receded into herself in her madness that they are only clues to what is in her mind when she sings. She is a speaker of old words, speaking from the verge of extinction, and Scott can let her speak, because she is already condemned.

Only Madge has an edge of wit to her, albeit she remembers fragments, and Madge has emblems of power—the switch, the baldric, the manners—although they are rags and tatters. What was Scott offering his women readers? He clearly offered Jeanie as a model of womanhood, not Effie, not Madge Wildfire. Yet he compromised his own model by his obvious fascination with Wildfire. The clearest message might be that the man who created Wildfire, an androgynous figure, with her clubbed hair and riding clothes, her masculine profile and lewd vocabulary, could only have drawn a heroic Jeanie who was equally masculine. Jeanie can be spared frills because she is poor, and she can be saved from foolish thought because she works.

Such a good daughter could never take up the role of mother, for motherhood entailed full control of the domestic empire, and that could not be in Scott's world of male-headed rural households, great or small. On the question of whether women might kill their own children, he had Effie voice the comforting wisdom that no mother could kill "her ain bairn," and allowed the half-mad Madge to greedily carry the child off. Perhaps most significantly, he traced Madge's insanity to the death of her own child, at her mother's hands. And he sent Effie and George into decline because they had no children. But he did not glorify Jeanie because she was a mother. It is an odd novel about infanticide, because there are no mothers in it. Scott was sufficiently repelled by infanticide to erase it from Isobell Walker's story, but he was also repelled by motherhood, presumably because both reeked of female dominion. And so Jeanie, for all her great domestic competence, is never shown off as a mother, but remains a young woman, possessed of competence and the courage to walk to London. Her reward is to live forever in Argyll, under the duke. "His grace's people" acknowledge his will, as he acknowledges their competence, as his newly hired English dairymaid discovers when she refuses to board a small boat, and threatens to sue the duke. " 'Madam,' said Archibald, with infinite composure, 'it's high time that you should know that you are in the Duke's country, and that there is not one of these fellows but would throw you out of the boat as readily as into it, if such were his Grace's pleasure' " (432). The Scots who know His Grace's pleasure live in a different world from that of the Englishwoman.

Scott's novel was an invitation to move back in time, and back to Argyll. Jeanie has not saved a half-sister; she has repaired a rent in the social fabric that began with the Porteous Riot, and was reiterated as infanticide. The real Jeanie, Helen Walker, may well have walked to London and sought some remedy in 1738, because Isobell Walker is pardoned by the Crown in July of 1738. If that "wily body," Helen, had anything to do with the pardon, her life still differed significantly from Jeanie's, for Helen Walker lived out her life as a cottager, unmarried, keeping chickens, knitting heels on stockings, and teaching young children. There was no reward, no benevolent duke, only a tombstone put up for Helen Walker, by Scott, identifying her as his Jeanie Deans. The novel succeeded where life failed. Helen and Isobell were not their father's daughters. Isobell lived with her mother, a widowed cottager, at the time she gave birth, and even if Helen was a legitimate half-sister to her, her mother was the only parent she had by 1738. Scott had structured their world differently, giving them a powerful duke and an indomitable father to establish order, even if Jeanie has to walk to London to reestablish ties that distance had strained, if not broken. As one of Scott's characters said after the Porteous Riot, " 'I dinna ken muckle about the law,' answered Mrs. Howden; 'but I ken, when we had a king, and a chancellor, and parliament-men o' our ain, we could aye peeble them wi' stanes when they werena gude bairns—But naebody's nails can reach the length o' Lunnon' " (49).

To "reach the length o' Lunnon" was the grand task Scott set Jeanie. Helen and Isobell and Isobell's mother also faced that problem, trying to survive in a world where the authority by which men ruled their domain, whether shire or cottage, was rapidly eroding, and where the resulting vacuum produced young female villagers who were of necessity canny, wily, and capable of doing what Isobell did, and perhaps whatever Helen may have done to procure Isobell's pardon. Scott was smart enough to understand that a vacuum, a moment of political anarchy, allowed women to act in public; he was innocent enough to believe that they would necessarily act as good women at those moments, restoring order, and helping him turn back the hands of time. But he did not recognize that by erasing the reality of infanticide, he was helping triumphant capitalist farming to obscure the changes he deplored in a hierarchical old order, where particular rights and duties pertained to persons in their various stations.[25]

By placing Jeanie Deans in the countryside, on a small tenant farm, and then on a prosperous tenant farm, Scott was surely invoking elements of the pastoral mythology that grew as men and women left the land, or found themselves wage laborers on it.[26] But Scott intended something very different, although his urban readers may have understood Jeanie's story in the context of rural mythologizing, for which the stage had been set by the collection of the ballads in Scotland.[27] He tied everything on the edge of extinction to the Old Town in Edinburgh: Madge Wildfire, her underworld confederates, Effie in her desire for Staunton the robber and rake. The urban world is old, corrupt, eroticized, seething with illegitimate will, the site of the Porteous Riot and the old Tolbooth where Effie was confined. Perhaps because Scott saw the old, late medieval Tolbooth dismantled while he was writing, it was easy for him to cast the city as old and dissolute. The countryside, on the contrary, offered progress: morality, work, agricultural improvement and the inevitable rise of Jeanie's family. It is a striking inversion, by which Scott erased the intellectual ferment of eighteenth-century Edinburgh, and the hardships of the agricultural revolution, and prepared to face down industrial capitalism itself, by subsuming bourgeois virtue within the sanctified social relations of the agricultural old order. Almost incidentally, he offered women a transition of their own: if they left behind the faded grandeur of Madge Wildfire, they might take on Jeanie's absolute competence, couched in a useful social life, lived in relation to others.

9

The Making of the Scots Bourgeoise

War is the great school both for acquiring and exercising this species of magnanimity. Death, as we say, is the king of terrors; and the man who has conquered the fear of death is not likely to lose his presence of mind at the approach of any other natural evil. In war, men become familiar with death, and are thereby necessarily cured of that superstitious horror with which it is viewed by the weak and unexperienced.[1]

—Adam Smith, 1759

Walter Scott might offer Jeanie Deans as a model, and Adam Smith might, tellingly, offer no model, but that did not mean that bourgeois women read these offerings uncritically. They also knew the world Adam Smith described. If, in *The Theory of Moral Sentiments*, Adam Smith displayed a profound sense of the power of our experience of the material world to form our character, women as well as men had some idea of what their material and imaginative world looked like. In that world, as Smith described it, women did not go to war, and thus could not hope to become self-possessed or heroic. Women did not figure in Smith's philosophy. There was no place in Smith's work for Jeanie Deans's long walk to London, and never, in describing his very material world, did he betray the slightest suspicion that women like Isobell Walker faced death in their own ways. Men went to war, and conse-

quently they alone might know how to keep their wits about them. If
women figured at all for Smith, it must have been as "the weak and
unexperienced."

Yet women faced death, even if it was rarely on the battlefield. They
faced death in childbirth, they faced the deaths of their children, and
their husbands, the temptation of infanticide, the accusations of the
witch hunters, and the choice of religious martyrdom. Women had already claimed a certain familiarity with death in the ballads, where
heroines fought back, and died violently, but did not pine away. Whatever Smith presumed, in the real world women stood up to landlords,
and joined in popular protest. In 1797 in a militia riot in Tranent,
women stood in the front ranks, and two women were among the
twelve persons cut down by mounted volunteers ordered to disperse
the crowd.[2] Death could be faced anywhere, and Smith did not draw
from life when he limited this experience to the battlefield, and some
women must have read him, and known this.

Late in the seventeenth century, the Scots bourgeoise could act with
formidable moral force, but she could not usurp the place and authority
of aristocratic women. Yet there were cracks in the armor, aristocratic
capitulations and compromises. By the end of the century, new ideas
of women's nature had appeared, as they did in the infanticide trials,
or in Scott's character Jeanie Deans. While these ideas were generally
flattering, and clearly saved some women from the gallows who were
more distraught than criminal, they were ultimately confining, as
Smith's premature description of a public world with no women in it
showed. And in their appeal to nature, they leveled social distinctions.[3]
For most of the eighteenth century, most women could not live in such
quiet domestication, even if they would have preferred it. Yet the values of those who had to manage their goods carefully, those, in other
words, who were not wealthy, and not distracted by the making and
unmaking of kings and national churches, had begun to creep into es-
teem by the end of the seventeenth century. Lady Grizel Hume Baillie,
whose Protestant family was forced into exile in the Netherlands during the 1680s, developed such a taste for doing the family's marketing
in Utrecht that in later life, restored to wealth and position in Scotland, she continued to keep accounts, and go to markets.[4]

As Lady Baillie, married to Baillie of Jerviswood, she managed the
affairs of her husband, at least one of her brothers, and her ailing fa-

ther. Her household account books were so thorough that the Scottish Historical Society published one as a monument to the complexity of the estate household. As her daughter later recalled, "She took in and settled her father's steward's accounts;—once at Kimmerghame, with a trouble and fatigue incredible, for two months, from five in the morning till twelve at night, that she scarce allowed herself time to eat or sleep, settling and taking them from one that had long had the charge of the business, till she half killed the whole family by attending her, though they kept not the hours she did."[5]

Visiting the Netherlands, many years after her family's exile, the intrepid Lady Baillie immediately remembered the language, "and made herself understood so as to do all the business necessary; and seemed delighted with the remembrance of things long past." She was particularly happy to be in Utrecht again, and showed her family "every corner of the town, which seemed fresh in her memory" (78–79). If that were not enough, shortly afterwards, at Naples, knowing not one word of Italian, "with only the help of a grammar and dictionary, she did the whole business of her family with her Italian servants, went to shops, bought everything she had occasion for, and did it so well, that our acquaintances who had lived many years there, begged the favour of her to buy for them when she provided for herself" (80). Yet Lady Baillie, in the words of her daughter, Lady Murray Stanhope, "had the bashfulness of a girl, and was as easily put out of countenance" (68). And she "often gave up her own opinion to that of others; not that it proved better, but that they were more positive and self-sufficient" (68–69). Lady Baillie knew something of both worlds, the country and the city, and she knew the city, not as a wealthy woman come for the season, but as housekeeper to her suddenly impoverished family during their exile in the 1680s.

Her eldest daughter, Lady Murray Stanhope, writing in 1749, three years after her mother's death, had much more to say about her mother than her father. It is hard to know how much of her mother's propriety was the product of her daughter's hindsight, but she seems to have been a fond, and, with all the difficulties of the word, truthful reporter. She claims never to have been away from her mother "above two months at a time," and said that her mother "treated my sister and me like friends . . . always used us with an openness and confidence which begat the same in us" (65). Yet her life differed considerably from her mother's. She married much earlier than her mother, at seventeen rather than twenty-seven, and separated from her husband four years later, because of his jealous rages. She was fashionable, noted by Alexander Pope, for a while a friend of Lady Mary Wortley Montagu, and for many years a friend of Montagu's sister, Lady Mar, and Lady Hervey. After the death of her husband, she became her parents' heir, and succeeded to the estate at her mother's death in 1746. She did not rule it with her mother's careful hand, but chose instead to live in family with her younger sister and nephews, where she died, thirteen years later, in 1759.

Lady Murray Stanhope was born just in time to profit from Scotland's new connection with England in 1707, and the range of her friendships greatly exceeded her mother's. She had been acknowledged by Pope as "The sweet-tongu'd Murray," and moved among a more worldly company than her mother, however daring her mother's rough-and-ready life in the 1680s may have seemed to her. Separated from an unpleasant husband by the time she was twenty-one, she followed as best she could in the ways of her bluestocking and educated English contemporaries, female and male alike.

Like her friends, she had money, and family. But unlike them, she was a Scot, and until her death "she was still accustomed to sing the native airs and ballads of her own country, with a delicacy and pathos quite peculiar to itself" (153). Whether these included traditional ballads, or only drawing room songs, like those of Elizabeth Cochrane or Elizabeth Dalrymple, is not clear. But it may have been a taste and skill acquired from her mother, who had written, while in Utrecht, "a book of songs," which Lady Murray Stanhope had kept. But her mother's penchant for household work must have interfered with her writing, for her daughter recorded that, "many of them [were] interrupted, half writ, some broke off in the middle of a sentence." It seems unlikely that these were traditional oral ballads, for if the young Lady Baillie had learned ballads, she might not have struggled so to write them down. But the book hardly precludes a knowledge of ballads, which might very well have prompted her to try her hand at songs. Lady Murray never published the songs, perhaps because her mother was to remain remarkable to her for those other books, "which she kept from the time of her marriage to the last, with the clear, strict exactness of a merchant."[6]

The Political Economy of Elizabeth Mure

In 1790 Elizabeth Mure wrote a memoir of changes she had seen in her long life, since 1700. In it, manners and textiles figured as prominently as liberty, rebellion, and gentlemen's rents. Born perhaps a decade after Lady Murray Stanhope, she was struck by the changes she had seen, and apologetic that she had not been "more in the world." But Mure was not daunted at having spent most of her life on an estate seven miles southwest of Paisley. She "had the principal charge of the Caldwell property during the minority and early youth of her nephew," and extricated the property from debts incurred by the "extensive improvements" of the previous proprietor, probably her father. While she did not admit to any of this in her memoir, her success with accounts and tenants must have helped her to pick up a pen and record her impressions.[7]

What she could recall makes one think of Lady Baillie's household accounts, kept with the "strictness of a merchant," not to mention Adam Smith's *The Wealth of Nations*:

> The 1727 is as far back as I can remember. At that time there was little bread in Scotland; Manefactorys brought to no perfection, either in linen or woolen. Every woman made her web of wove linen, and bleched it herself; it never rose higher than 2 shilings the yeard, and with this cloth was every body cloathed. . . . I remember in the 30 or 31 of a ball where it was agreed that the company should be dress'd in nothing but what was manufacture'd in the country. My sisters were as well dress'd as any, and their gowns were strip'd linen at 2s and 6d per yard. . . . A few years after this, wovers were brought over from Holland, and manefactorys for linen established in the West. (260)

She marked out three distinct periods within the eighteenth century, and she connected changes in manners with her own rudimentary sense of political economy and her interest in the increasing wealth that she saw. She began with her grandparents' generation, reciting what she knew of "those born betwixt the 60 and 70 in the last century," including their "feudle" manners and revered masters, as discussed in Chapter 4 (260).

Having listed the cheaper prices of provisions, the restraint in clothing, and the dirty pewter dishes but excellent linens of what seem to
be substantial lairds' households, Mure cited, as she would several
times, the "Rebellion in the forty five" as the point at which wealth
began to increase, although she had no explanation, other than to
dwell on the scarcity of currency: "Before the union, and for many
years after it, money was very scarce in Scotland. A country without
Trade, without Cultivation, or money to carrie on either of them, must
improve by very slow degrees. A great part of the gentlemen's rents
were payd in kind. This made them live comfortably at home, tho they
could not anywhere else" (262). Mure referred to this as the "small
Society," and described an inbreeding of opinions that led to "pride of
understanding, Bigotry of religion, and want of refinement in every
useful art" (262). Mure seems to have been progressive; she was probably the daughter of the improving proprietor who nearly ruined the
Caldwell estate. She also noted that "the Children of this small Society
were under a necessity of being companions to one another. This produced many strong friendships and strong attachments, and often very
improper marriages" (262). The separation of children and parents
early in the eighteenth century must have struck her, especially the
separation of girls from their mothers. "While the Parents were both
alive the mother could give little attention to her girls. Domestic affairs
and amusing her husband was the business of a good wife" (262). Aside
from learning to recite psalms, girls were left to their own devices:
"They were allow'd to rune about and amuse themselves in the way
they choiced even to the age of women, at which time they were generally sent to Edin[burgh] for a winter or two, to lairn to dress themselves and to dance and to see a little of the world" (263).

They must have learned something, however, for Mure also said that
as women, in the country, "their employment was in color'd work, beds,
Tapestry, and other pieces of furniture; imitations of fruits and flowers,
with very little taste. If they read any it was either books of devotion
or long Romances, and sometimes both" (263). Her account of life in
town early in the eighteenth century was extracted from her uncle's
papers, and suggests that women were as rowdy as men in the upper
ranks of early eighteenth-century Edinburgh society, gobbling ducks,
overturning chairs to pocket sweetmeats, and drinking from kegs. To
Mure's mind, this period lasted until 1730, and was at one, for her,
with the old "feudle" household of her grandfather.

Mure closed her account of these old manners by referring to religion as a practice liable to change, and much changed during her lifetime:

> I shall only observe, that while that reverence and Awe remain on the minds of man for masters, Fathers, and heads of Clans, it was then that the Awe and dread of Deity was most powerful. This will appear from the superstitious writing of the times. The fear of Hell and deceitful power of the Devil was at the bottom of all their religious sentiments. The established belief in witch-craft (for which many suffer'd) prevailed much at this time; Ghosts too and appearitions of various kinds were credit'd; few old houses was without a Ghost chamber that few people had courage to sleep in. (266)

She began her account of "The change of manners in the new genera-tion" with "The Court of Exchaquer" and the "Bourds of Customs." These offices for the collection of government money recalled the influx of English bureaucrats that followed the Act of Union in 1707; contact with the English brought not only new manners, but "a liberty of Trade we had not before" (266). The enlarged society struck her as an im-provement, but the immediate change of manner, especially young gentlemen's tours on the Continent, did not please her. Young men brought home "to Scotland Franch politeness grafted on the self impor-tance and dignity of their Fathers. May we not suppose it was at this time our nation acquired the Character of poverty and pride?" (267). Nonetheless, she found men's manners better than women's:

> The men's manners, tho stiff and evidently put on, yet were bet-ter than weman's, who were undelicate in their conversation and vulgar in their manners. As the awe and reverance for par-ents and elder friends wore off, they brought into company the freedom and romping they had acquired amongst their brothers and neer relations. Many of them threw off all restrent. Were I to name the time when the Scotch Ladys went farthest wrong, it would be betwixt the 30 and 40. (267)

This reference to the 1730s suggests that Mure remembered a gener-ation of women ahead of her own who struck her as rowdy. Or she may have simply been giving herself credit for a precocious niceness of

manners. But this rowdiness was unconnected, in her mind, with the
increasing freedom of discussion and of intellectual fashion that she so
clearly delighted in as a young woman:

> As everybody at this period went regularly to Church, I may
> justly mention ministers as teachers: Professor Hamilton and
> the two Mr Wisherts at Edin; Professor Hutchison; Craig, Clark,
> and Principal Leishman in the west; these taught that whoever
> would please God must resemble him in goodness and benevo-
> lance, and those that had it not must affect it by politeness and
> good manners. These lectures and Sermons were attended by all
> the young and gay. They were new and entertaining and matter
> for conversation and critisizm. . . . The regular teatables which
> commenced about the 20 was the meeting of all the young and
> gay every evening. There they pulled to pieces the manners of
> those that differed from them; every thing was matter of conver-
> sation; Religion, Morals, Love, Friendship, Good manners,
> dress. This tended more to our refinement than any thing ellse.
> The subjects were all new and all entertaining. (267–68)

These discussions pleased her; they were quite separate, to her, from
the phenomenon of daughters throwing off "all restrent" in the 1730s.
Yet despite her essentially social eye, the watershed came with the
Jacobite rebellion in 1745. Much had already changed, especially with
access to British trade. She noted that colonial fortunes were displac-
ing the old gentry, saw the old order losing its grip on Scots society,
and marked the '45 as giving rise to much discussion of liberty:

> Whether the dread of Arbitrary power disposed us for more lib-
> erty, or if another cause, I shall leave the more knowing to deter-
> mine, but surely it had powerful effects on the manners. It was
> then that the slavery of the mind began to be spocken off; free-
> dom was in every bodys mouth. The Fathers would use the Sons
> with such freedom that they should be their first friend; and the
> mothers would allow of no intimasies but with themselves. For
> their Girls the utmost care was taken that fear of no kind should
> inslave the mind; nurses was turned off who would tell the
> young of Witches and Ghosts. (270)

Slavery and liberty were to Mure equally applicable to the state and its miniature, the household, and she feared that this dissolution of rank, privilege, and distance was anarchic, if not ludicrous. She saw in these developing affective domestic bonds not the coming of a tightly knit family, but the dissolution of wider social bonds. She continued in her paragraph on liberty to calculate the losses: no more shared baskets of grouse, open hospitality, lengthy visits, friends and relatives anxious to help in any illness or disaster. Turning to the present, she turned a cool eye on liberty, which looked to her like the self-interest of her neighbors:

> What may be the effects none knows. May not even the love of Liberty become the disease of a State; and Men be enslaved in the worst way by their own passions? The word meniall becomes of leat years to be much used; every degree of denaying on's self to please others is meniall; and for fear of imputation of this we are in hazard of tricking ouselves out of the finest feelings of humanity; Devotion, Love, and Friendship; as in each of them theres a degree of self denyall. Nobody will at present share a family dinner with the friend they love for fear of being meniall. (270)

No doubt she was appalled by the coming of domestic privacy, for what she had valued in her life was conversation, long, late, rowdy, and always in mixed groups. Although she discussed reading, the real point, for her, was the discussion of whatever one read. Mure clearly knew of Addison, Pope, and Swift, and valued what might be called civic prose—sermons and history. These held sway in her mind over novelists or novels, none of which she bothered to distinguish by name. She often referred to novels as if they appeared on her horizon in an indistinguishable swarm. But she was not interested in listing what anyone read; she wanted to describe talking, not reading. What a woman read, or declined to read, contributed to her place in society and was as much a part of her appearance as her choice of clothing. Reading created conversation; whatever a woman read she had to be ready to discuss, and implicitly, defend, in mixed company (269).

The tea table conversations of the 1720s soon continued over into suppers, for "when the young people found themselves happy with one another they were loath to part." This Edinburgh habit created a want when these young people went back to the countryside, which was filled by the "collation after Supper, when the young people met in some one of their bed chambers, and had either tea or a posset, where they satt and made merry till far in the morning" (271). But the collation met its doom in the 1760s, when the English fashion of dining at three "took place." The women retired to tea when dinner was over, and "the men took their bottle." William Creech confirmed this, noting that in Edinburgh in 1763, "[i]t was the fashion for gentlemen to attend the drawing-rooms of ladies in the afternoons, to drink tea, and to mix in the society of and conversation of women." By 1783, the "drawing rooms were totally deserted," and men and women met only at dinner, "where an impatience was sometimes shewn, till the ladies retired."[8] Mure despaired. For Mure, it marked the end of those conversations she so much valued, and she wrote bitterly, describing what seemed to her to be the ramifications of those English dinners:

> The weman were all the evening by themselves, which put a stope to that general intercourss so necessary for the improvement of both sexes. . . . These leat dinners has entirely cut off the merry suppers very much regretted by the women, while the men passe the nights in the Taverns in gaming or other amusement as their temper leads them. Cut off in great measure from the Society of the men, its necessary the women should have some constant ammusement; and as they are likewise denied friendships with one another, the Parents provides for this void as much as possible in giving them compleat Education. . . . Besides this, shopes [are] loaded with novels and books of amusement, to kill the time. (272)

These are the last words of her memoir. They mark, at least in her experience of the world, a curious transition. Women who read little of the world were freer to discuss it earlier, while women who read and were educated competently had no audience outside themselves in 1790. Mure began and ended by describing varieties of female isolation, first with needlepoint, and later with books. She deeply regretted being denied the company of men, perhaps especially because she never married, and also regretted the loss of those "merry suppers" made up of both men and women. For all her dislike of what she found the pretension of learned ladies, and bluestocking culture, the late suppers, tea tables, and collations she took great delight in seem remarkably similar to salons. And for all her insistence on the greater knowledge that men had of books and the world, her memoir shows great skill, or an unconscious habit of mind, in placing manners within a political and economic framework, which if not the equal of Adam Smith's, is the work of a mind not alien to his.

Elizabeth Mure was an old woman nearing the end of a very long life in 1790. She had lived, by her account, somewhere between the "feudle" household of 1690, and the later home where novels "kill the time." She mourned the loss of society that domestic pleasure entailed, and blamed the new love of liberty that led people to indulge in privacy, free of the demands of what she had still been able to call intercourse. Her own most cherished liberty had been that of free discussion among her friends. And she was not the only old woman in Edinburgh piecing out for herself what it had meant to participate in "the classical public sphere" of the eighteenth century.[9]

The Free Speech of Menie Trotter and Suff Johnston

Henry Cockburn, a Whig contemporary of Walter Scott, recalled in his memoirs a string of Edinburgh's old ladies. He particularly singled out Miss Menie Trotter, whose "understanding was fully as masculine" as her attire. Cockburn, reaching middle age in 1810, found these old women a breed on the edge of extinction, and he gave one story to make his point: "On one of her friends asking her (Miss Trotter), not long before her death, how she was, she said, 'Very weel—quite weel. But, eh, I had a dismal dream last night! a fearfu' dream!' 'Aye! I'm sorry for that—what was it?' 'Ou! what d'ye think? Of a' places i' the world, I dreamed I was in heeven! And what d'ye think I saw there? Deil ha'et but thoosands upon thoosands, o' stark naked weans! That wad be a dreadfu' thing! for ye ken I ne'er could bide bairns a' my days!' "[10] Weans and bairns are children, or infants. Cockburn went on to say that "all these female Nestors" were truly pious, but would hardly be deemed so in his own day, for "the very freedom and cheerfulness of their conversation and views on sacred subjects would have excited the horror of those who give the tone on these matters at present."[11]

Henry, Lord Cockburn, was a leading Whig and noted
jurist.

If Elizabeth Mure was right to date a new fashion in childrearing to
1745, these old women of 1810 were quite possibly the result. As Mure
put it, "for their Girls the outmost care was taken that fear of no kind
should inslave the mind; nurses was turned off who would tell the
young of Witches and Ghosts" (268). Sophia Johnston, also known as
Suff or Suphy, was the product of one of those experiments in childrearing that Mure noticed as fashionable. The character of Sophia, who
was born too early to have been a reflection of Rousseau's Sophie, was
the result of an oath sworn by her parents, at her father's insistence
on the "great folly of education," that the child "never should be taught
anything from the hour of its birth, or ever have its spirit broken by
contradiction."[12] Her father was a small laird in Berwickshire, a proprietor of excellent arable land, and connected to an important family.
She was born about 1730 and "passed her youth in utter rusticity; in
the course of which, however, she made herself a good carpenter and a

good smith—arts which she practiced occasionally, even to the shoeing of a horse, I believe, till after the middle of her life."[13] Henry Cockburn, the author of one of two surviving accounts of her, knew her late in her life as a shrunken, but intellectually imposing, old woman living in an Edinburgh flat on a small income. She taught herself to read as an adult, and then read voraciously until the end of her life. To Cockburn she was a formidable conversationalist, welcome everywhere:

> Her dress was always the same—a man's hat when out of doors and generally when within them, a cloth covering exactly like a man's greatcoat, buttoned closely from the chin to the ground, worsted stockings, strong shoes with large brass clasps. And in this raiment she sat in any drawing-room, and at any table, amidst all the fashion and aristocracy of the land, respected and liked. For her dispositions were excellent; her talk intelligent and racy, rich both in old anecdote, and in shrewd modern obser-vation, and spiced with a good deal of plain sarcasm; her under-standing powerful; all her opinions free, and very freely expressed.

What Cockburn apparently did not know about her was that she was related to the Earl and Countess of Crawford, and lived with them in Balcarres, Fife, after the birth of their first child in 1750. From this period in her life we have the other account of her, written by Lady Anne Lindsay, later Lady Barnard. Lady Anne was that first child, and she was reported to have been entranced with her ballad-singing, horse-shoeing companion as a child, and to have preferred Johnston to the governess selected by her mother. Yet her own memoir in the fam-ily papers suggests that in later life she was embarrassed by Johnston and inclined to joke about or join in condemning her: "I scarce think any system of education could have made this woman one of the fair sex. Nature seemed to have entered into the jest and hesitated to the last whether to make her a boy or a girl. Her taste led her to hunt with her brothers, to wrestle with the stable boys and to saw wood with the carpenter. She worked well in iron, could shoe a horse quicker than the smith, made excellent trunks, played well on the fiddle, sung a man's song in a strong, bass voice, and was by many people suspected of being one."[14]

Sophia Johnston was both an imposing figure and a troubling one to Lady Anne. Nonetheless, she was familiar with Johnston's ballad singing, and in 1771, when she was twenty-one, she wrote a song of her own, "Auld Robin Grey." It earned her some small fame. Based on the tune of one of Johnston's ballads, the words were much more refined than those of the original.[15] Henry Cockburn, younger than Lady Anne, found much more to like about Sophia Johnston, citing with some relish the spectacle of Johnston's interrupting anyone she chose with "That's surely great nonsense, sir!" as she laid down whatever she was reading. How are we to judge Lady Anne's discomfort over the woman she termed nature's jest, when that same woman had lived with her parents for many years, and they had built a forge for her use? Even authorship was too much for Lady Anne, who had denied writing her ballad until Walter Scott persuaded her, just before her death, to set the record straight for Scottish antiquarians. Lady Anne's reluctance to publish her name was consistent with her rejection of Sophia, in that Sophia must have represented just where having a loud voice might lead a woman.

Women Denying Authorship

Female authorship was horribly problematic early in the nineteenth century, and the sight of women denying their own work was widespread enough to give the editor of Susan Ferrier's novels pause. Writing in 1897 for a late collected edition, he called her "dread of publicity, her shrinking from the fame and the responsibility of authorship" morbid and affected.[16] Yet he went on to describe the context of Ferrier's behavior:

> It was in truth a universal tradition, a superstition one might almost call it, which we find in full force among brilliant Scotswomen of that day, every whit as clear sighted and as fearless as Miss Ferrier. Lady Louisa Stuart is half beside herself with alarm and annoyance because a ballad with which Sir Walter had usually been credited, but which she had really composed, was being traced to its true author. Lady Ann Lindsay makes a mystery of the authorship of "Auld Robin Grey", and Lady Nairn, in whom courage, frankness, and strength of mind met

Caroline Nairne, a Jacobitical Highland
heiress, knew a good many ballads, and spent
much time on bowdlerizing them, under the
pen name of Mrs. Bogan of Bogan. Like many
women of her day, Nairne preferred to write
anonymously.

as they have met in few women, or men, would fain pass herself
off on her publishers as Mrs. Bogan of Bogan.[17]

These women wrote, sang, and composed polite songs on the skeletal
framework of ballads. And much like the genuine oral composer Anna
Gordon Brown in 1802, they preferred to do it anonymously. They
could not resist writing, but they grew profoundly uncomfortable with
their own productions, or at least with their identity as producers. The
act of writing had become tantamount to claiming property in oneself,
by first claiming property in one's work. If masculine intellect could at
any moment be transformed into the acquisition of property, like

Scott's baronial estate, or the claim to absolute property in oneself, women were less willing to make that claim once writing amounted to so much.[18]

The latter claim was revolutionary and few women anywhere in Europe, and perhaps none in Scotland, wished to emulate Mary Wollstonecraft, or Olympe de Gouges, once writing had been tainted irrevocably with revolutionary notions of independence and property. Those women whom Elizabeth Mure described as increasingly educated and increasingly isolated would have to backpedal energetically if they wished to write and avoid being thought freaks, trespassers on both masculine and political authority. In the end, many Scotswomen contented themselves with rewriting ballads, or bowdlerizing the old ones they remembered. Most are known for only one song. Jessie Findlay, writing in 1902, claimed that Lady Baillie had become a "Scottish songstress" by virtue of only one line: "Werena my heart licht, I would dee" (4). Following Lady Baillie were Jean Adam, Mrs. Cockburn, Miss Jean Elliot, Jean Glover, Lady Anne Lindsay, and Mrs. John Hunter, wife of the anatomist; Elizabeth Hamilton, the novelist, wrote one song, as did Mrs. Grant of Carron, and Mrs. Grant of Laggan. The titles of these songs tell all one needs to know. Jean Glover wrote *Ower the muir among the heather*, Elizabeth Hamilton wrote *My Ain Fireside*, and Mrs. Grant of Laggan, whom Cockburn noted as "an excellent woman and not too blue," wrote *O where, tell me where, does my Highland Laddie dwell* (4–6). Most of this work was done in imitation of traditional Scots ballads, as well as against the grain of them, to domesticate the harsh and dangerous ballad world. It would be easy enough to argue that Carolina Oliphant, Lady Nairne, had the skill, given a slightly different life, to rival Robert Burns, who worked with traditional ballads and local songs in much the same way. But she did not have access to Burns's life. She never ploughed fields, or heard all the singing, tragic, historical, foolish, and pornographic, that Burns must have.[19] As a young woman she learned a prodigious number of ballads, and she was cited by Child for the A.a text of *Bonnie House o Airlie*.[20]

Lady Nairne was born in Gask, Perthshire, in 1766, and her father, a surviving Jacobite laird, named her Carolina after King Charles. She was recognized as an authority on Scots songs; once, at dinner in the Edinburgh suburb of Ravelston, the evening's entertainment consisted of "the singing of ancient and modern Scottish songs."[21] Miss Helen

Walker of Dalry sang a ballad, and someone in the audience insisted that there were more verses, and pointed to Nairne, sitting in the back, as an infallible source (137). In 1798 she wrote *The Land o' the Leal*, which became a popular song. She long concealed her authorship, but near the end of her life, acknowledged it in her own words, thus: "Oh yes! I was young then. I wrote it merely because I liked the air so much, and I put these words to it, never fearing questions as to the authorship. However, a lady would know, and took it down, and I had not Sir Walter's art of denying. I was present when it was asserted that Burns composed it on his death-bed, and that he had it *Jean* instead of *John*; but the parties could not decide why it never appeared in his words as his last song should have done. I never answered" (127–28). Apparently writing a ballad offered little danger of labeling one "too blue," for ballads no doubt circulated anonymously. Imitation was safe. But it also offered the exciting possibility of hearing one's work mistaken for Burns's, all at no risk to oneself.

But Nairne's great task was not the production of *The Land o' the Leal*; it was "the purification of Scottish song" (138). One of her biographers, Jessie Findlay, could hardly contain herself as she revealed the young Lady Nairne's calling, discovered while driving through a Highland village during the annual fair. Seeing many villagers carrying a small yellow book, Lady Nairne sent her footman for a copy. It "proved to be a collection of old Scots songs and ballads, many of them so essentially gross in sentiment and diction that their dissemination was a positive danger to the song-loving peasantry of Scotland" (115). And so in 1793 Carolina Oliphant, later Lady Nairne, supposedly "resolved to purify those ribald national songs" (115).

The opportunity did not come until 1821, and it came through the daughters of David Hume, and Robert Purdie, a music publisher, who wished to publish "a collection of national airs with words suitable for refined circles" (137–39).[22] The Misses Hume turned to Nairne, among other women; a committee was formed, and operated in complete secrecy. Nairne agreed to contribute only if she could be screened, even from the publisher, and signed her pieces B. B., for Mrs. Bogan of Bogan, and S. M., for Scottish Minstrel. Purdie's *Scottish Minstrel* was published in 1824, when Nairne was fifty-eight, and dropped into relative obscurity, after some gossip over the identity of B. B.

Female authorship was fraught with such mystification. Nairne could not resist pushing her anonymity even further, and dressed as the elderly Highlander, Mrs. Bogan of Bogan, to visit her publisher, ostensibly to prevent anyone from suspecting that B. B. was Nairne. This practiced duplicity was not her own invention, but that of Clementina Stirling Graham of Duntrune, who dressed as an old, genteel, outspoken country woman and paid calls all over Edinburgh.[23] Graham seems to have taken great pleasure both in duping people, and in expressing opinions she clearly could not bring herself to claim as her own. That they both so enjoyed dressing up as old women was a stark comment on the limits imposed on women of their generation.

In the end, Lady Nairne, like the playwright Joanna Baillie, Lady Grisell Baillie of Mellerstain and Dryburgh, and the novelist Susan Ferrier, found Christ.[24] Before her conversion, Susan Ferrier published a novel in 1810, *Marriage*, in which the characters Lady Emily and Miss Mary played out a theme that had been developed in 1801. In that year, the Anglo-Irish novelist Maria Edgeworth published *Belinda*. Pairing the bourgeois heroine of that name with the witty, but decadent, and literally decaying, Lady Delacour, Edgeworth let the healthy, reasonable, and domesticated Belinda save the worldly Lady Delacour from a cancer, both real and symbolic, destroying her breast and her family.

Ferrier was twenty-eight when her novel was published, and the clash between the free, sarcastic, utterly aristocratic, and unhappy Lady Emily, and the almost superfluously good Miss Mary was now a classic device for portraying the transition from aristocratic to bourgeois values. Lady Emily in *Marriage*, Lady Delacour in *Belinda*, and Scott's Madge Wildfire, bumbling about in her tattered, spangled bits and pieces, all marked the passing of the old order. They did not fit. Lady Delacour was ill, Madge mad, and Lady Emily out of place, as she herself remarked: "[B]ut alas! I live in degenerate days. Oh! that I had been born the persecuted daughter of some ancient Baron bold, instead of the spoiled child of a good natured modern Earl! Heavens! To think that I must tamely, abjectly submit to be married in the presence of all my family, even in the very parish church! Oh, what detractions from the brilliancy of my star!"[25]

All three mimicked the older, spectacular confrontation between the Marquise de Merteuil and Madame de Tourvel in a French novel, Pierre Choderlos de Laclos's *Les Liaisons Dangereuses*, published in 1784. Although in Laclos's novel the contrast between the two women was not central, and Madame de Tourvel's virtues not fully developed, the later British novels, from 1801, 1810, and 1817, made the differences between aristocrat and bourgeoise very clear. Much as the Duke of Argyll admired Jeanie Deans in Scott's novel, virtue was transferred, countless times, to women who were dependable, honest, temperate, self-effacing, and resolutely moral. Some door had shut, and Henry Cockburn, writing his memoirs in the 1840s, knew the generation of outspoken old women who had come before him as a dying breed.

Those older women, born between what Mure described as the end of the "feudle" household, and the coming of women's isolation from men, had moved easily between rural and urban society. They may have mastered some, if not all, of the mysteries of the rural economy, and they entered into serious discussions with real pleasure. They were not bourgeois, but urbane, and negotiated places for themselves in a new world electrified by discussions of manners, customs, societies, and economy. If Anna Gordon Brown lived long enough to be embarrassed by her ballads in 1802, her mother and aunt had lived more freely in the earlier years of transition, as the ladies of Disblair. One married to stay in the country, while the other married into Aberdeen university life, and, typically in a world in which urbanity was still the sport of country people, they visited. Other women must also have used the land, and its attendant responsibilities as an apprenticeship; Baillie managed, Mure managed, Johnston roamed the grounds and took up blacksmithing, Graham impersonated landed women visiting Edinburgh to try cases. Even a more likely bourgeoise like Walter Scott's mother was solidly Jacobite and rural in her sympathies, despite the Whiggish urbanity of her husband.

These women force us to admit that in the eighteenth century there was no such homogeneous figure as the bourgeoise, at least in her familiar nineteenth-century form as the good middle-class woman. Nevertheless, a new model of womanhood, no longer aristocratic or queenly, was in the making.[26] New ideas about woman's nature must have had some effect on them. Not only did Menie Trotter dream with horror of a heaven filled with naked infants; Elizabeth Mure was viciously parodied by Susan Ferrier in *Marriage*, and Lady Anne became very uncomfortable with her memory of Sophia Johnston. The erasure of infanticide was real, and it surely mattered, for it meant that some very influential men preferred to see women as maternal, and therefore not dangerous. Walter Scott's creation of Jeanie Deans also mat-

tered, for she tells us that even Scott felt obliged to create a glowing
heroine who was not an aristocrat. But even though Sir Walter was
forced by his own carefully tuned cultural sensibility to make her a
commoner, and send Madge Wildfire to an early death, he could not
bring himself to make her particularly maternal, or even slightly helpless. Perhaps men listened more carefully than women to the new language used to describe women because, like William Hunter or Henry
Erskine, they could put that language to good use in their professions.

But women like Elizabeth Mure, Margery Cuthbert, or Sophia Johnston, if they heard the same ideas, apparently resisted or transformed
them. Indeed, it is hard to reconcile the lives of those stubborn, quirky,
intelligent women with the coming of new, and ultimately confining
and domesticating, ideas of women's nature. But we can measure the
coming of some new spirit in the exaggerated modesty of the female
poets of the later eighteenth century, each with her one or two ballad-
like works, and in Lady Nairne dressing herself as Mrs. Bogan of
Bogan. That she literally created a separate life for her pseudonymous
self, and tramped around Edinburgh as that other woman tells us just
how uncomfortable she was with the thought of herself as an author.
But then it was a period when various sorts of duplicity reigned, at
least for women. We can compare Lady Nairne and Clementina Stirling
Graham of Duntrune with those women who committed infanticide
after 1798, and knew that their private horror would be efficiently
erased in the courts. As the older, gregarious, outspoken women died
off, the silence would be broken by Clementina Graham, impersonat-
ing an old woman, or by the ballads, still eagerly bought up during
the 1820s, or by the occasional extraordinary outburst of a Euphemia
Hunter or a Jean McKay.

Scott had been right to put Jeanie Deans on the land. The land had
made some women, from the Duchess of Hamilton to Margery Cuthbert, figures of authority, and it had taught them to manage property
and other people's lives. For many more women, the land had held out
the promise of a living, and then the promise of a much better life, for
those who could make their way into the ranks of the new farmers, as
Agnes Walker's sister had done. If the coming of rural capitalism would
ultimately displace most of those women, it initially produced what
must sometimes have been an intoxicating chaos, especially as it combined with the political reordering of Scotland after 1707. Mure remembered the end of her grandparents' world, which she called

"feudle," as marking the beginning of her world, in which sermons, a little reading, and much conversation ushered in new manners and a new productivity. Those were also the years that produced Sophia Johnston, Menie Trotter, and Agnes Walker, and if we want to generalize about that transformation, we might say that capitalism never slams a door without somewhere breaking a window. Underneath all these changes in the large and small patterns and structures of life, the ballads we now have were being shaped, providing their singers and their bowdlerizers with the grimly pragmatic ballad heroine.

Appendixes

Appendix I: The Ballad *Mary Hamilton* (C.173.A.c) "from the lips of an old lady in Annandale"

This nicht the queen has four Maries,
Each fair as she can be;
There's Marie Seton, and Marie Beaton
And Marie Carmichael, and me.

Word's gane to the kitchen,
And word's gane to the ha,
That Marie Hamilton gangs wi bairn
To the hichest Stewart of a'.

He's courted her in the kitchen,
He's courted her in the ha,
He's courted her in the laigh cellar,
And that was warst of a'.

The bairn's tyed in her apron
And thrown intill the sea
"O sink ye, swim ye, bonny wee babe
You'll neer get mair o me.

"Oh I have born this bonnie wee babe
Wi mickle toil and pain;
Gae hame, gae hame, you bonnie wee babe
For nurse I dare be nane."

Then down cam Queen Marie,
Goud tassels tying her hair:
Saying, "Marie mild, where is the babe
That I heard greet sae sair?"

"There was nae babe intill my room
There was na babe wi me;
It was but a touch o a sair cholic,
Come oer my fair bodie."

The queen turned down the blankets fine,
Likewise the snae-white sheet,
And what she saw caused her many a tear,
And made her sair to greet.

"O cruel mither," said the queen,
"A fiend possessed thee:
But I will hang thee for this deed,
My Marie though thou be.

"O Marie, put on your robes o black,
Or else your robes o brown
For ye maun gang wi me the night,
To see fair Edinbro town."

"I winna put on my robes o black,
Nor yet my robes o brown;
But I'll put on my robes o white
To shine through Edinbro town."

And some they mounted the black steed,
And some mounted the brown,
But Marie mounted her milk-white steed,
And rode foremost through the town.

When she gaed up the Cannogate,
She laughd loud laughters three;
But when she cam down the Cannongate
The tear blinded her ee.

When she gaed up the Parliament stair,
The heal cam aff her shee;
And lang or she cam down again
She was condemned to dee.

When she cam down the Cannogate,
The Cannogate sae free,

Many a ladie lookd oer her window,
Weeping for this ladie.

"Ye need nae weep for me," she says,
"Ye need nae weep for me;
For had I not slain mine own sweet babe,
This death I wadna dee.

"Bring me a bottle of wine," she says,
"The best that eer ye hae,
That I may drink to my weil-wishers,
And they may drink to me.

"Yestreen the queen had four Maries,
The nicht she'll hae but three;
There was Marie Seton, and Marie Beaton,
And Marie Carmichael, and me."

Ye mariners, ye mariners,
That sail upon the sea;
Let not my father and mother wit
The death that I maun dee.

I was my parent's only hope,
They neer had ane but me;
They little thought, when I left hame,
They should nae mair me see.

Oh little did my mother think,
The day she cradled me,
What lands I was to travel through,
What death I was to dee.

Oh little did my father think,
The day he held up me,
What lands I was to travel through,
What death I was to dee.

Last nicht there were four Maries,
The nicht there'l be but three;
There was Marie Seton, and Marie Beaton,
And Marie Carmichael, and me.

Appendix II: Women Investigated and/or Prosecuted for Infanticide, 1661–1821

Year	Name	County*
1661	Jean Brown	
1661	Jonet Richmond	
1661	Christian Thom	Edinburgh
1662	Marion Lawson	
1662	Margaret Ramsay	
1662	Janet Gray	Selkirk
1663	Bessie Brebner	
1663	Barbara Smith	
1663	Margaret Taylor	
1665	Marion Smith	
1668	Christian Galloway	
1679	Mary M'Millan	Argyll
1680	Finvall N'Cannill	Argyll
1690	Grizell Walker	Lanark
1690	Agnes Wood	Lanark
1691	Catharin N'Inturnor	Argyll
1691	Catherine N'Keller	Argyll
1692	Agnes Porteous	Edinburgh**
1692	Janet Greig	Fife**
1692	Agnes Cross	Lanark
1692	Jannot Cross	Lanark**
1692	Margaret Craigie	Peebles
1692	Cirrill Brown	Peebles**
1692	Alison Beutson	Perth
1693	Euphan Colstoun	
1693	Helen Scot	
1693	Katharine Comrie	Stirling

*The county, or shire, names used are the nineteenth-century ones, to match the map included; hence the old Mid-Lothian appears as Edinburgh.

**These are attributions, when no county was clearly given in the records consulted. When no county appears, the information is either absent from the records or the woman's name and date come from indexes only.

Year	Name	County*
1694	Helen Bridges	Dumfries
1695	Christian Park	Dumfries
1698	Janet Alston	Lanark
1699	Janet Greenhill	Dumfries
1699	Margaret Wright	Edinburgh
1700	Margaret Mayne	Fife
1700	Agnes Scott	Forfarshire
1701	Christian Oliphant	Haddington
1701	Katharine Smith	Lanark
1701	Jannot Riddell	Roxburgh
1702	Janet Syme	
1702	Helen Watson	
1703	Marion Dalgleish	Edinburgh
1703	Margaret Drysdale	Haddington
1703	Marion Govan	Stirling
1704	Jean Doceal	
1704	Elizabeth Halyburton	Edinburgh
1704	Grizel Tullo	Fife
1704	Jean Riddell	Selkirk
1705	Margaret Campbell	Argyll
1705	Marie Nicoll	Roxburgh
1706	Bessie Mackross	Kinross**
1706	Elspie Mackross	Kinross**
1708	Margaret Thomson	Lanark
1708	Margaret Taylor	Perth
1708	Elizabeth Peacock	Stirling
1709	Christian Adam	
1709	Bessie Turnbull	
1709	Isobell Abernethie	Aberdeen
1709	Barbara Troup	Aberdeen
1709	Bessie ffisher	Ayr
1709	Elspeth Greenhill	Dumfries
1709	Christian Hodge	Fife
1709	Elspeth Laing	Forfarshire
1709	Margaret Campbell	Perth

Year	Name	County*
1709	Agnes Barr	Renfrew
—		
1710	More McVurich	Argyll
1710	Elizabeth Brown	Ayr
1710	Janet Shanks	Dumfries
1711	Isobel McFarland	Lanark
1712	Mary Paterson	
1712	Christian Strachan	
1712	Agnes Lecke	Lanark
1713	Margaret Anderson	
1714	Christian Low	Aberdeen
1714	Anna Hall	Perth
1715	Janet Philip	
1715	Elizabeth Johnston	Edinburgh
1715	Elizabeth Arrock	Haddington
1715	Ann McDonald	Inverness
1715	Jean Larry	Kincardine
1715	Magdalen Alexander	Lanark
1715	Elspeth Crichton	Perth
1717	Ann Crawford	
1718	Margaret Crooks	
1719	Mary McIver	Argyll
—		
1720	Ann Brown	
1720	Janet Hutchie	
1720	Helen Marshall	
1721	Mary McKinny	
1722	Helen Wilson	
1722	Margaret Bennet	Aberdeen
1723	Margaret Fleck	Lanark
1724	Sybilla Buie	
1724	Janet Gilchrist	Ayr
1724	Jean Alexander	Renfrew
1724	Margaret Dirkson	Roxburgh
1726	Katherine Bell	
1726	Jean Stirling	
1728	Elspeth Robertson	

Year	Name	County*
1729	Jean Davidson	
1729	Mary Jamieson	Fife
—		
1730	Margaret Craig	Fife
1731	Janet Ilay	Perth
1732	Katharine Gray	Perth
1733	Mary McLean	Argyll
1733	Janet Stewart	Elgin
1734	Janet Black	Perth
1734	Joan Cowan	Stirling
1735	Katharine Ross	Aberdeen
1735	Margaret Mitchell	Stirling
1736	Anna Durward	Aberdeen
1736	Janet McClellan	Inverness
1736	Sarah Clerk	Perth
1737	Jannet McIntire	Aberdeen
1737	Margaret White	Aberdeen
1737	Mary Douglas	Dumfries
1737	Isobell Walker	Dumfries
1738	Agnes McGuffock	Wigton
1739	Mary Craig	Renfrew
—		
1740	Janet Brown	
1742	Elizabeth Kempt	Aberdeen**
1742	Christian McCuian	Inverness
1743	Jannet Stevenson	
1743	Margaret Stewart	
1743	Margaret Rob	Aberdeen
1744	Alison Belishes	
1744	Mary Agnew	Dumfries
1746	Grizell McGuffock	
1746	Margaret Arnot	Kinross**
1747	Helen Wilson	Lanark
1748	Jean Black	
1748	Mary Pearson	Ayr
1748	Margaret Pearie	Banff
1749	Ann Philip	Kincardine

Year	Name	County*
1749	Margaret Gillespie	Stirling
—		
1751	Janet Stewart	Clackmannan
1751	Janet Bone	Lanark
1751	Janet Gardner	Renfrew
1751	Marion McQuarrie	Renfrew
1752	Christian Trin	Aberdeen
1752	Mary McChombie	Argyll
1752	Anne Chalmers	Ayr
1752	Sarah Quarrier	Dumfries
1753	Ann Earle	Ayr
1753	Margaret Minna	Berwick
1753	Mary Wallace	Fife
1754	Isobell Kilgour	Edinburgh
1754	Janet Anderson	Haddington
1755	Jannet Robertson	Edinburgh
1755	Margaret Burnet	Haddington
1756	Agnes Crocket	Edinburgh
1757	Jean Hendry	Forfarshire
1757	Nicolas Fotheringhame	Perth
1758	Margaret Young	
1758	Helen Mortimer	Aberdeen
1758	Isobel Baxter	Dumfries
1758	Anne Marr	Edinburgh
1758	Anne Morison	Edinburgh
1758	Kathrine McKinnel	Kirkcudbright
1758	Jean Finnie	Renfrew
1759	Margaret Graham	Stirling
—		
1760	Elspie McNuir	Argyll
1760	Anne Hastie	Haddington
1761	Janet Heatly	Edinburgh
1761	Mary Burgess	Perth
1762	Anne Davidson	
1762	Christian Scott	
1762	Marjory Russell	Aberdeen

Year	Name	County*
1762	Jean Campbell	Ayr
1762	Janet Thomson	Ayr
1762	Agnes Walker	Kirkcudbright
1762	Jean Tweedie	Peebles
1762	Helen Munro	Ross**
1763	Isobell McIntosh	
1763	Janet Nairn	Aberdeen
1763	Jean Cameron	Forfarshire
1763	Anne Miller	Inverness
1763	Agnes Constable	Perth
1763	Helen Frazier	Perth
1764	Ann Thomson	
1764	Margaret Douglas	Ross**
1766	Mary Lawson	Aberdeen
1766	Margaret McWhirter	Ayr
1766	Marion Davie	Edinburgh
1767	Marion Brown	
1767	Katherine Miller	Aberdeen**
1767	Margaret Douglas	Dumfries
1767	Janet Meldrum	Fife
1767	Mary MacKenzie	Ross**
1767	Christian Kerr	Wigtown
1768	Elspeth Dalgleish	
1768	Elizabeth Smeall	
1768	Margaret Gray	Aberdeen
1768	Janet Cooper	Ayr
1768	Margaret Boine	Elgin
—		
1771	Barbara Davidson	Aberdeen
1771	Janny Stewart	Edinburgh
1771	Bell, a servant or slave	Fife
1771	Jean Ewart	Haddington
1771	Janet Dunlop	Roxburgh
1771	Agnes McIntosh	Stirling
1772	Margaret Watt	Aberdeen

Year	Name	County*
1772	Grizel Ninian	Ayr
1773	Mary Thomson	Berwick
1774	Elizabeth Black	
1776	Anne Peter	Aberdeen
1776	Anne Mather	Haddington
1777	Marion White	Kinross**
1777	Janet Hislop	Lanark
1777	Joanna Dobson	Stirling
1778	Jean Hunter	Dumfries
—		
1781	Elizabeth Simond	Ayr
1782	Mary Blue	Argyll
1782	Margaret Scott	Lanark
1782	Margaret Comrie	Perth
1783	Margaret Falconer	
1783	Margaret Davidson	Perth
1783	Agnes Inglis	Stirling
1784	Ann Pringle	
1784	Margaret Black	Aberdeen**
1784	Mary Kilpatrick	Argyll
1784	Margaret McDonald	Inverness
1784	Jean Lindsay	Lanark
1784	Marie Norrie	Perth
1784	Jean Mailin	Perth**
1784	Marjory McIntosh	Ross**
1784	Marjory Charles	Stirling
1785	Jean McKinnon	Aberdeen
1785	Sarah Calder	Edinburgh
1788	Isobel Dalgardno	Aberdeen
1788	Mary Murray	Aberdeen
1788	Margaret Wallace	Berwick
1788	Margaret Smith	Elgin
1788	Agnes Corstorphin	Fife
1788	Isobel Tait	Haddington
1788	Mary MacEachan	Inverness
1788	Ann McLeod	Inverness
1788	Ann Napier	Kincardine

Year	Name	County*
1788	Ann Stewart	Perth
1788	Elizabeth Buntine	Renfrew
1788	Margaret Fenton	Stirling
1789	Elizabeth Anderson	
1789	Ann Nicol	Aberdeen
1789	Henrietta Manson	Caithness
1789	Mary McEachan	Inverness
1789	Isobel Smith	Perth
—		
1790	Isobel Sharpe	Berwick
1790	Margaret Thomson	Lanark
1792	Isabella Fleming	Berwick
1792	Janet Alexander	Clackmannan
1792	Christian Campbell	Inverness
1793	Ann Watts	Forfarshire
1793	Margaret Barron	Inverness
1793	Jean Bisset	Ross**
1795	Susan Bishop	Berwick
1796	Isobel Fead	Dumfries
1796	Elizabeth Elliot	Roxburgh
1798	Janet Ramsay	Berwick
1798	Catherine Bain	Caithness
1798	Isobel Scott	Forfarshire
1798	Isobel Perston	Lanark
1798	Janet Gray	Selkirk
1799	Mary Cork	
1799	Jean Nicholson	Aberdeen
1799	Helen Moir	Fife
1799	Mary Edwards	Forfarshire
1799	Janet Downie	Perth
1799	Margaret Gilruth	Perth
1799	Isobel Keir	Perth
1799	Christian Monro	Ross**
—		
1801	Janet Whiggham	
1802	Margaret Marshall	Stirling
1803	Katherine Chalmers	Banff

Year	Name	County*
1803	Elizabeth Burt	Fife
1803	Elizabeth Gibson	Fife
1803	Elizabeth Wishart	Fife
1803	Marjory Hedderwick	Forfarshire
1804	Katharine Sutherland	Caithness
1804	Marjory Dunsire	Fife
1804	Elizabeth Peggie	Fife
1804	Elizabeth Cameron	Inverness
1804	Agnes Davidson	Kincardine
1804	Barbara Jackson	Perth
1805	Janet Miller	
1806	Helen Marshall	
1809	Christian Murray	Aberdeen
1809	Joan Parkinson	Dumfries
1809	Isobell McMillan	Inverness
1809	Margaret Ferguson	Lanark
1809	Isobel Hood	Perth
—		
1810	Ann Mitchell	Banff
1810	Jane Aldridge	Kincardine
1810	Isobell Donald	Linlithgow
1812	Isabel Morice	Aberdeen
1812	Katherine Lowden	Fife
1812	Jean Ferrier	Forfarshire
1812	Elizabeth Wilkie	Forfarshire
1812	Jemima Baillie	Haddington
1812	Euphemia Hunter	Haddington
1812	Sarah Bridgeford	Kincardine
1812	Janett Sutherland	Kincardine
1812	Jean Gibson	Lanark
1812	Betty Collins	Renfrew
1813	Margaret Bookless	Edinburgh
1813	Sarah Dunsmuir	Kirkcudbright
1813	Ann Falconer	Nairne
1813	Margaret Bald	Stirling
1813	Margaret Lockhart	Wigtown

Year	Name	County*
1814	Margaret Bean	Argyll
1814	Lizy MacNichol	Argyll
1814	Katherine Ramsay	Clackmannan
1814	Margaret Aitken	Edinburgh
1814	Elizabeth Patterson	Haddington
1814	Jean McKay	Lanark
1814	Bessie MacKay	Sutherland
1815	Aurora MacLeod	Ross**
1816	Elizabeth Dalgleish	
1816	Agnes Johnston	Berwick
1817	Isobel Milne	Aberdeen
1817	Janet Reid	Aberdeen
1817	Isobel Pirrie	Lanark
1818	Jean Matheson	Aberdeen
1818	Sophia Ross	Aberdeen
1818	Ann Milwain	Ayr
1818	Janet Rae	Dumfries
1818	Janet Hannah	Kirkcudbright
1818	Janet Farquharson	Perth
1818	Margaret McLaren	Perth
1819	Margaret Gunn	Caithness
1819	Euphemia Henderson	Fife
1819	Euphemia Mill	Fife
1819	Margaret Hill	Lanark
1819	Ann Tayne	Ross**
1819	Isabella Halliday	Wigtown
1819	Mary Ann Wilson	Wigtown
—		
1820	Janet Burd	Aberdeen
1820	Christian Cruickshank	Aberdeen
1820	Agnes McNeil	Ayr
1820	Catherine McFarlane	Dumbarton
1820	Jean Pollock	Kirkcudbright
1820	Carolina Cameron	Lanark

Year	Name	County*
1820	Helen Law	Linlithgow
1820	Grizel Bryce	Perth
1820	Margaret Keir	Perth
1820	Margaret Marshall	Perth
1820	Janet McKenzie	Ross**
1820	Mary Brock	Stirling
1821	Ann Sommerville	
1821	Mary Brown	Edinburgh

Notes

Prologue

1. Thanks are due The Keeper of the Records of Scotland for permission to quote from these and all other court records; and thanks are due the staff of the Scottish Record Office, hereafter noted as SRO, as well. For Duncan Buy, see SRO JC 11/9; for Hector McLean, see SRO JC 11/21; for Margaret Craigie, see SRO JC 6/13; for Isobell Walker, see SRO JC 12/5, JC 26/127/D2049, JC 26/127/D2005; for Anne Morrison, see SRO JC 3/26. All were hanged except for Walker, who was mysteriously pardoned and later became the subject of a novel; see Chapter 8 for Isobell Walker's court record and fictional life.

Introduction

1. In only a few regions of Scotland, on large farms, were married farm servants sought, or tolerated; see T. M. Devine, "Introduction: Scottish Farm Service in the Agricultural Revolution," in T. M. Devine, ed., *Farm Servants and Labour in Lowland Scotland 1770–1914* (Edinburgh: John Donald Publishers, 1984). Presumably children also took over leases held by aged parents.

2. On illegitimacy, see especially Rosalind Mitchison and Leah Leneman, *Sexuality and Social Control* (New York: Blackwell, 1989), 1–15, for their overview; and Andrew Blaikie, *Illegitimacy, Sex, and Society: Northeast Scotland, 1750–1900* (Oxford: Clarendon Press, 1993). For the figure for Stirlingshire, and the national average, see Mitchison and Leneman, 136–37 and 164.

3. The Kirk is the great Church of Scotland, the work of the sixteenth-century reformer John Knox; it was much battered by the eighteenth century; see Rosalind Mitchison, *Lordship to Patronage: Scotland 1603–1745* (London: Edward Arnold, 1983), 174–75. Bruce Lenman made the point that Scots economic history after 1707 is the story of Scotland's integration into not simply the British economy, but the world economy; see Bruce Lenman, *An Economic History of Modern Scotland* (Hamden, Conn.: Archon, 1977), 7; see also Rondo Cameron, *A Concise Economic History of the World* (Oxford: Oxford University Press, 1993), 186. Cameron calls Scotland "a poor and backward" place at mid-century, but then points out that Scotland's growth as an industrial center was "even more spectacular" than England's.

4. On the outcome of Culloden, and the management of the Highlands, see what is still the standard introduction to modern Scotland, William Ferguson, *Scotland 1689 to the Present* (New York: Praeger, 1968), 152–56; and Hugh R. Trevor-Roper, "The Invention of Tradition," in *The Invention of Tradition,* Eric Hobsbawm and Terence Ranger, eds. (Cambridge: Cambridge University Press, 1983); John Prebble, *Culloden* (London: Penguin, 1967); and Bruce Lenman, *Integration, Enlightenment, and Industrialization:*

Scotland 1746–1832 (London: Edward Arnold, 1981); and on the Lowlander's decision to side with England, rather than with the Highlanders, see Eric Hobsbawm, "Capitalisme et Agriculture: Les Réformateurs Ecossais au XVIIIe Siècle," *Annales: Economies, Sociétés, Civilisations* 33:3 (1978): 580–601.

5. R. S. Neale, *Writing Marxist History: British Society, Economy, and Culture Since 1700* (Oxford: Basil Blackwell, 1985), 65–85.

6. For the court cases, both of which are discussed in later chapters, see SRO JC 12/11 for Agnes Walker, and SRO JC 12/5 for Isobell Walker. All SRO references are to the Scottish Record Office holdings. For consistency, the farm and the stream of Cludan or Cluden are given as Cluden throughout.

7. Illegitimacy has been discussed at length, and the debates detailed twice, with reference to the Scots context, with different biases but quite clearly, in two books: see Mitchison and Leneman, *Sexuality and Social Control,* 1–15, for their overview; see also their "Scottish Illegitimacy Ratios in the Early Modern Period," *Economic History Review,* 2d ser., 40:1 (1987): 41–63, and "Girls in Trouble: The Social and Geographical Setting of Illegitimacy in Early Modern Scotland," *Journal of Social History* 22 (Spring 1988): 483–89; and Blaikie, *Illegitimacy, Sex, and Society,* 9–31; Blaikie's bibliography of post-1900 books, 243–55, is also useful. On illegitimacy and infanticide, in Britain and in general, see the Bibliographical Essay at the end of this volume.

8. See the illegitimacy debate of the 1970s: Edward Shorter, *The Making of the Modern Family* (New York: Basic Books, 1975), and "Illegitimacy, Sexual Revolution, and Social Change in Modern Europe," in Robert I. Rotberg and Theodore K. Rabb, eds., *Marriage and Fertility: Studies in Interdisciplinary History* (Princeton: Princeton University Press, 1980); Louise Tilly, Joan W. Scott, and Miriam Cohen, "Women's Work and European Fertility Patterns," *Journal of Interdisciplinary History* 6:3 (1976): 447–76; and especially Cissie Fairchilds, "Female Sexual Attitudes and the Rise of Illegitimacy: A Case Study," *Journal of Interdisciplinary History* 8:4 (1978): 627–67.

9. For the Reverend Cole, see *The Blecheley Diary of the Rev. William Cole, 1765–67,* introduced by Helen Waddell; Francis Griffin Stokes, ed. (London: Constable, 1931), 41.

10. E. A. Wrigley, *Population and History* (New York: McGraw-Hill, 1969), and his "Family Limitation in Pre-Industrial England," *Economic History Review* 19 (1966); and on the evidence of female-specific infanticide from the English data used by Wrigley and his colleagues, see Ruth Wallsgrove, "Infanticide in Early Modern England" (M.A. thesis, University of London, 1983); and in general, Michael Flinn et al., eds., *Scottish Population History: From the Seventeenth Century to the 1930s* (Cambridge: Cambridge University Press, 1977); David Levine, *Family Formation in an Age of Nascent Capitalism* (New York: Academic Press, 1977); Peter Laslett, *The World We Have Lost* (New York: Scribner, 1965), *The World We Have Lost Further Explored* (Cambridge: Cambridge University Press, 1983), *Family Life and Illicit Love in Earlier Generations* (Cambridge: Cambridge University Press, 1977), and "The Bastardy Prone Sub-society," in Peter Laslett, Karla Oosterveen, and Richard M. Smith, eds., *Bastardy and Its Comparative History* (Cambridge: Harvard University Press, 1980); Keith Wrightson, "Infanticide in Earlier Seventeenth-Century England," *Local Population Studies* 15 (1975): 10–22, "Household and Kinship in Sixteenth-Century England," *History Workshop Journal* 12 (Autumn 1981): 151–58, and with David Levine, "The Social Context of Illegitimacy in Early Modern England," in Laslett et al., *Bastardy,* and also with Levine, *The Making of an Industrial Society: Whickam, 1560–1765* (New York: Oxford University Press, 1991).

11. One classic account of the agricultural transformation of Scotland is to be found in T. C. Smout, *A History of the Scottish People* (Glasgow: William Collins Sons, 1969); also useful to me have been James E. Handley, *Scottish Farming in the Eighteenth Cen-*

tury (London: Faber & Faber, 1953), and, more directly, accounts of estate practices, such as those in Henry Hamilton, ed., *Selections from the Monymusk Papers (1713–1755)* (Edinburgh: Scottish History Society, 1945), or in G. W. T. Omond, *The Arniston Memoirs: Three Centuries of a Scottish House, 1571–1838* (Edinburgh: David Douglas, 1887), 192–95. More recently, see sources cited in the first section of the Bibliographical Essay in this volume.

12. For Catherine McPhee, see Alexander MacKenzie, *The History of the Highland Clearances* (1883; reprint, n.p.: Melven Press, 1986), xxiv.

13. See Henry Hamilton, ed., *Selections from the Monymusk Papers.*

14. Margaret George, *Women in the First Capitalist Society: Experiences in Seventeenth-Century England* (Urbana: University of Illinois Press, 1988), 1.

15. On the Scots contribution to the American concept of republican motherhood described by Linda Kerber, see Rosemarie Zagarri, "Morals, Manners, and the Republican Mother," *American Quarterly* 44 (June 1992): 192–215; and more generally, Robyn Cooper, "Alexander Walker's Trilogy on Woman," *Journal of the History of Sexuality* 2:3 (1992): 341–64; and in a more roundabout way, Christina Larner, *Enemies of God: The Witch-hunt in Scotland* (Baltimore: The Johns Hopkins University Press, 1981). On shifting ideologies of womanhood, see the Bibliographical Essay at the end of this volume.

16. For Duncan Buy, see SRO JC 11/9, May 1736, Inverness. For Hector McLean and Isobell McEwan, see SRO JC 11/21, May 1757, Perth. See Mitchison and Leneman, *Sexuality and Social Control,* for the trail left in kirk session records by adulterers and fornicators.

17. Francis James Child, ed., *The English and Scottish Popular Ballads,* 5 vols. (1882–1898; reprint, New York: Dover Publications, 1965). Child's collection is primarily made up of traditional oral ballads, transcribed from singing in the late eighteenth and early nineteenth centuries; for broadside, or printed, ballads, see the preface to Hyder Edward Rollins, *The Pack of Autolycus or Strange and Terrible News* (1927; reprint, Port Washington, N.Y.: Kennikat Press, 1969). For the technical meaning of traditional orally composed ballad poetry, see David Buchan, *The Ballad and the Folk* (London: Routledge and Kegan Paul, 1972); for an intelligent introduction to Scots ballad collectors and their manuscripts, see William Montgomerie, "Bibliography of the Scottish Ballad Manuscripts: 1730–1825" (doctoral dissertation, Edinburgh University, 1956).

18. Records consulted include those of the Scottish High Court of Justiciary, held by the Scottish Record Office, Edinburgh, including the records of the High Court sitting at Edinburgh, the daybooks of the Circuit Courts for the 1690–1820 period, and the precognitions of HM Advocate, from 1800 to 1821; and the somewhat randomly surviving Small Papers of the High Court. Also, the records of the Justiciary of Argyll, a separate jurisdiction until 1746, published as John Cameron, ed., *The Justiciary Records of Argyll and the Isles, 1664–1705,* vol. 1 (Edinburgh: The Stair Society, 1949), and John Imrie, ed., *The Justiciary Records of Argyll and the Isles, 1705–1742,* vol. 2 (Edinburgh: The Stair Society, 1969); John Hill Burton, ed. and abr., *The Register of the Privy Council for Scotland, 1545–1689,* 36 vols. (Edinburgh: HM Register House, 1877–1933); and W. G. Scott-Moncrieff, ed., *The Records of the Proceedings of the Justiciary Court of Edinburgh, 1661–1678,* 2 vols. (Edinburgh: T. and A. Constable, 1905) have been used. I have used the years 1661–1821 because the statute developed out of Restoration legal practice, which was evident in the period covered by the *Register of the Privy Council* and the early published Justiciary records and continued through the period 1690–1809, when the statute was in force, and the pattern did not alter much, from women's perspective, when the statute was rewritten as a misdemeanor in 1809, which is apparent in the precognitions for 1800–1821.

19. The figure of 347 is based on all women named in the index to records of the High Court at Edinburgh, many of which have also been consulted in their entirety, and a sampling of the unindexed Circuit Courts, North, South, and West, in which I read two volumes and skipped two, from 1707 to 1810, plus the other sources cited in note 18, above.

Chapter 1: Ballad Singers and Ballad Collectors

1. Francis James Child, ed., *The English and Scottish Popular Ballads,* 5 vols. (New York: Dover Publications, 1965), vol. 1, vii. Republication of the Houghton Mifflin edition published in ten parts between 1882 and 1898.

2. For Francis James Child, see *The English and Scottish Popular Ballads.* For Child's life and character, see Francis James Child, *The Scholar-Friends: Letters of F. J. Child and James Russell Lowell* (Cambridge: Harvard University Press, 1952); and Jo McMurtry, *English Language, English Literature: The Creation of an Academic Discipline* (Hamden, Conn.: Archon Books, 1985). For broadside ballads, see the preface to Hyder Edward Rollins, *The Pack of Autolycus or Strange and Terrible News* (1927; reprint, Port Washington, N.Y.: Kennikat Press, 1969). For Percy, the most accessible modern version is the Dover reprint of Henry B. Wheatley's somewhat scholarly 1886 edition of Percy's work: Thomas Percy, D.D., *Reliques of the Ancient English Poetry, Consisting of Old Heroic Ballads, Songs, and Other Pieces of Our Earlier Poets, Together with Some Few of Later Date,* ed. Henry B. Wheatley, (1886; reprint, New York: Dover Publications, 1966). Percy's manuscript collection was for the most part not Scottish, and not traditional. For the technical meaning of traditional orally composed ballad poetry, see David Buchan, *The Ballad and the Folk* (London: Routledge and Kegan Paul, 1972); for an intelligent introduction to Scots ballad collectors and their manuscripts see William Montgomerie, "Bibliography of the Scottish Ballad Manuscripts, 1730–1825" (doctoral dissertation, Edinburgh University, 1956).

3. For the literacy debate in Scotland, see R. A. Houston, "Literacy, Education, and the Culture of Print in Enlightenment Edinburgh," *History* 78 (October 1993): 373–92, and "The Literacy Myth? Illiteracy in Scotland 1630–1760," *Past and Present* 96 (August 1982): 81–102; and T. C. Smout, "Born Again at Cambuslang: New Eighteenth-Century Scotland," *Past and Present* 97 (November 1982): 114–27.

4. Albert B. Lord, *Singer of Tales* (Cambridge: Harvard University Press, 1960), 5, for Lord's definition of oral poetry.

5. Lord, *Singer,* 4.

6. Percy, *Reliques,* 7.

7. Ballads are cited using Child's system: A ballad noted as C.13.C.22 is Child's ballad number 13, C text, stanza 22 only. A ballad noted as C.173.A.C would be the third version of the A text, meaning that several distinct versions of the A text had been recorded, usually from as many singers or printed copies. All notes to Child are to the Dover edition, and notes to material other than ballads are given by volume and page only.

8. For Rob Roy Macgregor, see SRO JC 3/29, for an account of the younger Macgregor's trial for bride stealing; he was indicted for rape, assault, and kidnapping.

9. Jane Porter, *The Scottish Chiefs* (1809; reprint, Philadelphia: J. B. Lippincott, 1879), 9–10; see "A Retrospective Introduction," written in 1831, pp. 9–20, and especially "These venerable ladies," p. 12.

10. On Macpherson, see James Macpherson, *Fingal, An Ancient Epic Poem, in Six Books, Composed by Ossian the Son of Fingal; Translated from the Galic* [sic] *Language,*

by James Macpherson (London: T. Becket and P. A. De Hondt, 1762); Hugh Blair, *A Critical Dissertation on the Poems of Ossian, the Son of Fingal* (London: T. Becket and P. A. De Hondt, 1763); Malcolm Laing, *The History of Scotland, from the Union of the Crowns on the Accession of James VI . . . to the Union of the Kingdoms in the Reign of Queen Anne . . . With Two Dissertations, Historical and Critical, on the Gowrie Conspiracy, and on the Supposed Authenticity of Ossian's Poems,* 2 vols. (London and Edinburgh: A Strahan for T. Cadell, Jr., and W. Davies, and Manners and Miller, 1800); Henry Mackenzie (Highland Society of Scotland), *Report of the Committee of the Highland Society of Scotland, Appointed to Enquire into the Nature and Authenticity of the Poems of Ossian* (Edinburgh: Edinburgh University Press, for Constable, 1805); Patrick Graham and William Richardson, *Essay on the Authenticity of the Poems of Ossian: In which the Objections of Malcolm Laing, Esq. Are Particularly Considered and Refuted. To which Is Added an Essay on the Mythology of Ossian's Poems, by Professor Richardson* (Edinburgh: P. Hill, 1807); James Grant, *Thoughts on the Origin and Descent of the Gael: . . . and Observations Relative to the Authenticity of the Poems of Ossian* (Edinburgh: A. Constable, 1814); William Livingston, *Duan Ghaelic: With a Brief Sketch Proving the Authenticity of Ossian's Poems* (Edinburgh: Maclachlan & Stewart, 1858); and more recently, Howard Gaskill, *Ossian Revisited* (Edinburgh: Edinburgh University Press, 1991); Hugh MacDiarmid, *Scottish Eccentrics* (New York: Johnson Reprint, 1972); George F. Black, *Macpherson's Ossian and the Ossianic Controversy: Contributions Towards a Bibliography* (New York: New York Public Library, 1926); T. Bailey Saunders, *The Life and Letters of James Macpherson* (New York: Macmillan, 1894); Alfred T. Nutt, *Ossian and the Ossianic Literature* (London: Nutt, 1910); J. S. Smart, *James Macpherson: an Episode in Literature* (Folcroft, Pa.: Folcroft Press, 1969).

On Lady Elizabeth Halket Wardlaw, see Thomas Percy, *Reliques,* vol. 2, 105–21, and vol. 1, xliv–lviii; and John Pinkerton, ed., *Scottish Tragic Ballads* (London: J. Nichols, 1781).

11. Little is known, but one source speculates that Macleod lived from 1588 to 1693, and composed most of her work after 1660, which suggests a career of lengthy proportion. See Alexander Mackenzie, "Mary Macleod," *Transactions of the Gaelic Society of Inverness* (22):43–66.

12. Susan Stewart, "Scandals of the Ballad," *representations* 32 (Fall 1990): 134–56. As MacEdward Leach remarked, "One expects that the quatrain came by way of the first collectors writing the ballad in this manner to avoid lines too long for the usual copy book." MacEdward Leach, *The Fireside Book of Ballads* (New York: Heritage Press, 1967), xviii; on Ritson, see J. A. Farrer, *Literary Forgeries* (New York and London: Longmans, Green, 1907).

13. On Jamieson, see Robert Jamieson, *Popular Ballads and Songs: And a Few Originals by the Editor* (Edinburgh: Archibald Constable, 1806), xv; Scott was quoted in J. A. Farrer, *Literary Forgeries,* 252; as was Cunningham, 261. On Child, see vol. 5 for the composite essay pieced together from his notes by Walter Morris Hart, "Professor Child and the Ballad," in the appendix; it was originally published in *Publications of the Modern Language Association of America* 21:4 (1906): 755–807.

14. For the publications of Percy, Herd, Ritson, Jamieson, Tytler, Fraser Tytler, Skene, and Scott, see William Montgomerie, "Bibliography."

15. Sir Walter Scott, *Minstrelsy of the Scottish Border* (Kelso: J. Ballantyne, 1802). For the manufacture of Scott's reputation as a folklorist, see William Montgomerie, "Bibliography," xxxii–xxxix. Scott's *Minstrelsy* of 1802 followed ten other collections, beginning with Percy's in 1765. But the *Minstrelsy* was the first to rely entirely on Scots traditional material. It was an instant success; by 1810, three other similarly Scots tra-

ditional collections appeared, exhausting the immediately available resources. On Scott, and Scots history, see Marinell Ash, *The Strange Death of Scottish History* (Edinburgh: Ramsay Head Press, 1980).

16. Scott was a highly political man. He started up a Tory journal, *The Quarterly Review,* and helped organize the Volunteer Cavalry between 1798 and 1808. James Skene recalled Scott's military zeal and patriotism as exceptional, not to mention laughable among Scott's fellow lawyers. For the political Scott, see Bruce Lenman, *Integration, Enlightenment, and Industrialization: Scotland 1746–1832* (London: Edward Arnold, 1981), 110–13, and throughout; John Prebble, *The King's Jaunt: George IV in Scotland, 1822* (London: Collins, 1988), esp. 176–79; Christopher Worth, " 'A very nice Theatre at Edinr.': Sir Walter Scott and Control of the Theatre Royal," *Theatre Research International* 17 (Summer 1992): 86–95; on cavalry, James Skene, *Memories of Sir Walter Scott* (London: J. Murray, 1909), 10–18; and on militia riots put down by the cavalry, see Kenneth J. Logue, *Popular Disturbances in Scotland 1780–1815* (Edinburgh: John Donald Publishers, 1979) 75–115; and William Henry Prescott, "Sir Walter Scott," in Prescott's *Biographical and Critical Miscellanies* (New York: Harper and Brothers, Publishers, 1845), 211–23.

17. No new ballad collections were published between 1810 and 1819; only one new ballad manuscript survives for the years 1808 through 1816. The first of the new collections to appear, in 1819, was from James Hogg, a protégé of Scott's.

18. These numbers are based on the identifications made by F. J. Child, and the further, more recent work of David Buchan on James Nichol's ballads; see David Buchan, *Ballad and Folk,* "The ballads of James Nicol," 223–46.

19. Montgomerie, "Bibliography," xxxix. Allan Ramsay's *Tea Table Miscellany* was first published in 1724.

20. On collectors' emendations and singers' corruptions, see Buchan, *Ballad and Folk,* 205-46.

21. See the debate over literacy, in note 3 above. On Lady Grizel Hume Baillie (1665–1746), the basic source is her daughter's memoir: Lady Murray Stanhope, *Memoirs of the Lives and Characters of the Right Honorable George Baillie of Jerviswood, and of Lady Grisell* [sic] *Baillie by Their Daughter* (Edinburgh: n.p., 1824); Robert Scott-Moncrieff, ed., *The Household Book of Lady Grizel Baillie, 1692–1733* (Edinburgh: Scottish History Society, 1911); see also the Reverend James Anderson, *Ladies of the Covenant: Memoirs of Distinguished Scottish Female Characters* (New York: A. C. Armstrong & Son, 1880) 428–58; and less seriously, Jessie P. Findlay, *The Spindle-Side of Scottish Song* (London: J. M. Dent, 1902), 7–25. Cunningham's edition of Burns, *The Poetical Works of Robert Burns,* edited with notes by Allan Cunningham (New York: Belford, Clarke, 1895), made clear Burns's use of ballads, tales, and broadside material in his poetry.

22. Montgomerie, "Bibliography," 2–11; Allan Ramsay's *Tea Table Miscellany* contained many parodies of ballads, as Montgomerie has called them, written for a literate audience.

23. Child agreed; see C.III.193. Three of Cochrane's four complete ballads did not definitely appear in print until well after 1730. The fourth, a Robin Hood ballad, had been in print through the first half of the eighteenth century.

24. For Elizabeth St. Clair Dalrymple, see Frank Miller, ed., *The Mansfield Manuscript* (Dumfries: Thos. Hunter, Watson, 1935). Cochrane and Creighton can be found in Montgomerie, "Bibliography." For another later example see the manuscript of Mrs. Creighton, copied down by her daughter-in-law in 1819: Montgomerie, "Bibliography," 312, and 287–88, which is a letter to Montgomerie from a descendant, Mrs. Williams, 29 March 1953.

25. For Thomas Gordon's letter to Fraser Tytler, 19 January 1793, see Montgomerie, "Bibliography," 144–45.

26. On Anna Gordon Brown, there have been numerous comments, but no full studies; see Buchan, *Ballad and Folk,* 62–73; and Montgomerie, "Bibliography," xxxi–xxxii. On her family, see David Johnson, "Musical Traditions of the Forbes Family of Disblair, Aberdeenshire," *Scottish Studies* 22 (1978): 91–94, and Alexander Walker, *Disblair 1634–1884* (Aberdeen: J. & J. P. Edmond & Spark, 1884); of great use in quickly assessing ballads, Brown, and other singers and collectors is the introduction in Montgomerie, "Bibliography." Again, see a reference to Thomas Gordon's letter on his daughter's ballad repertoire, 19 January 1793, given in Montgomerie, "Bibliography," 144–45. Disblair was a large house and estate, bought in 1695; both the Forbeses and the Gordons were old Aberdeen merchant families. See Alexander Walker, *Disblair 1634–1884,* 16–18. On Anna Gordon Brown, her grandfather's rather rakish pamphlets, from 1700 to 1704: William Forbes of Disblair, "The Renegado Whip't." and "Essay Upon Marriage in a Letter Adress'd to a FRIEND," in Edinburgh, at New College Library, J. d./7.

27. Montgomerie, "Bibliography," 144–45.

28. Montgomerie, "Bibliography," 1, 94; p. 1 refers to Ritson's complaint that her ballads were not ancient, p. 94 to Walter Scott's initial suspicion of Anna Gordon Brown, as a poetess, like Lady Wardlaw.

29. Lives of Walter Scott abound; the standard biography was done by Scott's son-in-law: J. G. Lockhart, *Memoirs of the Life of Sir Walter Scott, Bart.* (Boston: Otis, Broaders, 1837). Almost all have some reference to Scott's mother, who was one of the noted Misses Rutherford of her day.

30. See David Buchan, *Ballad and Folk,* 62–73; and Bertrand Bronson, "Mrs. Brown and the Ballad," *California Folklore Quarterly* 4 (1945): 129–40. Anna Gordon Brown's letters to Robert Jamieson, quoted here, are in Montgomerie, "Bibliography," 148–52.

31. Derived from F. J. Child's notes to ballad texts; the women can be identified by looking up the ballads in Child; for Marjory Johnston, see the following ballads: 63.H; 64.D; 52.B; for her great-aunt, see C.II.107.

32. See C.II.268, 274; for Mrs. Storie, see C.II.267.

33. See C.II.270–71, 274.

34. C.II.227; on *The Douglas Tragedy* by the Reverend John Home, see Ian Ross, *Lord Kames and the Scotland of His Day* (Oxford: Clarendon Press, 1972); Susan Staves, "Douglas' Mother," in John Hazel Smith, ed., *Brandeis Essays in Literature* (Waltham, Mass.: Department of English and American Literature, 1983), 51–67; and Lenman, *Integration,* 27–28.

35. Of the 40 women singers after 1832 only 8 knew more than one ballad, while 52 of the 130 earlier singers knew more than one ballad. Ballad collectors were motivated by profit as well as by curiosity, and probably did not miss much. For Kirkcudbright, see Robert and William Chambers, *The Gazetteer of Scotland,* vol. 2 (Edinburgh: Thomas Ireland, Junior, 1835), 662–68. Amelia Harris and Mrs. Gibb learned their ballads between 1790 and 1810, so they have been counted among the 130 singers of the early part of the century, even though the Harris Manuscript is from 1859, and the Gibb from 1860; see Montgomerie, "Bibliography," for Harris and Gibb; see also C.V.398, on Mrs. Gibb; C.V.398, on Amelia Harris; and C.V.266, 306, on Miss Jane Webster, aunt to the ballad collector William Macmath.

36. On Margaret Patterson, see C.IV.417. On William Laidlaw, there were useful extracts in Montgomerie, "Bibliography," but it is finally necessary to consult his "Recollections of Sir Walter Scott (1802–1804)," in *Hawick Archaeological Society's Papers* (1905). All other women mentioned here are from Child; many can also be found in fuller references in Montgomerie, "Bibliography."

37. Of women singers who mention their sources, there were 14 mothers or grand-
mothers, 10 unrelated women, 7 women servants, 6 aunts, 7 unrelated men, and 4 fathers; for men, there were 6 fathers, 2 women servants, 1 mother, 1 unrelated man, and
1 unrelated woman. Thomas Wilkie, Walter Scott's friend, sent Scott various battlefield
remains, and Scott got him an appointment as ship's surgeon in 1815, and advertised
Wilkie's health resort in his novel *St. Ronan's Well* in 1824. See also Robert Sim,
C.IV.227; and the chapter on James Nicol in Buchan, *Ballad and Folk,* 223–43.

38. The Pepys ballad was quoted in Child, V.113; on lewd songs, see also Thomas
D'Urfey, *Wit and Mirth: Or, Pills to Purge Melancholy* (London: printed for J. Tonson,
1719); and Peter Buchan, *The Secret Songs of Silence,* a "high-kilted," or pornographic,
manuscript collection now rare; see Buchan, *Ballad and Folk,* 211.

39. Ballads of Jane Webster, learned from women: C.99; C.17; C.3; C.12; C.75; C.90;
C.93; C.191; C.228; C.279; from men: C.100; C.170; C.275; C.278; C.279; C.299; and from
unknown source, C.188. *The Jolly Beggar* is C.279.

40. For the English bawdy tradition, see C.10.A. Seward's remembered version was
C.10.L; Seward's version has been quoted here, as in C.IV.448, where Seward's letter to
Scott of 25–29 April 1802 is excerpted.

41. The nine Scots singers of *The Twa Sisters* included Anna Gordon Brown C.10.B,
an old woman C.10.C, Mrs. Johnston C.10.D, Agnes Lyle C.10.F, Mrs. King C.10.G, M.
Kinnear C.10.I, Mrs. Lindores C.10.K, Mrs. A. F. Murison C.10.M; and Nancy Brockie,
C.IV.448–49; there was also a version recorded by a Mrs. W. W. Newell, from "an ignorant old woman in her dotage," at Long Island, C.I.137.

Chapter 2: The Ballad Heroine

1. See note 2, Chapter 1, for the citation system from Child. This version of *Babylon*
was collected from the recitation of Agnes Lyle of Kilbarchan in 1825; see Child I.174,
Agnes Lyle note to *Babylon.* She lived in Kilbarchan, a textile center; see Robert and
William Chambers, *The Gazetteer of Scotland,* vol. 2 (Edinburgh: Thomas Ireland, 1835),
619-21.

2. Dianne M. Dugaw, in *Warrior Women and Popular Balladry, 1650–1850* (Cambridge: Cambridge University Press, 1989), addressed the military ballads, mostly literary compositions rather than traditional, in which a woman disguises herself to join the
army or navy, to be with her lover or husband. For Little Red Riding Hood, see Jack
Zipes's brilliant study, *The Trials and Tribulations of Little Red Riding Hood* (South
Hadley, Mass.: Bergin and Garvey Publishers, 1983). Zipes argued that the vulnerable
Little Red Riding Hood was the creation of later collector-transcribers, like Perrault and
the Grimms, and offered a version of that tale in which the girl outwits the wolf by
herself as the likely "old" or peasant version, arguing that such self-sufficiency was more
valuable to villagers than helplessness. For directories of the repeated themes and characters, see Natasha Wurzbach, *English Motif Index of the Child Corpus* (New York: W.
de Gruyter, 1995).

3. See Nancy K. Miller, *The Heroine's Text* (New York: Columbia University Press,
1980); Carroll Smith-Rosenberg, "Misprisioning *Pamela:* Representations of Gender and
Class in Nineteenth-Century America," in *Michigan Quarterly Review* 26:i (1987): 9–28;
Cathy N. Davidson, *Revolution and the Word* (New York: Oxford University Press, 1986);
Marilyn Butler, *Jane Austen and the War of Ideas* (Oxford: Clarendon Press, 1987); and
in contrast to Butler, Claudia L. Johnson, *Jane Austen: Women, Politics, and the Novel*
(Chicago: University of Chicago Press, 1988). In *Babylon*'s E text, which Child thought
a late version, all three daughters choose death, but the last is saved when a brother

kills the robber, who is a stranger; it is closest to the Scandinavian tales suggested as analogues. See also *Lady Isabel and the Elf Knight* (C.4), and *Clerk Colvill* (C.42).

4. Bride stealing, if never a very common practice, was prosecuted in the eighteenth century; see the High Court of Justiciary case of Rob Roy Macgregor, SRO JC 3/29.

5. The last four stanzas commonly end later ballads, like *Bonny Barbara Allen* (C.84), in which sentimentalized deaths replace plots. As Zipes commented in *Little Red Riding Hood,* sentiment is not simply decorative, but evidence of the intrusion of new ideology. In this case, the real difficulties of marriage, property, and alliance are converted to vague personal misunderstandings, drawing on the old conceit that love is a sickness.

6. On magic, riddles, and incantation, see P. Lain-Entralgo, *The Therapy of the Word in Classical Antiquity* (New Haven: Yale University Press, 1970); and Peter Burke, *Popular Culture in Early Modern Europe* (New York: Harper & Row, 1978).

7. On "bourgeois transparency" and individualism, see Lynn Hunt, *Politics, Culture, and Class in the French Revolution* (Berkeley and Los Angeles: University of California Press, 1984); Joan B. Landes, *Women and the Public Sphere in the Age of the French Revolution* (Ithaca: Cornell University Press, 1988); and Elizabeth Colwill, " 'Women's Empire' and the Sovereignty of Man in *La Decade Philosophique,* 1794–1807," *Eighteenth-Century Studies* 29 (Spring 1996): 265–90. "Laws of Nature/Rights of Genius: The Drame of Constance de Salm," in Elizabeth Goldsmith and Dena Goodman, eds., *Going Public: Women and Publishing in Early Modern France* (Ithaca: Cornell University Press, 1995); and on individualism, see Elizabeth Fox-Genovese's introduction to *The Autobiography of Du Pont de Nemours* (Wilmington, Del.: Scholarly Resources, 1984). For a somewhat Scottish example of transparency, i.e., visible self-worth, see Dr. Gregory, *A Father's Legacy to His Daughters* (London: A. Strahan and T. Cadell, 1786), 26–28, where he discusses the social utility of blushing in women.

8. See also *Lord Saltoun and Auchanachie* (C.239).

9. These stanzas recall *Eppie Morrie* (C.223).

10. For *Willie o' the Winsbury,* see also the similar *Willie of Douglas Dale* (C.101).

11. Dr. Gregory, *A Father's Legacy to His Daughters,* 229–30; and Adam Smith, *The Theory of Moral Sentiments* (1759; reprint, Oxford: Clarendon Press, 1979); see especially sympathy, and the discussion of it in D. D. Raphael and A. L. Macfie's introduction to this edition.

12. See also *Mother's Malison* (C.216), *Willie's Lady* (C.6), and *The Lass of Roch Royal* (C.76).

13. The claiming of his son is reflected in Scandinavian ritual; see Oscar Helmuth Werner, *The Unmarried Mother in German Literature, with Special Reference to the Period 1770–1800* (New York: Columbia University Press, 1917), 21. Ballads resembling *Child Waters* are *The Lady of Livingston* (C.91), *Young Beichan* (C.53), *Gil Brenton* (C.5), and *The Lass of Roch Royal* (C.76). In *The Broom of Cowdenknowes* (C.217), or *The Rantan Laddie* (C.240), the young rakes return when they hear that the women are pregnant. Pregnancy occurs as a difficulty, not a moral flaw, and it is no more blameworthy than sexual prowess, as in *Earl Brand* (C.7.A). See Rosalind Mitchison and Leah Leneman, *Sexuality and Social Control* (Oxford: Basil Blackwell, 1989); and Andrew Blaikie, *Illegitimacy, Sex, and Society: Northeast Scotland, 1750–1900* (New York: Oxford University Press, 1994).

14. *Mary Hamilton* was recorded in twenty-nine versions, in more than twenty-nine texts; see also *Lord Thomas and Fair Annet; The Maid Freed from the Gallows* (C.95); *The Laird of Wariston* (C.194); and *Fair Janet* (C.64 and Child III.381). For one version of *Mary Hamilton,* see Appendix I.

15. For Scott's reference to Knox, see Child III.382.

16. The Old Lady of Annandale's version is C.173.A.c.11; Motherwell's unidentified singer's is C.173.B.11; and Mrs. Crum's is C.173.C.11. For the Old Lady of Annandale, see Child III.384; for the full text of her version of C.173.A, see Appendix I.

17. For Scott's complaint, see Child III.382; Child also discussed William Motherwell's and James Maidment's attempts to find historical analogues for the ballad. Child favored the Peter the Great explanation; see Child III.382–84. Child relied on J. B. Schérer, *Anecdotes Intéressants et Secrètes de la Cour de Russie* (London: 1792); he also noted that *Mary Hamilton* first appears as a ballad, on record, in 1790, which suggests that it was vaguely Jacobitical, countering French pamphleteering denouncing Marie-Antoinette at the beginning of the French Revolution.

18. Women in court records did indeed hide dead infants near themselves, in their beds, or under floorboards, were there any. See the cases of Janny Stewart, SRO JC 26/193/2, and Barbara Davidson, SRO JC 11/28; both were tried in 1771.

19. On Anderson and Harvey, see Rev. James Anderson, *The Ladies of the Covenant: Memoirs of Distinguished Scottish Female Characters* (New York: A. C. Armstrong & Son, 1880), 272–99.

20. See C.173.A.c.7; C.173.C.7; C.173.D.7.

21. The trial exists by allusion, variously taking place in Parliament; or, less accurately, in the Tolbooth, the Edinburgh jail; Parliament Close, a nearby alley; the Canongate; or the Netherbow Port. In subsequent versions, the trial, and much of the ballad heroine's public performance, have slipped away, to be replaced in the J, L, and M texts with a murdered child discovered in her bed.

22. Hangings and gallows speeches were very public occasions; see Walter Scott's account of the Porteous Riot in *The Heart of Mid-Lothian* for a description of these processions, and see Douglas Hay et al., *Albion's Fatal Tree* (New York: Pantheon, 1976); the sixth chapter of Edward P. Thompson, *Whigs and Hunters: The Origin of the Black Acts* (New York: Pantheon, 1975); David D. Cooper, *The Lesson of the Scaffold* (Athens: Ohio University Press, 1974).

23. For the Old Lady of Annandale, see C.III.384; for the full text of her version of C.173.A, see Appendix I. Infanticide, after 1809, was prosecuted as concealment of pregnancy in Scotland, barring the sort of direct evidence that would leave a woman liable to prosecution for murder; see "The Concealment of Birth (Scotland) Act," 49 George 3 AD 1809, in *The Statutes,* vol. 2, AD 1770–1821 (London: HMSO, 1950); the wording of the new act, identified by its short title above, virtually duplicated that of the old statute of 1690, but the punishment after 1809 was no more than two years in a local jail.

24. On the suicide note in the eighteenth-century popular press, see Michael MacDonald, "Suicide and the Rise of the Popular Press in England," *representations* 22 (Spring 1988): 36–55.

Chapter 3: Reconstructing Rural Infanticide

1. This version of the Mother Goose rhyme comes from the memory of the English illustrator Arthur Rackham; see Arthur Rackham, *Mother Goose Nursery Rhymes* (London: Pan Books, 1975); for a study of the implications of these stories, see D. R. Thelander, "Mother Goose and Her Goslings: The France of Louis XIV as Seen Through the Fairy Tale," *Journal of Modern History* 54 (September 1982): 467–96.

2. In Scotland, at least 347 women were investigated, and most of those prosecuted, between 1661 and 1821. For England, see the work of Peter Hoffer and N. E. H. Hull, *Murdering Mothers* (New York: New York University Press, 1981). For a brief introduc-

tion to the complex problems of culture, demography, economic survival, and morality that infanticide poses, see Keith Wrightson, "Infanticide in European History," *Criminal Justice History* 3 (1982): 1–20; E. A. Wrigley, *Population and History* (New York: Mc-Graw-Hill, 1979); and more recently, Jona Schellekens, "Courtship, the Clandestine Marriage Act, and Illegitimate Fertility in England," *Journal of Interdisciplinary History* 25 (Winter 1995): 433–44, discussing the complexity of household formation, and the difficulties of marriage. For fuller reference to infanticide see the Bibliographical Essay in this volume.

3. On illegitimacy in Scotland, there are two important books: See Rosalind Mitchison and Leah Leneman, *Sexuality and Social Control: Scotland 1660–1780* (New York: Basil Blackwell, 1989), and Andrew Blaikie, *Illegitimacy, Sex, and Society: Northeast Scotland, 1750–1900* (Oxford: Clarendon Press, 1993); Blaikie's bibliography of post-1900 books, pp. 243–55, is useful. For further references to population, illegitimate births, and sexuality, see the Bibliographical Essay in this volume.

4. See Wrightson, "Infanticide"; as he and others have noted, the care given to illegitimate children was often designed to destroy them, and the children represented a problem before and after the infanticide laws. But building an orphanage, no matter how many of its inmates die, is not the same as knocking a child over the head. See also Elizabeth Fox-Genovese's introduction and "Women and Work" in Samia I. Spencer, ed., *French Women and the Age of Enlightenment* (Bloomington: Indiana University Press, 1984), 1–32, 111–27; and Rachel Fuchs, *Poor and Pregnant in Paris: Strategies for Survival in the Nineteenth Century* (New Brunswick: Rutgers University Press, 1992); and the very useful review by Barbara Corrado Pope, "Female Troubles and Troubled Men in Eighteenth- and Nineteenth-Century France," *Journal of Women's History* 6:3 (1994): 126–31.

5. There is an enormous literature on the agricultural transformation in Scotland, probably because it was so swift, coming largely after the last Jacobite rising in 1745. Nonetheless, there are indications of regional transformation in the seventeenth century, as Bruce Lenman has particularly argued, and debate about the impact and timing of agricultural capitalism in Scotland has been heated. See T. C. Smout, *A History of the Scottish People* (Glasgow: William Collins Sons, 1969); and Bruce Lenman, *Integration, Enlightenment, and Industrialization: Scotland 1746–1832* (London: Edward Arnold, 1981), and *An Economic History of Modern Scotland 1660–1976* (Hamden, Conn.: Archon, 1977). For further references, see the Bibliographical Essay.

6. There are many ways to investigate these guises. One is through the now old debate over causes of rising illegitimacy in the eighteenth and nineteenth centuries, as it developed in women's history in the 1970s; see Edward Shorter et al., in the note directly below. Another would be to read the love poems of Robert Burns, or the letters he exchanged with Agnes M'Lehose; see Amelia Josephine Barr, ed., *Sylvander and Clarinda: The Love Letters of Robert Burns and Agnes M'Lehose* (New York: George H. Doran, 1917); or to examine what Lord Kames had to say about women, or what James Boswell said. There is also fiction, which had a good deal to say about sex in the eighteenth century; see especially Nancy K. Miller, *The Heroine's Text: Readings in the French and English Novel, 1722–1782* (New York: Columbia University Press, 1980).

7. See the 1970s debate: Edward Shorter, "Illegitimacy, Sexual Revolution, and Social Change in Modern Europe," *Journal of Interdisciplinary History* 2:2 (1971): 237–72; Louise A. Tilly, Joan W. Scott, and Miriam Cohen, "Women's Work and European Fertility Patterns," *Journal of Interdisciplinary History* 6:3 (1976): 447–76; and Cissie Fairchilds, "Female Sexual Attitudes and the Rise of Illegitimacy," *Journal of Interdisciplinary History* 8:4 (1978): 627–67.

8. Men and women may well have had very different ideas of what was possible, for them, in their village, while we have little to guide us in guessing whether men or women would have taken greater risks for those possible prizes.

9. See Mitchison and Leneman, *Sexuality and Social Control;* Blaikie, *Illegitimacy;* and the comparative study of Britain and New England, which established the eighteenth-century paradigm of infanticide committed by a single woman who was often an agricultural servant, Peter Hoffer and N. E. H. Hull, *Murdering Mothers;* and for a New England example, see James A. Henretta and Gregory H. Nobles, "The Crisis of American Colonial Society 1740–1765," in Henretta and Nobles, *Evolution and Revolution: American Society 1600–1820* (Lexington, Mass.: D. C. Heath, 1987), 103–24. It is from this latter essay that I have borrowed the idea of parental control declining in colonial society as parents had less land for children to inherit, and could consequently exercise less control over their courtships and sexual practices.

10. The absence of prosecutions between 1798 and 1809 came in the wake of an important appeal, for Janet Gray in 1798, when a circuit court jury refused to convict in the usual terms. There were no successful prosecutions before the high court, or in the 50 percent of the circuit court records that I have seen for those years, and it appears that the statute fell into desuetude, to use the legal term, or disuse, until it was rewritten as a misdemeanor in 1809. For Janet Gray, see [Scottish Record Office, Edinburgh] SRO JC 12/22, JC 3/49, and JC 26/295.

11. See note 18, Introduction.

12. The mains tenants were tenants on an estate's biggest, main farm; as such, they would have made some money if they knew what they were doing, although their house may not have been much different from the houses of other tenants in the eighteenth century. For an example, see the mains tenants in Henry Hamilton, ed., *Selections from the Monymusk Papers (1713–1755)* (Edinburgh: Scottish History Society, 1945).

13. These numbers don't add up to 347 because in some cases, notably banishments, no information about a woman was recorded other than her name and the year.

14. For Agnes Walker, see SRO JC 12/11, 1762; all subsequent references are to this record, of the South Circuit Court.

15. See Rosalind K. Marshall, "Birth of a Profession," *Nursing Mirror* (November 30, 1983): i–vii.

16. Confronting the murderer with the corpse, and then waiting for the corpse to show signs to the living is part and parcel of traditional beliefs, traditional trial, and justice.

17. A very useful study of village shaming and mechanisms of moral force is N. Z. Davis's "The Reasons of Misrule: Youth Groups and Charivaris in Sixteenth-Century France," *Past and Present* 50 (February 1971): 41–75; see also Helen Lynd, *On Shame and the Search for Identity* (New York: Harcourt Brace, 1958).

18. For roads and paths in the southwest of Scotland, see A. R. B. Haldane, *The Drove Roads of Scotland* (London: Thomas Nelson and Sons, 1951).

19. J. Leopold, "The Levellers Revolt in Galloway in 1724," *Journal of the Scottish Labor History Society* 14 (1980): 4–29.

20. Loretta Timperly, *A Directory of Landownership in Scotland c. 1770* (Edinburgh: Scottish Record Society, 1976), 201–2. John Maxwell is listed as owning Halmyre, and a Mr. Maxwell as owning Kirkland; whether they were related or the same man is impossible to tell. In 1758, a James Maxwell of Barncleugh was foreman of the jury at Kathrine McKinnel's trial; she was from Bridgend of Dumfries, and was unanimously found guilty; see SRO JC 12/9. The Maxwell influence is hard to identify, but the family owned much land, and may have been Jacobitical and unfriendly to the kirk. Maxwell of Barncleugh also had the right to present clergy for the parish of Kirkpatrick-Irongray, Isobell

Walker's territory; the Maxwells of Terregles used Lincluden College as their burying place; see Hugh Scott, D.D., *Fasti Ecclesiae Scoticanae: The Succession of Ministers in the Church of Scotland from the Reformation,* vol. 2 (Edinburgh: Oliver & Boyd, 1917).

21. For Isobell Walker, see SRO JC 12/5, 1737.

22. Nathaniel McKie was "noted for his simplicity of character, plain uncultivated manners, superstitious credulity, and great eccentricity"; see Scott, vol. 2, *Fasti,* 405.

23. The four parishes in question are Crossmichael, Terregles, Irongray, and New Abbey, in Dumfriesshire.

24. For Jean Larry, see SRO JC 11/3, 1715.

25. For Christian Low, see SRO JC 11/3, 1714.

26. Anna Hall, SRO JC 11/3, 1714; ministers play a part in a number of cases; see Janet Thomson, JC 12/10; Sara Quarrier; JC 12/3, Helen Budges, JC 6/13; Christian Park, JC 6/13; Margaret Maynes, JC 6/14; Agnes McGuffock, JC 13/7.

27. On ministers, testimonial certificates, and the mobility of servants, especially women, see R. Houston, "Geographical Mobility in Scotland, 1652–1811: The Evidence of Testimonials," *Journal of Historical Geography* 11:4 (1985): 379–94; mobility, combined with the kirk's ability to censure, probably account for the lack of evidence of charivari, or rough music, in Scotland. For Margaret Minna, see SRO JC 12/7, Roxburgh, 1753.

28. It is not clear where she was coming from, or if she had any goal, only that she arrived in Eckford, claimed to be headed north, was escorted in that direction, and returned south, to Eckford. She may have been headed for England all along, or had no plan, or had gotten lost.

29. For Janet Stewart, see SRO JC 26/122/D, 1733.

30. No record of Janet Stewart alias McOmas is in the records of the North Circuit or the High Court of Justiciary; preceding account is based on documents in the Small Papers, SRO JC 26.

31. For Agnes McGuffock, see SRO JC 13/7, 1738.

32. For Margaret Main or Mayne, see JC 6/14, 1700.

33. For Sarah Quarrier, see SRO JC 12/7, 1752.

34. In towns or cities, a magistrate or physician was much more likely to be first consulted.

35. For Jannet Heatly, see SRO JC 3/32, 1761.

36. For Isobell Walker, see SRO JC 12/5; JC 26/127/D2049 and D2005.

37. For Christian Trin, see SRO JC 11/17, 1753.

38. Midwives remained authorities in rural areas. As doctors appeared in the court records, most were surgeons, few were physicians.

39. For Jannet Heatly, see SRO JC 3/32, 1761.

40. Most women indicted after the 1740s were banished without trials, and no record survives, other than that of indictment and then the acceptance by the A.D. (or advocate depute, the representative of the lord advocate, or chief prosecutor, at circuit court sittings) of a petition requesting banishment; unless fragments survive in the boxes of Small Papers (SRO JC 26) in the Scottish Record Office.

41. For Janny or Jean Stewart, see SRO JC 26/193.

42. For Adam Wilson, see SRO JC 7/26, August 1747.

43. For Adam Wilson, see SRO JC 7/26, August 1747; testimony of Margaret Arnot.

44. For Adam Wilson, see SRO JC 7/26, August 1747; testimony of David Ireland.

45. For Adam Wilson, see SRO JC 7/26, August 1747; testimony of David Ireland.

46. For Adam Wilson, see SRO JC 7/26, August 1747; testimony of Mr. James Bennet of Briggs of Gairnie. This was a respectable community; both Bennet and Wilson owned

land. They could all sign their names legibly, except for Arnot, who could not write. One sign of stress is David Ireland, who at thirty still lived with his parents, tenant farmers. If Wilson was as old as his second cousin, Ireland, and also unmarried, it suggests something awry in local society. And one of the tenants in Wester Balgeddie, of which Wilson was a portioner, was a forty-six-year-old unmarried woman with children, Jannet Miller.

47. Variously referred to as corn yard and barnyard. Two other men were tried for helping dispose of children; both had exposed children, in 1758 and 1803; neither was in much danger of being severely punished; see John Brown JC 11/21, and James Wilson JC 11/47, and also Alison Beutson, who was indicted for infanticide and incest with a shepherd, JC 6/13.

48. Only 35 women of the 132 who came from working farms were in service to the gentry, or to tenants recorded as farmers, rather than the older, usual words, "tenant in."

49. For Isobell Kilgour, see SRO JC 3/29, 1754. See also Elizabeth Mure, "Some Remarks on the Change of Manners in My Own Time: 1700–1790," in William Mure, ed., *Selections from the Family Papers Preserved at Caldwell: 1696–1853* (Glasgow: Maitland Club, 1854).

50. For Ann McLeod, see SRO JC 26/249, and JC 11/38, 1788; for Marjory Russell, see JC 11/24, 1763; for Mary Mackenzie, see JC 11/24, 1764, Ross; for Mary Pearson, see JC 12/5, 1748, Ayr; for Isobell Walker, see JC 12/5, and JC 26/127/D2049, 1736, Kirkcudbright; and for Bessie ffisher, see JC 13/1, 1709.

51. For Anne Mackie or Mather (James Gray), see SRO JC 3/39, 1776, Haddington; Mungo Ochiltree was mentioned in testimony, see Jannet Heatly, JC 3/32, 1761, Edinburgh; Barbara Davidson named the father of her child and he purged himself by oath, see Barbara Davidson, JC 11/28, 1771, Aberdeen; and for Katherine Ramsay, see AD 14/14/50, 1814, Clackmannan.

52. Much has been written about the redefinition of woman's nature during the eighteenth century, especially in the contexts of the American and French Revolutions; work particularly important to me has been: Linda K. Kerber, who coined and developed the phrase "republican mother" in *Women of the Republic: Intellect and Ideology in Revolutionary America* (New York: W. W. Norton, 1986), and in "The Republican Mother—Women and the Enlightenment: An American Perspective," *American Quarterly* 28 (1976): 187–205; and on ideas of female nature discussed in the Scots Enlightenment and its aftermath, see Jane Rendall, *The Origins of Modern Feminism* (Chicago: Lyceum Books, 1985); and Robyn Cooper, "Alexander Walker's Trilogy on Woman," *Journal of the History of Sexuality* 2:3 (1992): 341–64; and in a more roundabout way, for the early modern period, Christina Larner, *Enemies of God: The Witch-hunt in Scotland* (Baltimore: The Johns Hopkins University Press, 1981); for the development of the same ideas in England, see Margaret George, *Women in the First Capitalist Society;* Susan D. Amussen, *An Ordered Society: Gender and Class in Early Modern England* (New York: Basil Blackwell, 1988); and Michael McKeon, "Historicizing Patriarchy: The Emergence of Gender Difference in England, 1660–1760," *Eighteenth-Century Studies* 28:3 (1995): 295–322.

Chapter 4: Women's Work in The Transformation of the Scottish Economy

1. The first sentence echoes that in Elizabeth Fox-Genovese's "Women and Work," in Samia I. Spencer, ed., *French Women and the Age of Enlightenment* (Bloomington: Indiana University Press, 1984).

2. I have been influenced by James E. Handley, *Scottish Farming in the Eighteenth Century* (London: Faber & Faber, 1953), 234–35. This work is now somewhat out of date, and must be supplemented by more recent research, but his pithy judgments are useful; see also the Bibliographical Essay in this volume for agriculture.

3. For Ann Blair, see SRO JC 12/20, 1792. For Henrietta Manson, see SRO JC 11/38; for Hector McLean, see JC 11/21.

4. Handley, *Scottish Farming,* see especially chapter 3; and Henry Hamilton, ed., for the Scottish History Society, *Selections from the Monymusk Papers (1713–1755),* 3d ser., vol. 39 (Edinburgh: T & A Constable, 1945), xv–xvii; for a better-off tenant's standard of living, see T. C. Smout, *A History of the Scottish People, 1560–1830* (London and Glasgow: William Collins Sons, 1969), 282–85, on the Lothian "gudeman."

5. Handley, *Scottish Farming,* 75.

6. Peter Hume Brown, ed., *Early Travellers in Scotland* (Edinburgh: David Douglas, 1891), 231.

7. Handley, *Scottish Farming,* 82.

8. Thomas Pennant, *A Tour in Scotland in 1769* (Warrington: W. Eyers, 1774), 117, quoted in Handley, *Scottish Farming,* 82. For my understanding of it I am indebted to Elizabeth Colwill; Pennant's other remarks on women are also instructive; see p. 193.

9. One pound Scots was equal to approximately one-twelfth pound sterling; see Ian Donnachie and George Hewitt, *A Companion to Scottish History* (New York: Facts on File, 1989), 245. The inventory also mentions "the men's room," suggesting that the nicer rooms were already, in 1738, associated with women. See the house belonging to the Bairds of Gartsherrie in Smout, *Scottish People,* facing p. 272. For another inventory, see that of Alexander Robertson of Faskally, a Highland gentleman who died in 1731; see Leah Leneman, *Living in Atholl: A Social History of the Estates 1685–1785* (Edinburgh: Edinburgh University Press, 1986), 45, 71–73; and Hamilton, ed., *Monymusk Papers,* 10–12.

10. Tenants paid most of their rents in goods, plus labor services—plowing, harvesting, carrying—even when they were reckoned in cash. Only leases converting all this to a cash payment allowed tenants to master their holdings, or lose them altogether. There is debate over the point at which money rent became cash, rather than a way of establishing the value of produce collected. Handley, *Scottish Farming,* 83–85.

11. Hamilton, ed., *Monymusk Papers,* 45–46. Subsequent citations for Grant given in text are to this edition.

12. Hamilton, ed., *Monymusk Papers,* 38–42, Todlachy (or Todlachie), and 56, William Herd.

13. Hamilton, ed., *Monymusk Papers,* see map facing p. 104, the mains farm, and pp. 70–71. On subtenancy, see Leneman, *Living in Atholl,* 58–61: Cottars were considered undesirable in Atholl from 1750.

14. Widows remarried; only further research can show whether men often married into a holding, and whether landlords commonly accepted marriage as transferring the lease to the husband. See Janet Taylour, in the trial of William Selbie, note 19 below.

15. For the Widow McInroy, see Leneman, *Living in Atholl,* 54, and Hamilton, ed., *Monymusk Papers,* 15–17. The network of financial obligations within which village women found themselves was complex. Besides the landlord's demands, there was also the kirk's measure, landlords' special expenses for a marriage or a son's commission, and the landlords' millers, whom tenants were obliged to use.

16. R. A. Gailey, "Mobility of Tenants on a Highland Estate in the Early Nineteenth Century" *Scottish Historical Review* 40 (1961): 136–45; the phrase "new farmers" is from Smout, *Scottish People,* 287–94; for evidence of turnover among tenants, see Leneman, *Living in Atholl,* 48–49.

17. On the witch hunts, see Christina Larner, *Enemies of God* (Baltimore: The Johns Hopkins University Press, 1981), 120–33.

18. For William Selbie, see SRO JC 11/17, Aberdeen 1753. Graystane was in the parish of Tullynessel (Tillienessel) in Aberdeenshire.

19. For William Selbie, see SRO JC 11/17, Aberdeen, 1753; see testimony of Janet Taylour, Elspet Webster.

20. For William Selbie, see SRO JC 11/17, Aberdeen, 1753; see testimony of Elspet Webster.

21. I am indebted to my students at Drake and Bucknell in "Sex and Power in Peasant Society" for reading this case with me every spring. No accusation of witchcraft was forthcoming, perhaps because it had become a misdemeanor in 1736, but the fear of the milk expressed by Selbie's dependents suggests the tenacity of older beliefs. Copulating with animals was also an attribute of witches; see Major Weir, in Robert Chambers, ed., *Domestic Annals of Scotland,* vol. 2 (Edinburgh: W. & R. Chambers, 1863), 332.

22. Smout and Fenton's phrase, "need to import," includes famine. See T. C. Smout and A. Fenton, "Scottish Agriculture Before the Improvers: An Exploration," *Agricultural History Review* 13 (1965, part 2): 73–93.

23. Moving grain to distant markets exacerbated local shortages, and led to grain riots. On exports, see Bruce Lenman, *An Economic History of Modern Scotland 1660–1976* (Hamden, Conn.: Archon, 1977), 37–40; on Scots grain riots, see Kenneth J. Logue, *Popular Disturbances in Scotland, 1780–1825* (Edinburgh: John Donald Publishers, 1979). The populations of Edinburgh and Glasgow may in fact have trebled; see Smout and Fenton, "Scottish Agriculture," 80.

24. In the last serious famine to strike Scotland, lasting from 1695 to 1699, there were imports of 26,000 bolls of grain in 1699. Compared with Scotland's export of 103,000 bolls from the northeast to Scandinavia in 1685, the difference is striking, but perhaps Scots could not afford to buy more. On population and food production, see Smout and Fenton, "Scottish Agriculture," 81–82; also generally useful is William Ferguson, *Scotland, 1689 to the Present* (New York: Frederick A. Praeger, Publishers, 1968). On wage regulation, see Hamilton, ed., *Monymusk Papers,* xxxvi. The impact of improved nutrition on the age of menarche, and hence on population, has been studied: See Peter Laslett, "Age at Menarche in Europe since the Eighteenth Century," in Robert I. Rotberg and Theodore Rabb, eds., *Marriage and Fertility: Studies in Interdisciplinary History* (Princeton: Princeton University Press, 1980), and also Laslett's *The World We Have Lost* (New York: Charles Scribner's Sons, 1971); this is the second edition. Also, in general, see E. A. Wrigley, *Population and History* (New York: McGraw-Hill, 1969); N. L. Tranter, *Population and Society, 1750–1940* (London: Longman, 1985); and Robert I. Rotberg and Theodore K. Rabb, *Hunger and History* (Cambridge: Cambridge University Press, 1983).

25. Smout and Fenton, "Scottish Agriculture," 73. That those cattle sometimes accounted for half of Scotland's exports in a given year does not reveal how small those exports were. Scotland's export of sheep and cattle on the hoof show one way to make up for poor roads. See chapter 8 in S. G. E. Lythe and J. Butt, *An Economic History of Scotland 1100–1939* (Glasgow: Blackie, 1975), for a quick survey; and Bruce Lenman, *An Economic History of Modern Scotland.* Also on black cattle, see Smout and Fenton, "Scottish Agriculture," 80; and G. Whittington, "Agriculture and Society in Lowland Scotland, 1750–1870," in G. Whittington and I. D. Whyte, ed., *An Historical Geography of Scotland* (New York: St. Martin's Press, 1973): T. Tucker's excise report, 1655, in Peter Hume Brown, ed., *Early Travellers in Scotland* (Edinburgh: David Douglas, 1891), 231.

26. For grain prices, see T. C. Smout and A. Fenton, "Scottish Agriculture," 73–93.

27. Elizabeth Mure's memoir, "Some Remarks on the Change of Manners in My Own

Time, 1700–1790," can be found in William Mure, ed., *Selections from the Family Papers Preserved at Caldwell, 1696–1853* (Glasgow: Maitland Club, 1854), 260.

28. Mure, "Some Remarks," 266.

29. Rosalind K. Marshall, *The Days of Duchess Anne: Life in the Household of the Duchess of Hamilton, 1656–1716* (New York: St. Martin's Press, 1973), and *Virgins and Viragos: A History of Women in Scotland from 1080 to 1980* (London and Glasgow: William Collins Sons, 1983). Walter Scott, in *The Heart of Mid-Lothian,* grounded the agricultural aspirations of the Deans family in the very paternal power of the Duke of Argyll, and made clear that the Duke's interest was also served by good tenants like David Deans.

30. Marshall, *The Days of Duchess Anne,* 22.

31. See Rev. James Anderson, "Lady Baillie of Jerviswood," in *The Ladies of the Covenant: Memoirs of Distinguished Scottish Female Characters* (New York: A. C. Armstrong & Son, 1880), 441; also, Lady Murray Stanhope, *Memoirs of the Lives and Characters of the Rt. Hon. George Baillie of Jerviswood, and Lady Grisell* [sic] *Baillie* (Edinburgh: n. p., 1824); and Robert Herbert Story, *William Carstares: A Character and Career of the Revolutionary Epoch, 1649–1715* (London: Macmillan, 1874).

32. Anderson, *Ladies of the Covenant,* 446.

33. Anderson, *Ladies of the Covenant,* 434, 446, 453; Lady Murray Stanhope, *Memoirs,* 31–105.

34. For Margaret Cuthbert and her daughters, Marjory and Jean Gair, see SRO JC 11/7, North Circuit Court, 1729, p. 62.

35. For page numbers given in text, see SRO JC 11/7. The estates of Damm and Ankervile are both in Ross, in the coastal parish of Nigg, in an area rapidly improved after 1750.

36. How, and with what success, they were using the seashells is not clear; they are not a good source of agricultural lime, although they were heated over peat fires to produce building lime early on. See Smout and Fenton, "Scottish Agriculture," 83.

37. Handley, *Scottish Farming,* 169.

38. Handley, *Scottish Farming,* 220. See Ian R. M. Mowatt, *Easter Ross 1750–1850: The Double Frontier* (Edinburgh: John Donald Publishers, 1981), 28–86. Mowatt describes a community of improving lairds, many of them Edinburgh lawyers, and the development of roads and shipping; the estate of Ankervile figures prominently. But he describes nothing as early as 1729. On roads, see pp. 74–82; roads appeared in Easter Ross on Roy's map of 1747. See also Mowatt's map on p. 239, showing roads and ferries; and pp. 28-29 on density of lawyers in Nigg; and p. 256 on valuations.

39. John Millar, ed., *A History of the Witches of Renfrewshire* (Paisley: Alexander Gardner, 1877), 18.

40. Millar, *Witches of Renfrewshire,* 20.

41. Said of Grant of Monymusk, Hamilton, ed., *Monymusk Papers,* liii.

42. See Alaistair J. Durie, "Linen-spinning in the North of Scotland, 1746–1773," *Northern Scotland* 2 (1975): 37–55. Durie discusses the British Linen Bank, and correspondence with landowners, Grant of Monymusk included.

43. See Durie, "Linen-spinning," for a discussion of the technology of spinning. See also W. R. Scott, ed., *The Records of a Scottish Cloth Manufactory at New Mills, Haddingtonshire 1681–1703,* vol. 46 (Edinburgh: Scottish History Society, 1905).

44. Elizabeth Mure, "Some Remarks," 260; for Katherine McKinnel, see SRO JC 12/9, the South Circuit Court at Dumfries, 1758; for Margaret Gillespie, see SRO JC 13/9, West Circuit Court, 1749; for Janet Thomson, see SRO JC 12/10, South Circuit Court, 1761; for Agnes Walker, see SRO JC 12/11, South Circuit Court, 1762; for Margaret Comrie see SRO JC 11/34.

45. For Grizzel Buchanan, see SRO JC 26/178; for Margaret Cusine, see SRO JC 11/35.

46. For Margaret Denoon's story, see SRO JC 11/34, North Circuit, May 1783, Jean Craig and Margaret Elder.

47. For Jean Craig and Margaret Elder, see SRO JC 11/34, North Circuit, May 1783. For the previous conviction, see the same volume, September 1783; for the trial of Jean Craig and Elspeth Reid, see SRO JC 11/35, North Circuit, May 1784, Jean Craig and Elspeth Reid.

48. The Reverend Dr. Alexander Carlyle, "Parish of Inveresk," in vol. 2, Sir John Sinclair, ed., *The Statistical Account of Scotland 1791–1799,* Donald J. Withrington and Ian R. Grant, eds. (Wakefield, Eng.: E P Publishing, 1975), 278–329. This is a republication of the original, and significantly reorganized; the reference in the original, known now as the Old Statistical Account, or OSA, is vol. 16, 1–49, 642–43. Hereafter noted as Carlyle, OSA republication, and citations in text are to this edition. Carlyle, OSA republication, 294. See also John Hill Burton, ed., *The Autobiography of Dr. Alexander Carlyle of Inveresk 1722–1805* (London: Foulis, 1910).

49. A report from 1830 discussed a similar phenomenon among the fishwives of Newhaven, but the minister filing a parish report in the 1790s made no mention of them. T. C. Smout, introduction to OSA republication, 12–18.

50. See Durie, "Linen-spinning"; and R. A. Houston, "Women in the Economy and Society of Scotland, 1500–1800," in R. A. Houston and I. D. Whyte, eds., *Scottish Society, 1500–1800* (Cambridge: Cambridge University Press, 1989), 118–47.

51. I am indebted to Lorna Davidson, Education Officer at the New Lanark Conservation Trust, for providing the information from records preserved there; see especially the pamphlet *Mr. Owen's Establishment at New Lanark: A Failure! as Proved by Edward Baines Esq. M.P.* (Leeds, 1838); for Robert Owen's journal entry, see Ref. No. UGD/42 31/17, Gourock Ropework Co. Mss. The Baines pamphlet mentions 240 women as heads of families. For Dundee, see W. M. Walker, *Juteopolis: Dundee and Its Textile Workers 1885–1923* (Edinburgh: Scottish Academic Press, 1979).

52. Much has been written on women's work; Joan Scott and Louise Tilly, in *Women, Work, and Family* (New York: Metheun, 1987), argue for continuities in the kind and condition of women's work that erase the significance of the coming of capitalism; for a rebuttal see Bridget Hill, "Women's History: A Study in Change, Continuity, or Standing Still?" *Women's History Review* 2:1 (1993): 5–22.

Chapter 5: Making the Legal Machinery to Prosecute Infanticide

1. *The Acts of the Parliaments of Scotland,* vol. 9 (Printed by command of His Majesty King George the Fourth, 1822), "Act Anent Murdering of Children," session 2, parliament 1, William and Mary. The English statute is 21 James I c.27 (1623). See also, more exactly, *An Account of the Proceedings of the Estates in Scotland 1689–1690,* vol. 2 (Edinburgh: Scottish History Society, 1955), 234. The entire record reads: "Act for preventing and hindering Common Women from murthering their Infants after their Birth." It apparently passed on Saturday, 19 July 1690. Its various titles have been modernized to Act Anent Child Murder, for consistency.

2. William Ferguson, *Scotland 1689 to the Present* (New York: Frederick A. Praeger, Publishers, 1968), 164–65. See also Rosalind Mitchison, *Lordship to Patronage* (London: Edward Arnold, 1983), 86.

3. *The Register of the Privy Council of Scotland, 1545–1689* (Edinburgh: H M General Register House, 1877–1933), 445–50; see particularly the cases of Grizell Walker and Agnes Wood, for incest and adultery. See also W. G. Scott-Moncrieff, introduction to *The Records of the Proceedings of the Justiciary Court, Edinburgh, 1661–1678,* vol. 1 (Edinburgh: Scottish History Society, 1905), vii–xxxiii; and also John Imrie, preface to *The Justiciary Records of Argyll and the Isles 1664–1742,* vol. 2 (Edinburgh: The Stair Society, 1969), v–xviii.

4. Robert Chambers, *Domestic Annals of Scotland,* vol. 3 (Edinburgh: W. & R. Chambers, 1861), 39–41.

5. George W. T. Omond, *The Lord Advocates of Scotland,* vol. 1 (Edinburgh: David Douglas, 1883), 219; see also Rosalind Mitchison, *Lordship to Patronage* (London: Edward Arnold, 1983), 90; Chambers, *Domestic Annals,* 397.

6. See The Right Honorable Lord Thankerton, "The Statutory Law," in *An Introduction to the Sources and Literature of Scots Law,* vol. 1 (Edinburgh: The Stair Society, 1958), 3–15; see also Ferguson, *Scotland 1689,* 164.

7. Scott-Moncrieff, *Proceedings of the Justiciary,* 28. Citations in text in this chapter are to this volume.

8. For Christian Park, see SRO JC 6/13, 1695; on disclosure, see Benjamin Robert Bell, ed., *Commentaries on the Law of Scotland, Respecting Crimes,* vol. 1, by Hon. David Hume, Baron of Exchequer, with Bell's Supplement (Edinburgh: Bell and Bradfute, 1844), 285.

9. For Christian Park, see SRO JC 6/13, 1695; for Elizabeth Arrock [Orrock], and Elizabeth Johnstoun, see SRO JC 7/7, 1715; and for Isobell Taylor, Johnston [*sic*], and Orrock [*sic*], see Bell, *Commentaries,* 294–95.

10. For Jannot Greig, Cirrill Beaton or Beutson, see HCJ SRO JC 6/13, 1692.

11. For proclamations, see Imrie, *Justiciary Record of Argyll,* vol. 2, 353, Mary McIver.

12. Chambers, *Domestic Annals,* vol. 2, on stagecoach, 391.

13. Chambers, *Domestic Annals,* vol. 2, on paperworks, 398; the elephant, 410; the roads, 409.

14. Chambers, *Domestic Annals,* vol. 2, 430; in a note to Provost Dickison.

15. On women and protest, see J. Leopold, "The Levellers Revolt in Galloway in 1724," *Scottish Labour History Society Journal* 14 (1980): 4–29; James D. Young, *Women and Popular Struggles* (Edinburgh: Mainstream, 1985); Kenneth J. Logue, *Popular Disturbances in Scotland 1780–1815* (Edinburgh: John Donald, 1979); on burgh food production, see Mitchison, *Lordship,* chapter 5; and Malcolm I. Thomis and Jennifer Grimmett, *Women in Protest 1800–1850* (London: Croom Helm, 1982).

16. Imrie, *Justiciary Record of Argyll,* vol. 1, 196.

17. Imrie, *Justiciary Record of Argyll,* vol. 1, 198.

18. Imrie, *Justiciary Record of Argyll,* vol. 1, 198; note that court sits in Inverary.

19. For Margaret Anderson, see SRO JC 7/6, 1713.

20. For Margaret Anderson, see SRO JC 7/6, 1713.

21. John Shaw, *The Management of Scottish Society* (Edinburgh: John Donald Publishers, 1983), 18–40; the Privy Council was dissolved by the first Parliament to meet after the union; see Alexander Murdoch on Omond's mistake in *The People Above: Politics and Administration in Mid-Eighteenth-Century Scotland* (Edinburgh: John Donald Publishers, 1983), 8.

22. Shaw, *Management,* 21–22, and chapter 2; Gordon Donaldson, "The Legal Profession in Scottish Society in the Sixteenth and Seventeenth Centuries," *Juridical Review,* n.s., 21 (1976): 1–19. G. W. T. Omond, *The Arniston Memoirs: Three Centuries of a Scot-*

tish House, 1751–1838 (Edinburgh: David Douglas, 1887), describes the rise of the Dundas dynaasty.

23. For Katharine Smith, see SRO JC 6/14, 1701; all subsequent references are to this record.

24. The so-called Scotch verdict of not proven may mean little. It was not a third choice, but the remains of an old choice: proven or not proven. In 1728 Robert Dundas secured the right of the jury to return a finding of guilt or innocence, which extended the implications of their decision considerably. But after 1728, verdicts varied, apparently on no principle, except the hazily grasped one that findings of guilt or innocence asserted the jury's power, and those of proven or not proven acknowledged the terms set by the state's prosecutor; see Omond, *The Arniston Memoirs,* 78.

Chapter 6: The Demise of the Act Anent Child Murder

1. The statute specified that "it shall be sufficient ground for them to return their verdict finding the lybell proven and the mother guiltee of murder tho there is no appearance of wound or bruise upon the body of the childe[.]" *The Acts of the Parliaments of Scotland,* vol. 9 (Printed by command of His Majesty King George the Fourth, 1822), "Act Anent Murdering of Children," session 2, parliament 1, William and Mary. The English statute is 21 James I c.27 (1623). See also E. W. M. Balfour-Melville, ed., *An Account of the Proceedings of the Estates in Scotland 1689–1690,* vol. 2 (Edinburgh: Scottish History Society, 1955), 234. The entire record reads, "Act for preventing and hindering Common women from murthering their Infants after their Birth." It apparently passed on Saturday, 19 July 1690.

2. For Agnes Walker, see SRO JC 12/11, October 1762; Minute Books of the South Circuit Court.

3. Agnes Walker, SRO JC 12/11, October 1762. All subsequent references are to this record of Agnes Walker's case unless otherwise noted.

4. See Katharine Eisaman Maus, "Proof and Consequences: Inwardness and Its Exposure in the English Renaissance," *representations* 34 (Spring 1991): 29–52.

5. Their insistence that the law was little known was a ploy, for less than thirty years earlier Isobell Walker had narrowly missed hanging for the same crime, in the parish next to Terregles. On Scots verdicts, see Mr. Maclaurin, *Arguments, and Decisions in Remarkable Cases* (Edinburgh: J. Bell at Addison's Head, 1774), xviii–xxi.

6. See W. F. Bynum and Roy Porter, eds., *William Hunter and the Eighteenth-Century Medical World* (Cambridge: Cambridge University Press, 1985); and the old essay in the noted 11th edition of *Brittanica* by Sir Alexander Russell Simpson, Emeritus Professor of Midwifery, Edinburgh University, "Obstetrics," in *The Encyclopedia Brittanica,* vol. 19 (New York: Encyclopedia Brittanica Company, 1911) 962–65. For an example of a case in which surgeons and midwives testify, see Katharine McKinnel, SRO JC 12/19, Dumfries 1758; and in the U.S. literature, Laurel Thatcher Ulrich, *A Midwife's Tale: The Life of Martha Ballard, Based on Her Diary, 1785–1812* (New York: Knopf, 1990).

7. William Hunter, "On the Uncertainty of the Signs of Murder, in the Case of Bastard Children," *Medical Observation and Inquiries* 6 (1784): 266–90. Hunter was physician to Queen Charlotte, and member of The Royal Academy of Sciences at Paris. He read the paper to The Medical Society on 14 July 1783, shortly before his death that year; it was published posthumously. For a recent biography of William Hunter see Bynum and Porter, *William Hunter and the Eighteenth-Century Medical World;* also see Samuel Foart Simmons, *William Hunter 1718–1783: A Memoir* (Glasgow: University of

Glasgow Press, 1983). By 1811, Hunter would be quoted as an authority in John Burnett's *A Treatise on Various Branches of Criminal Law of Scotland* (Edinburgh: G. Ramsay, 1811); by 1826, P. J. Martin, in "Observation on Some of the Accidents of Infanticide," *Edinburgh Medical and Surgical Journal* 26 (July 1826): 34–37, would complain that even the most blatant murders were excused. In 1814, a reviewer of Christopher Johnson's translation of Dr. P. A. O. Mahon's *An Essay on the Signs of Murder in New Born Children* complained of "the erroneous opinions . . . propagated by Dr. William Hunter, which are not first controverted in the English language," *Edinburgh Medical and Surgical Journal* 10 (July 1814): 394. By 1811, Hunter had become orthodoxy, of a sort, as his citation by Burnett attests. John Burnett was a crown hatchet man in the Scots sedition trials of the 1790s, and his work on criminal law was denounced by Henry Cockburn, an arch-Whig, as "bad." See [Henry] Lord Cockburn, *An Examination of the Trials for Sedition,* vol. 1 (Edinburgh: David Douglas, 1888), 96.

8. The statute of 1690 was replaced in 1809 by a very similar statute, but reducing the penalty to no more than two years' imprisonment; see *The Statutes Revised* 49 Geo. 3.c.14, "The Concealment of Birth (Scotland) Act."

9. See "Child-Murder-Obstetric Morality," *The Dublin Review* 45 (September 1858): 71. In an English case, the judge directed the jury to acquit, saying that the accused woman could not be guilty if she was unconscious at the time, disregarding evidence that she had cut the child's throat from ear to ear.

10. Elizabeth Fox-Genovese has remarked, "With the triumph of bourgeois individualism, the self—individual right—became the basic unit of social organization, the source of political legitimacy, and the self-conscious locus of first knowledge and, ultimately, of truth." It seems ironic that Hunter claimed exactly that personal knowledge for himself only in a posthumous pamphlet. See Elizabeth Fox-Genovese, *The Autobiography of Du Pont de Nemours* (Wilmington, Del.: Scholarly Resources, 1984), 6; see also Elizabeth Colwill, " 'Women's Empire' and the Sovereignty of Man in *La Decade Philosophique,* 1794–1807," *Eighteenth-Century Studies* 29 (Spring 1996): 265–90.

11. Janet Black, SRO JC 11/9, Perth 1734.

12. Janet Gray's case was first heard on the South Circuit with that of Janet Ramsay; the jury returned a verdict for Ramsay that concluded, "But considering that the prooff of her Guilt arose solely from her own confession The Jury unanimously recommend The Pannell to Mercy." For Ramsay and Gray, see SRO JC 12/22, Jedburgh, April 1798; and also SRO JC 26/295. Ramsay's jury consisted chiefly of landowners, while the information against her had been brought mainly by the elders of the kirk; and the two law lords, Swinton and Dunsinnan, refused to sentence, and referred the case back to the High Court. Janet Gray, servant to a substantial tenant, was found guilty under the act by all, but a plurality found "that the actual Murder of the Child mentioned in the Indictment is not proven." SRO JC 12/22, April 1798. This chapter draws on the appeal, specifically of Gray's case, heard by the High Court, SRO JC 3/49, 1798. "Mr. Burnet" is John Burnett; see note 7 above. Gray's case was mentioned in *The Edinburgh Magazine* (July 1798): 315.

13. On Erskine's career, see Alexander Ferguson, *The Hon. Henry Erskine* (Edinburgh: William Blackwood and Sons, 1882), 353–64; and G. W. T. Omond, *The Arniston Memoirs: Three Centuries of a Scottish House 1571–1838* (Edinburgh: David Douglas, 1887), 245; and see also Michael Fry, *The Dundas Despotism* (Edinburgh: Edinburgh University Press, 1992). Henry Cockburn, a young Whig at the time, also had much to say about Erskine and Dundas; see his *An Examination;* also Henry, Lord Cockburn, *Memorials of His Time* (Edinburgh: Robert Grant & Son, 1946); and Karl Miller, *Cockburn's Millenium* (Cambridge: Harvard University Press, 1976). To understand Dun-

das's position, and patronage politics, see John M. Simpson, "Who Steered the Gravy Train, 1707–1766?" in Rosalind Mitchison and N. T. Phillipson, eds., *Scotland in the Age of Improvement* (Edinburgh: Edinburgh University Press, 1970), 47–72; and John Dwyer and Alexander Murdoch, "Paradigms and Politics: Manners, Morals, and the Rise of Henry Dundas, 1770–1784," in John Dwyer, Roger U. Mason, and Alexander Murdoch, eds., *New Perspectives on the Politics and Culture of Early Modern Scotland* (Edinburgh: John Donald Publishers, n.d.), 210–48. See also John Stuart Shaw, *The Management of Scottish Society* (Edinburgh: John Donald Publisher, 1983).

14. The younger Dundas had enjoyed his uncle's patronage; see Omond, *Arniston,* 212–300; his father and grandfather had both been lord president of the Court of Session, the civil court.

15. Cockburn, *Memorials,* 99.

16. Cockburn, *Memorials,* 99; on the King's Birthday Riot, see Omond, *Arniston,* 231.

17. The image of the gravy train comes from Simpson, "Who Steered the Gravy Train?" On Henry and his brothers, see Ferguson, *Henry Erskine,* 339–48.

18. The quotes are from Ferguson, *Henry Erskine,* 343; see also 356–57.

19. Citations given in text for Janet Gray are from the record of the High Court appeal, SRO JC 3/49, July 1798. The page numbers given are mine, and refer only to her case.

20. For Jean Bisset, SRO JC 11/40, 1793; Anne Mackie or Mather, JC 26/210, and JC 3/39, 1776.

21. I consulted the High Court index, some of the High Court cases, half the books of the High Court circuit sittings, and various published sources. The complete records would undoubtedly yield even higher numbers.

22. This was part of Dundas's "Information," the written arguments presented by a lawyer in the Scots courtroom; they did not preclude verbal arguments, but constituted most of an appeal, which was decided by judges, not a jury.

23. Dundas lectured the lords like a schoolmaster, saying that "here no discretion can be exercised"; Janet Gray, SRO JC 3/49, p. 15. On the growth of the jury's rights in returning verdicts, see Omond, *Arniston,* 78. It was Dundas's grandfather, the first lord president, who secured the right of the Scots jury to find in general terms of guilty or not guilty. Before this, they found only in terms of proven or not proven; the famous Scots verdict of not proven was sometimes used later, and has been taken to imply an unprovable guilt, but may only indicate deference to the court on the jury's part. This right was secured for English jurors in Fox's libel bill, 1792; see John W. Derry, *Charles James Fox* (New York: St. Martin's Press, 1972), 316. See also Maclaurin, *Arguments,* xviii–xxi.

24. The list of jurors was part of the record of the sitting of the South Circuit Court: Janet Gray, SRO JC 12/22, 10 April 1798.

25. On the maternal in Scotland, see Susan Staves, "Douglas's Mother," in John Hazel Smith, ed., *Brandeis Essays in Literature* (Waltham, Mass.: Department of English and American Literature, Brandeis University, 1983), 51–67.

26. The parliamentary record referred to "Common Women"; see note 1 above.

27. It is worth noting that the English statute was not nearly as harshly written as the Scots, and consequent interpretations of it were not really relevant to the Scots statute. But Erskine quoted plentifully from "the Writers upon the Law of England." Janet Gray, SRO JC 3/49, p. 41.

28. Blackstone's *Commentaries* was first published in 1769.

29. Erskine was quoting from Barrington's *Observations on the Statutes,* published in 1766.

30. Janet Gray, SRO JC 3/49, pp. 45–64.

31. Barrington clearly had a few presumptions of his own about women. Note his extraordinary idea that there is a "proper" place for concealing a dead infant. See Ann-Louise Schapiro, "Disordered Bodies/Disorderly Acts: Medical Discourse and the Female Criminal in Nineteenth-Century Paris," *Genders* 4 (Spring 1989): 68–86.

32. J.-J. Rousseau was many things, but for women he was the author of *Emile,* and particularly of the fifth book of *Emile,* "Sophie." Dr. Gregory was a late-eighteenth-century Edinburgh divine, and a popularizer of Rousseau; see his *A Father's Legacy to His Daughters* (London: A. Strahan and T. Cadell, 1786). On bourgeois realism, see Linda Nochlin, *Realism* (New York: Penguin, 1971).

33. The surgeon, P. J. Martin, had also remarked that judges and juries sympathized with the women accused, and surgeons were left to sympathize with the children; P. J. Martin, "Observations," 34–37.

34. The act was still in effect, but it seems unlikely that the circuits would have heard a case, when there were no indictments before the High Court.

35. In 1809 the statute was replaced by another; see *The Statutes Revised* 49 Geo.3.c.14, "The Concealment of Birth (Scotland) Act."

Chapter 7: Confessing to Child Murder

1. For Margaret Craigie, see SRO JC 6/13; references to Craigie are interspersed with others for 1692, and pages are unnumbered. Craigie is also mentioned in Robert Chambers, *Domestic Annals of Scotland,* vol. 3 (Edinburgh: W. & R. Chambers, 1861), 19–20; Chambers gives the location of Jedderfield.

2. For Elizabeth Brown, see SRO JC 13/3. Brown was hanged. So was Craigie, but only after rotting in prison in Edinburgh for three years, having been accused in 1689, during the Glorious Revolution, or "the present surcease of justice," as one sheriff put it; see Chambers, *Domestic Annals,* vol. 3, 20.

3. Few women confessed, and seventeenth-century court records, especially for infanticide, were poorly kept. For Katharine Comrie, see SRO JC 6/13. On guilt I have been guided by the distinction between guilt, in modern societies, and shame, in precapitalist societies, in Helen M. Lynd, *On Shame and the Search for Identity* (New York: Harcourt, Brace, 1958); on individualism, see Elizabeth Fox-Genovese, introduction to *The Autobiography of Du Pont de Nemours* (Wilmington, Del.: Scholarly Resources, 1984).

4. For Grissel Tullo, see SRO JC 7/1.

5. For Mary Pearson, see SRO JC 12/5. Pearson's position was no doubt complex; she had had arguments with Hunter's daughter, to whom she referred as "a bold Imperious woman"; the elders of the kirk were also on the scene when she was questioned. Her farm, North Barshair, was in the parish of Old Cumnock. For the phrase of Washington's, "entangling alliance," used below in this context, I am indebted to my colleague Mary Hill at Bucknell University who used it in a lecture on Charlotte Perkins Gilman.

6. For Janet Ramsay, see SRO JC 3/49; JC 12/22; and for the quotation from her declaration, JC 26/295. It is possible that Ramsay's remorse was calculated; for a skeptical view of women's confessions in Germany, see Susanne Kord, "Women as Children, Women as Childkillers: Poetic Images of Infanticide in Eighteenth-Century Germany," *Eighteenth-Century Studies* 26 (Spring 1993): 449–66.

7. For Anne Morison, see SRO JC 3/26.

8. For Euphemia, or Effy, Hunter, see the precognitions, or materials submitted to

the lord advocate to determine if a prosecutable offense has been committed; SRO AD 14/12/26, *Precognition for Euphemia Hunter.*

9. For the ballad, see Francis James Child, ed., *The English and Scottish Popular Ballads,* 5 vols. (1882–98; reprint; New York: Dover Publications, 1965); *The Cruel Mother* is C.20.

10. This and what follows is from the *Precognition of Jean McKay,* SRO AD 14/14/8. The precognition contains letters that passed between officials, and notes, but the body of it, numbered at the time, consists of statements taken from all concerned. All further references are given in the text using those page numbers; the speaker is clear from context.

11. Not all surgeons, at least, came from the middle class. Walter Scott helped a young man, Thomas Wilkie, to a place as ship's surgeon. Wilkie had attended Edinburgh University without graduating; his father was a village blacksmith. This may have been typical of some surgeons, who did not command the fees or status of physicians.

12. The estimate of ten to twenty beds per ward is based on the information that McKay's bed was sixth from the water closet, and there were beds on both sides of hers, and possibly another row opposite.

13. SRO AD 14/14/8, Jean McKay's *Declaration.* It is a separate document in the file, and has no page numbers.

14. Of course the distance or propriety with which McKay describes her body was probably exaggerated by the copyist.

15. For Mary Toft, see Susan Bruce, "The Flying Island and Female Anatomy: Gynaecology and Power in Gulliver's Travels," *Genders* 2 (Summer 1988): 60–76.

16. Henry Home Drummond's note survives as a loose paper in the bundle of precognition papers for McKay, SRO AD 14/14/8; the italics are mine. Drummond was a good Tory servant of the Crown, and sat in Parliament; see George W. T. Omond, *The Lord Advocates of Scotland,* vol. 2 (Edinburgh: David Douglas, 1883) 242–46, 271.

Chapter 8: The Bourgeois Novel of Infanticide

1. Sir Walter Scott, letter to Daniel Terry, November 12, 1816, in John Gibson Lockhart, vol. 5, *Memoirs of the Life of Sir Walter Scott, Bart.* (Boston: Houghton, Mifflin, 1910), 122. In a letter of May 16, 1818, Scott remarked, "I think we could hammer a neat little *comèdie bourgeoise* out of The Heart of Mid-lothian." See Lockhart, *Memoirs,* 235.

2. On the character of Jeanie Deans, and the connection to Helen Walker, see W. Crockett, *The Scott Originals* (Edinburgh: T. N. Foulis, 1912), 227–40.

3. For Isobell Walker, see SRO JC 12/5, May 1737, Dumfries; the pages are unnumbered. The date was given as Thursday before Hallowmas, which fell on November 1 or in late October in 1736, old style calendar.

4. If the ripe, meaning full-term, child found on the sandbank was hers, she would of course have become pregnant in February or March, which Emelia Walker and the other women in that room must have known. David Stott, the father, would later admit to "carnal dealings" on February 2.

5. These men may represent the elders of the kirk session in her parish; her "judicial confession" was recorded then or shortly thereafter by "Colliestoun Chappell Provost Ewart" and three justices of the peace.

6. W. E. K. Anderson, ed., *The Journal of Sir Walter Scott* (Oxford: Clarendon Press, 1972), xxii–xxiii; the ex-proprietor of Toftfield, which Scott bought, would become Scott's tenant. See also Lockhart, *Memoirs,* 222.

7. Lockhart, *Memoirs,* 221–22.

8. Lockhart, *Memoirs,* 179–80.

9. Lockhart, *Memoirs,* 223.

10. Anderson, *Journal,* xxxi–ii.

11. Scott acknowledged women novelists. "The ladies, in particular, gifted by nature with deep powers of observation and light satire, have been so distinguished by these works of talent, that, reckoning from the authoress of Evelina to her of Marriage, a catalogue might be made, including the brilliant and talented names of Edgeworth, Austin [*sic*], Charlotte Smith, and others, whose success seems to have appropriated this province of the novel as exclusively their own." See the introduction to *St. Ronan's Well,* written in 1832, in Sir Walter Scott, *The Waverley Novels,* vol. 8 (Philadelphia: J. B. Lippincott, 1861), 299.

12. See Jane Rendall, *The Origins of Modern Feminism* (Chicago: Lyceum Books, 1985), 7–72.

13. For changed family relations, see Randolph Trumbach, *The Rise of the Egalitarian Family: Aristocratic Kinship and Domestic Relations in Eighteenth-Century England* (New York: Academic Press, 1978); Leonore Davidoff and Catherine Hall, *Family Fortunes: Men and Women of the English Middle Class, 1780–1850* (Chicago: University of Chicago Press, 1987); and Catherine Hall, "The Early Formation of Victorian Domestic Ideology," in S. Burman, ed., *Fit Work for Women* (New York: St. Martin's Press, 1979).

14. Hannah More, a moralizing ex-bluestocking, had a remarkable career in the early nineteenth century, riding on the coattails of Methodism. In 1809, *The Edinburgh Review* found her *Coelebs in Search of a Wife* largely humorous, but despised any hint of "the trash and folly of Methodism," *Edinburgh Review* 14 (April 1809): 145–51. See also Kathryn Kish Sklar, *Catherine Beecher: A Study in American Domesticity* (New York: Yale University Press, 1973).

15. On Effie's unsociable wildness, see Julia Douthwaite, "Rewriting the Savage: The Extraordinary Fictions of the 'Wild Girl of Champagne,'" *Eighteenth-Century Studies* 28:2 (1994–95): 163–92.

16. Lockhart, *Memoirs,* 223.

17. *HM,* xii; no dates given except for Jeffrey, January 1820. And there was cage-rattling from Jacksonian America; see *HM,* xii; and The *New York Review* said nothing of elevation, or moral inspiration, instead comparing "that unadorned peasant woman, Jeanie Deans" to Cordelia, Desdemona, et al. See *New York Review* 13:8 (July 1840): 165.

18. *HM,* vii–ix. See also James Howe, ed., *Lady Louisa Stuart: Selections from Her Manuscripts* (New York: Harper & Brothers, 1899), 217–60.

19. See Elaine Showalter, *The Female Malady: Women, Madness, and English Culture, 1830–1980* (New York: Penguin Books, 1985).

20. Much of David Deans's covenanted ranting can be found in print, where Scott found it. See the anonymous *Waverly Anecdotes* (London: George Routledge and Sons, n.d.), 409. Scott once remarked in a letter to Daniel Terry, "I'll tickle ye off a Covenanter as readily as old Jack could do a young Prince"; see Lockhart, *Memoirs,* 121.

21. Adam Smith, *The Theory of Moral Sentiments,* ed. D. D. Raphael and A. L. Macfie (1759; reprint, Oxford: Clarendon Press, 1976). See their discussion of sympathy in the introduction.

22. On the plots of Whig and Tory novels, see Marilyn Butler, *Jane Austen and the War of Ideas,* 2d ed. (Oxford: Clarenden Press, 1987), xvi; and the new introduction, ix–xlvi.

23. Much of the debate over aristocratic and bourgeois culture wars has been done in French history, and on the French Revolution; see Elizabeth Colwill, " 'Women's Empire' and the Sovereignty of Man in *La Decade Philosophique,* 1794–1807," *Eighteenth-*

Century Studies 29 (Spring 1996): 265–90; and Joan B. Landes, *Woman and Public Sphere in the Age of the French Revolution* (Ithaca: Cornell University Press, 1988).

24. I do not mean this literally, as Scott had sons. Figuratively, she might have been a son he would have admired.

25. The language of particular rights is from Elizabeth Fox-Genovese, *Within the Plantation Household* (Chapel Hill: University of North Carolina Press, 1988), 242–89, on Louisa McCord.

26. The idealization of the countryside has been ably described by Raymond Williams, *The Country and the City* (New York: Oxford University Press, 1973), and Leo Marx, *The Machine in the Garden* (London: Oxford University Press, 1964), but without attention to gender. Quite different is the work of Annette Kolodny, *The Lay of the Land* (Chapel Hill: University of North Carolina Press, 1975), equalled in Britain, only unconsciously, by Thomas Hardy in his novels.

27. The stage was also set by other novelists, like Elizabeth Bond, whose *Letters of a Village Governess* (London: printed for the author, 1814) was dedicated to Walter Scott.

Chapter 9: The Making of the Scots Bourgeoise

1. Adam Smith, *The Theory of Moral Sentiments,* ed. by D. D. Raphael and A. L. Macfie (1759; reprint, Oxford: Clarendon Press, 1979), 239. Smith's understanding of the power of the material world was endemic to the Enlightenment, invoking Locke's *tabula rasa* to focus on the importance of environment, or circumstance. On circumstance, see a review of Thomas Broadhurst's "Advice to Young Ladies on the Improvement of the Mind," *Edinburgh Review* 16 (1810): 299–315; and on circumstance as a variety of (circumstantial) direct evidence, see Alexander Welsh, "The Evidence of Things Not Seen: Justice Stephen and Bishop Butler," *representations* 22 (Spring 1988): 60–88.

2. See Kenneth J. Logue, *Popular Disturbances in Scotland, 1780–1815* (Edinburgh: John Donald Publishers, 1979); Malcolm I. Thomis and Jennifer Grimmet, *Women in Protest* (London: Croom Helm, 1982); and James D. Young, *Women and Popular Struggles* (Edinburgh: Mainstream, 1985); for studies of public protest, riot, assembly, and collective actions. See Dianne M. Dugaw, *Warrior Women and Popular Balladry 1650–1850* (Cambridge: Cambridge University Press, 1989), and Simon Shepherd, *Amazons and Warrior Women: Varieties of Feminism in Seventeenth-Century Drama* (Sussex: The Harvester Press, 1981), for information on women in the military, facing death the more recognized way.

3. On some of this wrestling with female nature, see Ruth Perry, "Colonizing the Breast: Sexuality and Maternity in Eighteenth-Century England," *Journal of the History of Sexuality* 2 (October 1991): 204–34; Felicity Nussbaum, " 'Savage' Mothers: Narratives of Maternity in the Mid-Eighteenth Century," *Cultural Critique* 20 (Winter 1991): 123–51; and Susan Staves, "British Seduced Maidens," *Eighteenth-Century Studies* 14 (1980): 109–34; for more on women's nature, see the Bibliographical Essay in this volume.

4. Both the Duchess of Hamilton and Lady Baillie make good examples of something like a work ethic moving up through the ranks of society, and they were not similarly Protestant; see Tony Dickson and Hugh McLachlan, "Debate: Scottish Capitalism and Weber's Protestant Ethic Theses," *Sociology* 17:4 (November 1983): 560–68.

5. Lady Murray Stanhope, *Memoirs of the Lives and Characters of the Right Honorable George Baillie of Jerviswood, and of Lady Grisell* [sic] *Baillie* (Edinburgh: n.p., 1824), 74–75; this was the second edition of a privately printed volume; unless indicated

otherwise, citations for Lady Baillie are to this volume. See also Robert Scott-Moncrieff, ed., *The Household Book of Lady Grizel Baillie 1692–1733* (Edinburgh: Scottish History Society, 1911).

6. Lady Murray Stanhope, *Memoirs,* 49, 87; and Robert Scott-Moncrieff, ed., *The Household Book of Lady Grizel Baillie 1692–1733.*

7. Elizabeth Mure, "Some Remarks on the Change of Manners in My Own Time," in William Mure, ed., *Selections from the Family Papers Preserved at Caldwell: 1696–1853* (Glasgow: Maitland Club, 1854), 259–72. References in text for Mure are to this volume.

8. William Creech, *Letters, Addressed to John Sinclair* (1793, Edinburgh; reprint, New York: AMS, 1982), 33–36.

9. Terry Eagleton, *The Function of Criticism* (London: Verso, 1984), 75.

10. Henry Cockburn, *Memorials of His Time,* ed. Karl F. Miller (Chicago: University of Chicago Press, 1974), 61.

11. Henry Cockburn, *Memorials,* 62.

12. Henry Cockburn, *Memorials,* 55.

13. Henry Cockburn, *Memorials,* 54–57.

14. See Alexander William Crawford Lindsay, 25th Earl of Crawford, *Lives of the Lindsays; Or, A Memoir of the House of Crawford and Balcarres* (London: J. Murray, 1849); Lady Anne Lindsay, later Lady Barnard, his daughter, contributed at least one section, "Sophia (Suff) Johnston of the Hilton Family."

15. Jessie P. Findlay, *The Spindle-Side of Scottish Song* (London: J. M. Dent, 1902), 95.

16. John A. Doyle, ed., *Memoir and Correspondence of Susan Ferrier, 1782–1854* (New York: Arno Press, 1979), 23.

17. John A. Doyle, *Memoir,* 23.

18. The argument about property and writing has been made by Elizabeth Colwill, "Laws of Nature/Rights of Genius: The Drame of Constance de Salm," in Elizabeth Goldsmith and Dena Goodman, eds., *Going Public: Women and Publishing in Early Modern France* (Ithaca: Cornell University Press, 1995); see also Carla Hess, "Enlightenment Epistemology and the Laws of Authorship in Revolutionary France, 1777–1793," *representations* 30 (Spring 1990): 109–37.

19. For writing to match against Burns's see the letters of Robert Burns and Agnes M'Lehose, in Amelia Josephine Burr, ed., *Sylvander and Clarinda: The Love Letters of Robert Burns and Agnes M'Lehose* (New York: George H. Doran, 1917). They exchanged not only letters, but verses, some of which survive, both in English and Scots.

20. Francis James Child, ed., *The English and Scottish Popular Ballads,* 5 vols. (1882–98; reprint, New York: Dover Publications, 1965), V.252.

21. Jessie P. Findlay, *The Spindle-Side of Scottish Song,* 136; subsequent citations in text, unless indicated otherwise, are to this volume. Ravelston was no doubt still a farm in the early nineteenth century; in 1843 the occupant was Lady Keith, according to James Findlay, *Directory to Gentlemen's Seats, Villages in Scotland* (Edinburgh: W. P. Kennedy, 1843), 113.

22. On Carolina Oliphant, Lady Nairne, see Mrs. R. A. Simpson, *The Scottish Songstress, Caroline Baroness Nairne* (Edinburgh: Oliphant Anderson & Ferrier, 1894); and T. L. Kingston Oliphant, Esq., *The Jacobite Lairds of Gask* (London: Charles Griffin, 1870), 433–39.

23. Clementina Stirling Graham of Duntrune, *Mystifications,* ed. Dr. John Brown (Edinburgh: printed privately, 1859); and also on Clementina Graham, see John A. Doyle, *Memoir,* 18.

24. For Lady Nairne, see Jessie P. Findlay, *The Spindle-Side of Scottish Song.* See

also Margaret Spufford, *Small Books and Pleasant Histories: Popular Fiction and Its Readership in Seventeenth-Century England* (Athens: University of Georgia Press, 1981); and Jacqueline S. Bratton, *The Victorian Popular Ballad* (Totowa, N.J.: Rowman and Littlefield, 1975). Religion was endemic; the great-great-granddaughter of Grizel Hume Baillie, Lady Grisell Baillie of Mellerstain and Dryburgh, found Christ in 1848, as did her brother in 1849; see D. P. Thomson, *Scotland's First Deaconess: Lady Grisell Baillie of Mellerstain and Dryburgh* (Galashiels: Printed for the Presbytery Campaign Committee by A. Walker Son, 1946).

25. Susan Ferrier, *Marriage, A Novel* (London: Oxford University Press, 1971), 448–50.

26. See Leonore Davidoff and Catherine T. Hall, *Family Fortunes: Men and Women of the English Middle Class, 1780–1850* (Chicago: University of Chicago Press, 1987); and the Bibliographical Essay, on womanhood.

Bibliographical Essay

This is not a comprehensive bibliography, but a short and occasionally descriptive list of works that have been useful to me, on Scots agricultural history, Scots women and ideas of women's nature, illegitimacy, and infanticide.

The shortest introduction to the economy of Scotland in this period is in T. C. Smout, *A History of the Scottish People, 1560–1830* (London and Glasgow: William Collins Sons, 1969); and Bruce Lenman, *Integration, Enlightenment, and Industrialization: Scotland, 1746–1832* (London: Edward Arnold, 1981) and *An Economic History of Modern Scotland, 1660–1976* (Hamden, Conn.: Archon Books, 1977). Smout has argued that agriculture was primitive at the outset of the eighteenth century, while Lenman has countered with evidence that it was already developing; see Smout, *Scottish People,* 223–29, and Lenman, *Modern Scotland,* 17–43. Both have written extensively on this matter, and their other works should also be consulted. See also, on the making of a traditional Scots culture through violent watersheds, Hugh R. Trevor Roper, "The Invention of Tradition," in Eric Hobsbawm and Terence Ranger, eds., *The Invention of Tradition* (Cambridge: Cambridge University Press, 1983), and his "The Highlander Myth," *Wilson Quarterly* (Summer 1984): 105–20; John Prebble, *Culloden* (London: Penguin, 1967); and Alexander MacKenzie, *History of the Highland Clearances* (1883; reprint, n.p.: Nelven Press, 1986). On the outcome of Culloden, and the management of the Highlands, see what is still the standard introduction to modern Scotland, William Ferguson, *Scotland 1689 to the Present* (Edinburgh: Mercat Press, 1990). Also useful on economy and society in the eighteenth century are William Creech, *Letters, Addressed to John Sinclair, Bart. . . .* (1793; reprint, New York: AMS Press, 1982); and Elizabeth Mure's memoir, "Some Remarks on the Change of Manners in My Own Time: 1700–1790," in William Mure, ed., *Selections from the Family Papers Preserved at Caldwell: 1696–1853* (Glasgow: Maitland Club, 1854). If there has been some agreement on the general pattern of agricultural improvement after 1750, there has been debate over what came before 1750, and whether the degree of change was indeed dramatic; see the debate that appeared in the "Comment" section of *Area,* starting with G. Whittington, "Was There a Scottish Agricultural Revolution?" *Area* 7:3 (1975): 204–6; D. Mills, no title, *Area* 8:3 (1976): 237–39; Ian H. Adams, "The Agricultural Revolution in Scotland: Contributions to the Debate," *Area* 10:3 (1978): 198–203; and I. D. Whyte, *Area* 10:3 (1978): 203–5. Otherwise, see David Turnock, *The Historical Geography of Scotland Since 1707* (Cambridge: Cambridge University Press, 1982); Robert A. Dodgshon, *Land and Society in Early Scotland* (Oxford: Clarendon

Press, 1981), which contains a good bibliography, and his article, "Farming in Roxburghshire and Berwickshire on the Eve of Improvement," *SHR* 54:2 (1975): 140–54; also M. L. Parry and T. R. Slater, eds., *The Making of the Scottish Countryside* (London: Croom Helm, 1980); T. C. Smout, "The Landowner and the Planned Village, 1730–1830," in N. T. Phillipson and Rosalind Mitchison, eds., *Scotland in the Age of Improvement* (Edinburgh: Edinburgh University Press, 1970); J. B. Caird, "Patterns of Rural Settlement, 1700–1850," in Chalmers M. Clapperton, ed., *Scotland: A New Study* (London: David & Charles, 1983); Ian H. Adams, "The Urban Scene, 1760–1980," in Clapperton, and his earlier article, "Economic Process and the Scottish Land Surveyor," *Imago Mundi* 27 (1975): 13–18; and E. J. Hobsbawm, "Capitalisme et Agriculture: Les Réformateurs Ecossais au XVIII Siècle," *Annales: Economies, Sociétés, Civilisations* 33:3 (1978): 580–601. More particular or local studies are: A. J. Durie, "Linen-spinning in the North of Scotland, 1746–1773," *Northern Scotland* 2 (1975): 37–55; R. H. Gailey, "Mobility of Tenants on a Highland Estate in the Early Nineteenth Century," *SHR* 40 (1961): 136–45; Ian Carter, "Dorset, Kincardine, and Peasant Crisis," *Journal of Peasant Studies* 2:4 (1975): 483–87; and David Craig, "A Reply to Ian Carter," *Journal of Peasant Studies* 2:4 (1975): 488–89. The standard works are worth consulting, especially Smout's *Scottish People* and Ferguson's *Scotland,* as are these more specific studies: G. Whittington and I. D. Whyte, eds., *An Historical Geography of Scotland* (New York: St. Martin's Press, 1973); Ian R. M. Mowatt, *Easter Ross 1750–1850: The Double Frontier* (Edinburgh: John Donald Publishers, 1981); and the now dated, but still pithy, James E. Handley, *Scottish Farming in the Eighteenth Century* (London: Faber & Faber, 1953); Leah Leneman, *Living in Atholl 1685–1785* (Edinburgh: Edinburgh University Press, 1986); T. C. Smout and A. Fenton, "Scottish Agriculture Before the Improvers: An Exploration," *Agricultural History Review* 13 (1965, part 2): 73–93; the invaluable introduction to the workings of an estate, and the difficulties facing improvers and their tenants, edited by Henry Hamilton, *Selections from the Monymusk Papers (1713–1755)* (Edinburgh: Scottish History Society, 1945); T. M. Devine, ed., *Farm Servants and Labour in Lowland Scotland 1770–1914* (Edinburgh: John Donald Publishers 1984); Eric Richards, *A History of the Highland Clearances,* vol. 2, *Emigration, Protest, Reasons* (London: Croom Helm, 1985); A. R. B. Haldane, *The Drove Roads of Scotland* (New York: Nelson, 1952); J. Leopold, "The Levellers' Revolt in Galloway in 1724," *Scottish Labour History Society Journal* 14 (1980): 4–29; and Loretta R. Timperley, "The Pattern of Landholding in Eighteenth-Century Scotland," in Parry and Slater, eds., *The Making of the Scottish Countryside;* she discusses power and land. These contain a wealth of information, combining information about landlords and tenants with descriptions of agricultural practices.

On Scots women, women's nature, and women's work, much has been written, but largely on Anglo-American and western European women, and much less on Scots women; see a recent review article by Jane McDermid, "Placing Women in Scottish History," *Journal of Women's History* 4:2 (1992): 180–88. Briefly, for English studies of women's work, see the classic works discussed in Bridget Hill, "Women's History: A Study in Change, Continuity, or Standing

Still?" *Women's History Review* 2:1 (1993): 5–22, especially Alice Clark's *Working Life of Women in the Seventeenth Century* (1919; reprint, London: Routledge and Kegan Paul, 1982); Ivy Pinchbeck, *Women Workers and the Industrial Revolution, 1750–1850* (London: Routledge, 1930); M. Dorothy George, *England in Transition: Life and Work in the Eighteenth Century* (Melbourne: Penguin, 1953); Eileen Power, *Medieval Women* (New York: Cambridge University Press, 1975); and, more recently Margaret George, *Women in the First Capitalist Society* (Urbana: University of Illinois Press, 1988); see also Joan Thirsk's introduction in Mary Prior, ed., *Women in English Society, 1500–1800* (London: Methuen, 1985); and on France, the very useful essays by Elizabeth Fox-Genovese, the introduction and "Women and Work," in Samia I. Spencer, ed., *French Women and the Age of Enlightenment* (Bloomington: Indiana University Press, 1984). A great deal has been written on women's work, and rural communities, and I will cite only a few articles and books that have been most useful to me: R. A. Houston, "Women in the Economy and Society of Scotland, 1500–1800," in R. A. Houston and I. D. Whyte, eds., *Scottish Society, 1500–1800* (Cambridge: Cambridge University Press, 1989); Barbara A. Hanawalt, *The Ties That Bound: Peasant Families in Medieval England* (New York: Oxford University Press, 1986); Margaret Spufford, *Contrasting Communities* (London: Cambridge University Press, 1974), and her earlier *A Cambridgeshire Community: Chippenham from Settlement to Enclosure* (Leicester: Leicester University Press, 1965); Karen Sayer, "Field-faring Women: The Resistance of Women Who Worked in the Fields of Nineteenth-Century England," *Women's History Review* 2:2 (1993): 185–98; and one French study using folklore, Martine Segalen, *Love and Power in the Peasant Family: Rural France in the Nineteenth Century* (Chicago: University of Chicago Press, 1983). On women in popular protests, and the point at which disorderly behavior became folklore, see Malcolm I. Thomis and Jennifer Grimmet, *Women in Protest* (London: Croom Helm, 1982) and James D. Young, *Women and Popular Struggles* (Edinburgh: Mainstream, 1985); Dianne M. Dugaw, *Warrior Women and Popular Balladry, 1650–1850* (Cambridge: Cambridge University Press, 1989); Simon Shepherd, *Amazons and Warrior Women: Varieties of Feminism in Seventeenth-Century Drama* (Sussex: The Harvester Press, 1981). On women in Scotland, there are recent studies, and a variety of older published sources. See Rosalind K. Marshall, *The Days of Duchess Anne: Life in the Household of the Duchess of Hamilton, 1656–1716* (New York: St. Martin's Press, 1973), and her *Virgins and Viragos: A History of Women in Scotland from 1080 to 1980)* (London and Glasgow: William Collins Sons, 1983); Leneman's *Living in Atholl;* the older and dated, but sometimes suggestive, work by Marion Lochhead, *The Scots Household in the Eighteenth Century* (Edinburgh: Moray Press, n.d.); on nonconforming Calvinist women during the Restoration, see the Reverend James Andersen, *The Ladies of the Covenant: Memoirs of Distinguished Scottish Female Characters Embracing the Period of the Covenant and the Persecution* (New York: A. C. Armstrong & Son, 1880); Robert Scott-Moncrieff, ed., *The Household Book of Lady Grizel Baillie 1692–1733* (Edinburgh: Scottish History Society, 1911); Lady Murray Stanhope, *Memoirs of the Lives and Characters of the Rt. Hon. George Baillie of Jerviswood, and Lady Grisell Baillie* (Edinburgh, n.p., 1824); and Elizabeth Mure, "Some Remarks";

Lady Louisa Stuart: Selections from Her Manuscripts, ed. James Howe (New York and London: Harper & Brothers, 1899); Jessie P. Findlay, *The Spindle-Side of Scottish Song* (London: J. M. Dent, 1902); Clementina Stirling Graham of Duntrune, *Mystifications,* ed. Dr. John Brown (Edinburgh: printed privately, 1859); and also on Clementina Graham, see John A. Doyle, ed., *Memoir and Correspondence of Susan Ferrier 1782–1854* (New York: Arno Press, 1970), 18; and Mrs. R. A. Simpson, *The Scottish Songstress, Caroline Baroness Nairne* (Edinburgh: Oliphant Anderson & Ferrier, 1894). On ideas of female nature, which were certainly discussed in the Scots Enlightenment, see Jane Rendall, *The Origins of Modern Feminism* (Chicago: Lyceum Books, 1985); Robyn Cooper, "Alexander Walker's Trilogy on Woman," *Journal of the History of Sexuality* 2:3 (1992): 341–64; and in a more roundabout way, Christina Larner, *Enemies of God: The Witch-hunt in Scotland* (Baltimore: The Johns Hopkins University Press, 1981); for the development of those same ideas in England, see Margaret George, *Women in the First Capitalist Society;* Susan D. Amussen, *An Ordered Society: Gender and Class in Early Modern England* (New York: Basil Blackwell, 1988); Michael McKeon, "Historicizing Patriarchy: The Emergence of Gender Difference in England, 1660–1760," *Eighteenth-Century Studies* 28:3 (1995): 295–322; Mary Lyndon Shanley, "Marriage Contract and Social Contract in Seventeenth-Century English Political Thought," *Western Political Quarterly* 32 (1979): 79–91; Frances E. Dolan, "Home-Rebels and House-Traitors: Murderous Wives in Early Modern England," *Yale Journal of Law & the Humanities* 4:1 (1992): 1–31; Leonore Davidoff and Catherine Hall, *Family Fortunes: Men and Women of the English Middle Class, 1780–1850* (Chicago: University of Chicago Press, 1987); Leonore Davidoff, *The Best Circles: Society, Etiquette, and the Season* (London: Croom Helm, 1973); Mary Poovey, *Uneven Developments: The Ideological Work of Gender in Mid-Victorian England* (Chicago: University of Chicago Press, 1988). And for the development of ideas of woman's nature in France, see Elizabeth Colwill, "Just Another *Citoyenne?* Marie-Antoinette on Trial, 1790–1793," *History Workshop* 28 (Autumn 1989): 63–87; Elizabeth Colwill, " 'Women's Empire' and the Sovereignty of Man in *La Decade Philosophique,* 1794–1807," *Eighteenth-Century Studies* 29 (Spring 1996): 265–90; and "Laws of Nature/Rights of Genius: The Drame of Constance de Salm," in Elizabeth Goldsmith and Dena Goodman, eds., *Going Public: Women and Publishing in Early Modern France* (Ithaca: Cornell University Press, 1995); Elizabeth Fox-Genovese and Eugene D. Genovese's essay on ideology and domestic economy, "The Ideological Basis of Domestic Economy: The Representation of Women and the Family in the Age of Expansion," in their *The Fruits of Merchant Capital: Slavery and Bourgeois Property in the Rise and Expansion of Capitalism* (New York: Oxford University Press, 1983), 299–336; Joan B. Landes, *Women and the Public Sphere in the Age of the French Revolution* (Ithaca: Cornell University Press, 1988); on the United States, see the work of Linda K. Kerber, who coined the phrase "republican mother": *Women of the Republic: Intellect and Ideology in Revolutionary America* (New York: W. W. Norton, 1986), and Kerber's "The Republican Mother—Women and the Enlightenment: An American Perspective," *American Quarterly* 28 (1976): 187–205; Jeanne Boydston, *Home and Work: Housework, Wages, and the Ideology of Labor in the Early Republic* (New York: Oxford University Press, 1990), and Boydston's "To Earn Her Daily Bread:

Housework and Antebellum Working-Class Subsistence," *Radical History Review* 35 (1986): 7–25.

On illegitimacy in Scotland, there are two important books: see Rosalind Mitchison and Leah Leneman, *Sexuality and Social Control: Scotland 1660–1780* (New York: Basil Blackwell, 1989), and Andrew Blaikie, *Illegitimacy, Sex, and Society: Northeast Scotland, 1750–1900* (Oxford: Clarendon Press, 1993). Blaikie's bibliography of post-1900 books, pp. 243–55, is also useful. The following references are meant to suggest briefly the nature of the work that has been done on Scotland. Specifically on Scotland, see Michael Flinn et al., eds., *Scottish Population History: From the Seventeenth Century to the 1930s* (Cambridge: Cambridge University Press, 1977); Leah Leneman, "The Study of Illegitimacy from Kirk Session Records: Two Eighteenth-Century Perthshire Parishes," *Local Population Studies* 31 (Autumn 1983): 29–33, "Girls in Trouble: The Social and Geographical Setting of Illegitimacy in Early Modern Scotland," *Journal of Social History* 22 (Spring 1988): 483–89, and with Rosalind Mitchison, "Scottish Illegitimacy Ratios in the Early Modern Period," *Economic History Review,* 2d ser., 40:1 (1987): 41–63. See also T. C. Smout, "Aspects of Sexual Behavior in Nineteenth-Century Scotland," in A. A. MacLaren, ed., *Social Class in Scotland: Past and Present* (Edinburgh: John Donald, 1976); and A. Roberts, "Illegitimacy in Catholic Upper Banffshire," *Scottish Journal of Sociology* 3 (April 1979): 213–24. For the most cheerful argument about the rise of illegitimacy, as evidence that people found new pleasure in sex, see the work of Edward Shorter, *The Making of the Modern Family* (New York: Basic Books, 1975), and "Illegitimacy, Sexual Revolution, and Social Change in Modern Europe," in Robert I. Rotberg and Theodore K. Rabb, eds., *Marriage and Fertility Studies in Interdisciplinary History* (Princeton: Princeton University Press, 1980). On the impact of industrialization, and for illegitimacy as implying frustrated courtship, see David Levine, *Family Formation in an Age of Nascent Capitalism* (New York: Academic Press, 1977), especially 127–45, "Illegitimacy: Marriage Frustrated, Not Promiscuity Rampant"; and in general, Peter Laslett, *The World We Have Lost* (New York: Scribner, 1965), *The World We Have Lost Further Explored* (Cambridge: Cambridge University Press, 1983), *Family Life and Illicit Love in Earlier Generations* (Cambridge: Cambridge University Press, 1977), and "The Bastardy Prone Sub-society," in Peter Laslett, Karla Oosterveen, and Richard M. Smith, eds., *Bastardy and Its Comparative History* (Cambridge: Harvard University Press, 1980); and on the upper classes, Lawrence Stone, *The Family, Sex, and Marriage in England, 1500–1800* (New York: Harper & Row, 1979), and Randolph Trumbach, *The Rise of the Egalitarian Family* (New York: Academic Press, 1978). For those who have been more suspicious of illegitimacy, writing in direct response to Shorter and forming the beginnings of the illegitimacy debate, see Louise Tilly, Joan W. Scott, and Miriam Cohen, "Women's Work and European Fertility Patterns," *Journal of Interdisciplinary History* 6:3 (1976): 447–76; and especially Cissie Fairchilds, "Female Sexual Attitudes and the Rise of Illegitimacy: A Case Study," *Journal of Interdisciplinary History* 8:4 (1978): 627–67. Much of the debate was collected in R. I. Rotberg and T. K. Rabb, eds., *Marriage and Fertility*. Also important is the work of Keith Wrightson; see his "Infanticide in European History," *Criminal Justice History* 3 (1982): 1–20, "Infanticide in Earlier Seventeenth-Century England," *Local Population Studies* 15 (1975): 10–22, and "Household and Kinship in Sixteenth-Century England," *History Workshop Journal* 12 (Autumn 1981): 151–58, and with David Levine, "The Social Context of Illegitimacy in Early Modern England," in Laslett et al., eds., *Bastardy,* and also with Levine, *The Making of an Industrial Society: Whickam, 1560–1765* (New York: Oxford University Press, 1991). And for the argument that French attitudes to illegitimacy varied with local wealth, see Martine Segalen, *Love and Power in the Peasant Family,* 20–22. And see also Rachel Fuchs, *Poor and Pregnant in Paris: Strategies for Survival in the Nineteenth Century* (New Brunswick: Rutgers University Press, 1992).

The study of infanticide as a feature of demographic structure, rather than personal tragedy, crystallized with T. R. Malthus and is now linked with studies of population, female criminality, childbirth, illegitimacy, marriage, and the household economy. See, in general, John Boswell, *The Kindness of Strangers* (New York: Pantheon, 1988); Peter Hoffer and N. E. H. Hull, *Murdering Mothers* (New York: New York University Press, 1981); Mark Jackson, *New-Born Child Murder: Women, Illegitimacy and the Courts in Eighteenth-Century England* (Manchester: Manchester University Press, 1996); Lionel Rose, *The Massacre of the Innocents* (London: Routledge and Kegan Paul, 1986); Barbara A. Hanawalt, *Crime and Conflict in English Communities, 1300–1348* (Cambridge: Harvard University Press, 1979); J. M. Beattie, *Crime and the Courts in England, 1660–1800* (Princeton: Princeton University Press, 1986); and more technically, the older quantitative literature on population: E. A. Wrigley, *Population and History* (New York: McGraw-Hill, 1969), and his "Family Limitation in Pre-Industrial England," *Economic History Review* 19 (1966); and on the possibility of teasing out evidence of female-specific infanticide from the English data used by Wrigley and his colleagues, Ruth Wallsgrove, "Infanticide in Early Modern England" (M.A. thesis, University of London, 1983); N. L. Tranter, *Population and Society, 1750–1940* (New York: Longman, 1985); Robert I. Rotberg and Theodore K. Rabb, eds., *Population and Economy* (Cambridge: Cambridge University Press, 1986); and Michael Flinn et al., eds., *Scottish Population History: From the Seventeenth Century to the 1930s* (Cambridge: Cambridge University Press, 1977). Useful articles on Britain include: J. M. Beattie, "The Criminality of Women in Eighteenth-Century England," *Journal of Social History* 8 (Summer 1975): 80–116; R. W. Malcolmson, "Infanticide in the Eighteenth Century," in J. S. Cockburn, ed., *Crime in England, 1500–1800* (Princeton: Princeton University Press, 1977); J. A. Sharpe, "Domestic Homicide in Early Modern England," *Historical Journal* 24:1 (1981): 29–48; R. H. Helmholz, "Infanticide in the Province of Canterbury During the Fifteenth Century," *History of Childhood Quarterly* 2 (Winter 1975): 379–90; Barbara A. Kellum, "Infanticide in England in the Later Middle Ages," *History of Childhood Quarterly* 1 (Winter 1974): 367–88; Catherine Damme, "Infanticide: The Worth of an Infant Under Law," *Medical History* 22 (1978): 1–24; Ann R. Higginbotham, " 'Sin of the Age': Infanticide and Illegitimacy in Victorian London," *Victorian Studies* 32 (Spring 1989): 319–37; P. E. H. Hair, "Homicide, Infanticide, and Child Assault in Late Tudor Essex,"

Local Population Studies 9 (1972): 43–45; Keith Wrightson, "Infanticide in Earlier Seventeenth-Century England," and his "Infanticide in European History"; R. Sauer, "Infanticide and Abortion in Nineteenth-Century Britain," *Population Studies* 32 (1978): 81–93; D. Seaborne Davies, "Child-Killing in English Law," *Modern Law Review* (December 1937): 203–23; and an older document, William Hunter, "On the Uncertainty of the Signs of Murder, in the Case of Bastard Children," *Medical Observations and Inquiries* 6 (1784): 266–90; on the kind of description Hunter, an obstetrician, offered, and which occurs in trial records of infanticide, see Thomas W. Laqueur, "Bodies, Details, and the Humanitarian Narrative," in Lynn Hunt, *The New Cultural History* (Berkeley and Los Angeles: University of California Press, 1989). Outside Britain, see Rene Leboutte, "Offense Against Family Order: Infanticide in Belgium from the Fifteenth Through the Early Twentieth Centuries," *Journal of the History of Sexuality* 2 (October 1991): 59–85; Emily Coleman, "Infanticide in the Early Middle Ages," in Susan M. Stuard, ed., *Women in Medieval Society* (Philadelphia: University of Pennsylvania Press, 1976), and her "L'infanticide dans le haut Moyen Age," *Annales: Economies, Sociétés, Civilisations* 29:2 (1974): 315–35; Keith Wrightson, "Infanticide in European History"; W. L. Langer, "Infanticide: A Historical Survey," *History of Childhood Quarterly* 1 (1973): 353–54; Eve Levin, "Infanticide in Pre-Petrine Russia," *Jahrbücher für Geschichte Osteuropas* 34 (1986): 215–24; Richard Trexler, "Infanticide in Florence: New Sources and First Results," *History of Childhood Quarterly* 2 (1975): 98–117; Y.-B. Brissaud, "L'infanticide à la fin du moyen âge, ses motivations psychologiques et sa repression," *Revue historique de droit français et étranger* 50 (1972): 229–56; Richard Lalou, "L'infanticide devant les tribunaux français (1825–1910)," *Communications* 44 (1986): 175–200; James M. Donovan, "Infanticide and the Juries in France, 1825–1913," *Journal of Family History* 16:2 (1991): 157–76; Regina Schulte, "Infanticide in Rural Bavaria in the Nineteenth Century," in Hans Medick and David Warren Sabean, eds., *Interest and Emotion: Essays on the Study of Family and Kinship* (Cambridge: Cambridge University Press, 1984), 77–102; Susanne Kord, "Women as Children, Women as Childkillers: Poetic Images of Infanticide in Eighteenth-Century Germany," *Eighteenth-Century Studies* 26 (Spring 1993): 449–66; Kristen Ruggiero, "Honor, Maternity, and the Disciplining of Women: Infanticide in Late Nineteenth-Century Buenos Aires," *Hispanic American Historical Review* 72 (August 1992): 353–73; David E. Stannard, "Recounting the Fables of Savagery: Native Infanticide and the Functions of Political Myth," *Journal of American Studies* 25 (December 1991): 381–417; Avner Galadi, "Some Observations on Infanticide in Medieval Muslim Society," *International Journal of Middle East Studies* 22 (May 1990): 185–200; Stephen Wilson, "Infanticide, Child Abandonment, and Female Honor in Nineteenth-Century Corsica," *Comparative Studies in Society and History* 30 (October 1988): 762–83; on the "dark number," or the unprosecuted, in criminal history, see Michael Stephen Hindus, "The Contours of Crime in Massachusetts and South Carolina, 1767–1878," *American Journal of Legal History* 21 (July 1977): 214 n. 3; and indirectly concerning infanticide, Magdalene Schultz, "The Blood Libel: A Motif in the History of Childhood," *Journal of Psychohistory* 14:1 (1986): 1–24; June K. Burton, "Human Rights Issues Affecting Women in Napoleonic Legal Medicine Textbooks," *History of European Ideas* 8:4/5 (1987): 427–34.

Index

abortion, 88, 173
Act Anent Child Murder, xx, 2, 5, 66, 69, 127–29, 131, 133, 136, 137, 139–60
  common women, 266 n. 1
  desuetude, 156
  repeal of, 159–60
Act of Union, 3–4, 136, 204, 216–17
Adam, Jean, 226
agricultural transformation, 2–12, 71, 79, 82, 95–96, 100, 106–8, 114, 209–10, 215, 257 n. 5
  Cuthbert, Margaret, 109–15, 118, 230
  farms, single-tenant, 79, 100, 140
  Galloway levelers' riot, 133
  Gellan, Christian, 103
  Peebles Riot, 132–33
  population growth, 6–7
  rural markets, growth of, 106
  seashell lime, 263 n. 36
Anderson, Margaret, 135–36
androgyny, 207
Anne, Queen, 132
Argyll, Duke of, 194, 203–4, 208
Arnot, Megg, 88–91
Arrock, Elizabeth, 131

Babylon, 39–41, 48, 51
Bagehot, Walter, 198
Baillie, Lady Grizel Hume, 26, 108–9, 212–14, 226, 229
  account books, 214–15
  book of songs, 214
  Stanhope, Lady Murray, 213–15
ballads, 3, 9, 10, 12, 17, 207, 209, 214, 226–27, 231
  collection of, 251 n. 15
  female collectors of, 26–33; Baillie, Lady Grizel Hume, 26, 212–15, 226, 229; Cochrane, Elizabeth, 26–27, 214; Dalrymple, Elizabeth St. Clair, 27
  female singers, 26–37; Brown, Anna Gordon, 10, 14–16, 18, 23–24, 27, 29–31, 35; Cochrane, Elizabeth, 26–27; Crum of Dumbarton, Mrs., 57; Dalrymple, Elizabeth St. Clair, 27; Farquarson, Anne Forbes, 14–16, 28; Gentles, Mrs., 57–58, 63; Gordon, Lillias Forbes, 14–16, 28; Hamilton, Nancy, 57–58, 63; Johnston, Suff, 224; Macqueen, Jean, 57; Michael, the Widow, 31–32; Nairne, Lady Caroline, 10; Patterson, Margaret, 31–32; Old Lady, 23, 27, 30; old lady in Annandale, 57–58, 63; Storie, Mrs. William, 31; Thomson, Mrs., 31–32; Trail, Mrs., 57; Webster, Jane, 32–34
  female writers, 30, 224–226; Lindsay, Lady Anne, 224
  heroine, 9–11, 37, 39–67, 231; gallows speech, 61, 64
  male collectors of: Beattie, James, 29; Buchan, Peter, 24; Chambers, Robert, 29; Child, Francis James, 10–11, 22, 36; Christie, William, 32; Cunningham, Allan, 22; Gordon, Thomas, 28, 29; Herd, David, 22, 27; Hogg, James, 29; Jamieson, Robert, 22–23, 29–30; Kinloch, George, 24, 29, 57; Laidlaw, William, 25, 29; Macmath, William, 29, 33–34; Motherwell, William, 24, 30, 32–33, 57; Percy, Thomas, 14, 17, 21; Pitcairn, Robert, 24, 29; Ritson, Joseph, 22–23, 26–27, 29; Robertson, Joseph, 29; Scott, Walter, 8–9, 10, 16, 22–24, 27, 29, 36, 56–57, 136, 179–80, 191, 196–210, 211–12; Sharpe, Charles Kirkpatrick, 29; Skene, James, 23–24; Tytler, Alexander Fraser, 23, 29; Tytler, William, 23, 29; Wilkie, Thomas, 29–30, 33
  male singers, 32; Lyle, Agnes (father), 32; Nicol, James, 25, 33; Sim, Robert, 33